Child Care and adult crime

In memory of Mary Minty

Child Care and adult crime

Brian Minty
with the assistance of Colin Ashcroft

Manchester University Press

Published by Manchester University Press,
Oxford Road, Manchester M13 9PL, UK

Distributed exclusively in the USA and Canada
by St. Martin's Press, Inc., 175 Fifth Avenue, New York 10010, USA

British Library cataloguing in publication data

Minty, Brian
    Child Care and adult crime.
    1. Crime and criminals – Social aspects –
    England
    I. Title   II. Ashcroft, Colin
    364.2′56′0924   HV6155

Library of Congress cataloging in publication data applied for

ISBN 0 7190 2469 2 *hardback*

Photoset in Linotron Plantin with Rockwell
by Northern Phototypesetting Co., Bolton
Printed and bound in Great Britain by
Biddles Ltd, Guildford and King's Lynn

Contents

Preface and acknowledgements

This is a book written by a practitioner for other practitioners, although it will be read equally (I hope) by academics and service managers. It is written for social workers, child psychiatrists, clinical and educational psychologists, paediatricians, general practitioners, health visitors and teachers, as they struggle to help unhappy and disadvantaged children. For some readers the argument through Chapters 4 to 10 may seem at times heavily statistical, but mathematics is the language of science and, therefore, their use is unavoidable. The figures are presented as simply as possible, so that even those unversed in statistics will see the drift of the argument.

Indirectly, this book is written for parents and children, even though I suspect that only a minority of parents, and an even smaller minority of children, will read it(!). Our findings suggest that with more caring parenting many children and young people would cause less serious trouble to others and themselves as they grow up, and that, judged by the criterion of adult convictions, some children from very inadequate homes would benefit from being placed long term in substitute care. At first sight, this conclusion may seem not only somewhat preposterous but even offensive to many social workers, and hostile to some natural parents. The book is not intended to be anti-parent. Few tasks in our society are assessed with such severity as that of parenthood. It is one of life's most difficult and exacting roles. Yet we expect all parents to be good parents, or at least, 'good enough'. In spite of its severe demands, few parents are excused a task they may find themselves demoralised by, or even quite unfitted for. Even if they require temporary respite, unless they have good relatives, friends or money, they will find that, at least in Britain, official help will be given grudgingly and sparingly, and often at the price of their being stigmatised. In a recent study of admissions to Care in two English towns by Packman, Randall and Jacques (1986), it was found that parents were put through hoops in an effort to prevent admission, with few services provided if admission was refused. Parents saw the local authority's refusal to admit their children into Care in 'purely negative terms'. Nothing helpful had been offered in its place, and some 'parents were left with a very real sense of despair'. For many, the sense of dissatisfaction remained just as strong six months later. A considerable minority of parents felt that the decision not to admit their child to state-provided care (henceforward to be described in this book as Care with a capital C) had been the wrong decision for the family. Parents seeking help for their children, because they feel they are themselves unable to cope, come up against a powerful ideology among social workers, and members of some of the other helping professions: that admitting a child to Care is nearly always the worst of all possible alternatives. They also face a widespread moral assumption: that the duties of parenthood are such categorical imperatives that parents and families can only be relieved of these duties when their desperation and inability to cope are only too apparent.

The origins of this study

My first practice of social work in relation to children and families took place in a traditional Child Guidance Clinic set in the middle of a deprived inner city area in the North of England (Northtown). My initial interest in following up children, especially severely disadvantaged and disturbed children, arose when I discovered at the clinic well-documented files on children who had first been seen there in the late 1940s and early 1950s. It seemed both socially important and scientifically fascinating to discover how these children turned out as young adults. At the time I had not yet discovered Robins' superb follow-up of adolescents seen at the St Louis Child Guidance Clinic (Robins, 1966), and when I did, I was interested to find that her study had begun in exactly the same way.

The introduction of genericism into social work in Britain in the early seventies led me to face for the first time the enormously painful human and moral dilemmas of whether to seek to remove children altogether from their homes when their parents seemed quite unable to give them adequate care, affection and understanding, or the effects of the parent's hostility or rigidity seemed quite destructive to a child. When I attempted to help parents at the end of their tether, or protect children rejected and neglected by their parents, I found all too often that the predominant philosophy in child care practice was that of the prevention of the admission of children to Care at almost all costs.

Genericism also provided me with access to the files of children who had come into the Care of the local authority immediately after the establishment of Children's Departments, following the Children Act of 1948. The children in Care were drawn from the same deprived inner-city area, and were of the same social stratum as the poorest and most disadvantaged children seen at the clinic, a majority of whose clients were referred from schools rather than through their general practitioners. With the exception of Ferguson's study of twenty-year-olds who had been brought up in the Care of Glasgow, there appeared to be, at that time, hardly any major long-term outcome study of children brought up in public Care in Britain (Ferguson, 1966).

It seemed possible to select a group of children who had been in Care for an appreciable period of time, and compare and contrast them for outcome with a group of children, matched for age, sex and social class, about whom there appeared to be very sound social, psychological and psychiatric descriptions and assessments.

Still later, in what proved to be an abortive search for the results of the eleven-plus examination, which all these children would have taken to decide which type of secondary school they should enter, I discovered files of chronic school non-attenders held by the Education Department of Northtown. These were of at least equal antiquity to the other two collections of files, and appeared to describe children living in as much material and social disadvantage as that experienced by the children entering Care. Although these files lacked the professional competence and amount of information as the other two sets of records, they meticulously recorded the (often changing) composition of these families, the health and social problems associated with their children's school non-attendance, the father's occupation – if he had one – and the extent of the children's absence from school, with the alleged reasons for that absence. The reason why these details were so meticulously recorded was that the records had to form a basis for possible prosecution of the parents for their child's persistent failure to attend school. There were similar pressures on Children's Officers to see that accurate records were maintained in relation to applications for 'Fit Person Orders', whereby the local authority attempted to establish in Court the need to remove a child from his or her parents. Children's Committees also needed to be convinced of the necessity for the local authority to obtain parental rights over children admitted to Care who appeared to have no effective parents.

What the study lacked was a group of contemporaneous children who might have been assumed to be problem-free and not particularly disadvantaged as children. This proved impossible to find. I made attempts to find such a group through: (a) school health records, only to discover that these had been systematically destroyed when children reached their eighteenth birthdays, and (b) through a general practice situated in the inner city, and which had been established well over a generation ago. Unfortunately, Northtown has experienced considerable emigration of its population from the more deprived areas to leafy suburbs as a result of slum clearance programmes. It would have been an unrepresentative population that had remained.

I also attempted to obtain a further contrast group of contemporaries who first came to the attention of the 'authorities' through convictions. I approached: (c) the Probation and After-care Service, but found that they also systematically destroyed their records of probationers ten years after the case had been closed. Finally: (d) I was given permission by the local bench of magistrates to follow up a group of young men sentenced in the Courts, but was unable to pursue this offer, since the Court registers did not contain information as to the social class of the parents, and often failed to record a date of birth, so that identification would have been very problematical.

Theoretical assumptions behind the research

This research was planned ten years ago, and its design inevitably reflected the main author's assumptions at the time in relation to child development and parent-child interactions. These assumptions might be described as a mixture of what Sameroff and Chandler (1975) describe as a 'main effects' view, and an 'interactional' view, of parent-child relationships. Both these views are in line with traditional scientific assumptions about causes having direct effects, the 'main effects' view stressing the impact of parents on their children's development, and the 'interactionist view' stressing that children also have an impact on their parents. We assumed (and still do, to an appreciable extent) that parents with marked personal problems, illnesses and inadequacies, especially if they lived in conditions of severe poverty and disadvantage, would be less likely to provide adequate care for their children, and this would manifest itself in conduct and emotional problems. Quinton and Rutter (1984) have shown that boys brought up by parents with mental disorders are much more likely to have conduct problems or a mixture of conduct and emotional problems than the rest of the population.

On the other hand, I would like to make three points about my position in relation to these matters. Firstly, it is well established, and was well-known when I planned this study, that children are born with markedly different temperaments, some of which are more difficult to manage than others. It follows that a child's innate temperament might well affect the quality of early parent–child relationships. This was shown in the work of Thomas, Chess and Birch (1968). It was also becoming clear that young children with high activity levels, and children with language delays are more likely to present later with behavioural problems, although Richman and Stevenson's follow-up study was not published until the mid-eighties (Richman, Stevenson and Graham, 1982).

Secondly, there is perhaps a further 'time warp' in that it is impossible to get behind the assumptions of the professional workers who wrote the original records a generation earlier. There was recognition then, as now, that problems in intelligence and in learning could make things very difficult for the child, and the psychometric and educational testing was done very thoroughly. A majority of the boys in our child-guidance sample who had conduct problems were specifically retarded, by between two to four years, in relation to reading and arithmetic. However, their general assumptions were 'main effects'.

The third point is that I would go along with the view that what is sometimes referred to as the 'child guidance model' of parent–child relationships is seriously deficient, and often unfair and demoralising to parents. It is true that rejecting and overprotective parents, and parents with serious personality problems tend to 'produce' children who are both troubled and troublesome. In fact, all that we, as a society, have learned about child abuse over the past twenty-five years confirms that parents can be extremely destructive to their children's well-being and development. It is the corollary that is so often unfair and untrue: that difficult children must be the product of parental rejection, overprotection and general incompetence. Perhaps the only really good parents are those who have successfully coped with children who have considerable problems, illnesses and handicaps!

In our study we found there were strong associations between descriptions of critical and hostile parents, or parents who were generally arguing, and sons who later become delinquent. It is possible that these attitudes and arguments were to some extent the consequence of the family's wretched position in society, or even of parental failures to understand or cope with their child. All the records give is a two-dimensional picture at a particular point (or points) in time. They only approximate to the reality. It does not follow that their view is totally false, or that research done on 'main effects' assumptions is worthless. To take an analogy from physics, much worthwhile work could still be done, I presume, on Newtonian principles.

Conduct problems

To some extent, this research depends on the assumption that certain types of childhood behaviour are socially unacceptable. There is usually no problem about agreeing over this in relation to most socially unacceptable behaviour. The list of behavioural problems I eventually settled for is given in Appendix II. The items I am not altogether happy with are the following: overactivity, self-poisoning, and temper tantrums over the age of five years. At the time I designed the study, it seemed to me better to include these items than to omit them. Eleven boys were described by a child psychiatrist as 'overactive', six severely so. They all had other behavioural problems. Only two adolescent boys took overdoses, at least, that were recorded. One of these was a chronic 'repeater'. Eleven boys were described by parents, house-parents or foster parents as being prone to frequent temper outbursts after the age of five.

Delays in publication

This study has been a very part-time effort by a busy social work practitioner and teacher living through a period of considerable organisational upheaval in social work. In addition, time and energy have had to be 'diverted' to unexpected family stresses: the need to foster the adolescent daughters of friends who died, coping with serious illness in a child, and caring for my wife in her terminal illness, and for our children after her death. She would have dearly wanted to see this book published, for a variety of reasons(!). It is dedicated to her memory.

Finally, there has been a delay of about two years, owing to the fact that one reviewer for an esteemed scientific journal felt that the work could not be accepted in the form in which it was then submitted. He argued that a fault had crept into the design because we discovered a considerable overlap in our original groups. Very careful searching through registers and files revealed that many children not in the original long-term Care sample had in fact spent some time in Care – usually for relatively short periods. Our original solution to this problem had been to include these cases as being in Care when it came to making comparisons within the Care group, but our reviewer pointed out that this was suspect, since they were not known to be representative of any group of children in Care. As a result, Colin Ashcroft and I redid most of the computations excluding the additional cases. We were pleased to find that the significant associations we had originally discovered usually still remained significant. In fact, we have often given both sets of findings, since we feel that the shift in the picture that comes from looking at both sets of findings underlines the general drift of our argument. We are, therefore, grateful to our anonymous reviewer, since he has enabled us to put right a possible error in our work. The delay has also meant that we have had the benefit of comparing our work with that of at least seven major pieces of research relating to children entering and leaving Care which have been published within the past two and a half years – mostly within the past year. We refer to the studies by: (a) Rowe *et al.* (1984), (b) Triseliotis and Russell (1984), (c) Milham *et al.* (1986), (d) Packman, Randall and Jacques, (1986), and (e) Fisher *et al.* (1986), Vernon and Fruin (1986) and Stein and Carey (1986). Although our work comes after them, it does not replicate them in any way, and we have had the benefit of reading them before submitting our work for publication.

This monograph would not have been possible without the considerable help and encouragement of many people. It is difficult to thank some adequately, and yet I am anxious there may still be shortcomings in the research from which it might be kinder to distance my friends(!). Responsibility for the methods, findings and interpretation in this study lies entirely with the authors.

I am most grateful to the Education and Social Services Departments of Northtown for their agreement to allow us to use their records. The NHS Records Office have helped us very considerably by tracing which subjects had died or emigrated and which were known still to be in the United Kingdom. The help of the local

Criminal Records Office and the national CRO was quite invaluable.

I owe a debt of gratitude to Dr P Maguire, Senior Lecturer in Psychiatry, who provided supervision when this study started as an MSc project, and Professor S. Brandon who encouraged me (a long time ago) to embark on this marathon. Professor D. Taylor has provided me with a great deal of encouragement and help. He read through the first draft of this book, and made many detailed and useful suggestions. Dr K. Pease has been generous with time and ideas – which we have not always followed. Dr. J. Erulkar, Dr P. Ainsworth and Dr I Goodyer have clarified my thinking over the years about the nature of conduct disorder. I owe to both Professor Taylor and Dr Goodyer many ideas about the nature of parental psychodynamics and child development.

Dr V. Hillier and Mr A. Gibb in the Department of Community Medicine, Manchester University, have been generous with their expertise and time in relation to statistics and computation. We must thank Dr M. Vaughan, Miss R. Morrison and Dr P. Huxley for their help, and Dr S. Wolkind for his encouragement.

Finally, we are greatly indebted to Mrs Margaret Barrett, Mrs Dorothy Welch, Mrs Freda Johnson and Mrs S. David who undertook the considerable labour of typing this book, and to Dr P. Brien who helped with the final editing.

Brian Minty, March 1987.

1

The background to this study

The child is father of the man.
Wordsworth.

This book aims to describe, in terms of adult crime, the outcome of a group of children who nearly all grew up in conditions of considerable material deprivation. The majority had, in addition, experienced inadequate parenting. They were all brought up in an inner-city area of a large English industrial conurbation ('Northtown') in the period following the Second World War. A century before their birth, Engels had described the geographical area in which they grew up as 'the classic slum'. The living conditions and the social milieu in which the grandparents of our subjects had lived in Edwardian times and during the First World War have been eloquently described by Robert Roberts (1971).

Two-fifths of the parents of our boys were known to be living at or below the National Assistance Benefit level, which was at that time the official criterion for poverty. Most of them lived in tightly-packed rows of 'two-up, two-down' terraced houses, often in overcrowded conditions, sometimes grotesquely so. Half of the boys in our study had three or more brothers and sisters, and a third had at least five.

A majority of them would be regarded as having experienced some degree of inadequate parenting. Just over half of the boys (fifty-four per cent) and just under half of the girls (forty-five per cent) had been admitted to the Care of the local Children's Department and, in many cases, this had been for appreciable periods of time, e.g. almost two-fifths of all the boys and nearly a third of all the girls had been in Care for periods of a year or more.

Child Care and Child Guidance records often contained a professional assessment of the quality of parenting received by these children. A fairly definite assessment had been put in writing for nearly two-thirds of the boys. In fewer than one-eighth of these cases was an assessment made that both parents were providing adequate care, although for a third of the children in which comments were recorded, it appeared that at least one parent was providing affectionate care and adequate control. In the other cases, where comments were recorded, either both parents or a single mother (in the case of one-parent families) had been described as 'neglectful', 'hostile', 'rejecting' or 'ambivalent', or 'unconcerned' or unable, because of illness or other personal handicaps (including alcohol abuse), to provide adequate care. Just over one-third of all the mothers had been described as neglectful and this meant either that the child had been admitted to the care of the authority for neglect or that a Co-ordinating Committee on Child Neglect, or a Child Care Officer, had recorded that a child was being neglected. Since over two-fifths of the boys and girls had been reported to the local education committee for persistent non-attendance at school, usually recorded over several periods, a considerable minority of our sample also lacked adequate schooling, as well as suffering from economic hardship and various forms of emotional deprivation. A particular form of emotional deprivation, or perhaps more correctly emotional 'abuse', for children is having to live in an atmosphere of marked disharmony and hostility between their parents. For almost three-fifths of the boys in this study, the records described the quality of the parental marriage. In nearly three-quarters of the cases described there were comments to the effect that there were at least considerable overt difficulties in the parents' relationship, and sometimes (in a third of the cases) the relationship seemed to be almost entirely discordant or acrimonious. It follows that although it would be wrong to suppose that the childhoods of our subjects were a constant round of misery, grinding poverty and unhappy relationships for everybody all the time, nevertheless, within the general hardship, a considerable minority of children were severely neglected, harshly treated or caught up in constant arguments and even marital violence. Some were doubtless physically abused by their parents but, since this was not recognised at the time, it could not be recorded.

One of the assumptions of this study is that, crudely speaking, the worse a child's environment and the longer he remains within it, the worse his outcome. Virtually all parents hope that their children will grow up to achieve some degree of success and contentment as adults; in relationships with other people, particularly in marriage and in their parenting of their own children, in work – although, sadly, this is not always available – and in leisure. Parents sometimes worry that their children may disgrace themselves when grown up, by shameful or seriously criminal behaviour, and they would feel that their children's subsequent social failure and shame would reflect badly on their parenting. Whether this assumption is correct or not, it is widely held and needs to be tested. It also raises questions as to what kinds of inadequate parenting have the worst consequences.

We have used only one index of outcome: convictions for indictable and other serious offences over the age of sixteen. We have examined their frequency, seriousness and nature (e.g. theft, breaking and entering or violent crime). There are other equally valid criteria, such as psychosocial adjustment, including mental health, or the abuse of alcohol or drugs, or the quality of parenting offered to the next generation. None of these measures is entirely satisfactory in itself, or along with the others, as a measure of the quality of parenting received. In the first place, constitutional factors in the child contribute to the manner in which the child copes with, and grows by, experience. Secondly, nearly all adult behaviour is likely to be affected by current circumstances. An attempt to describe the contributions of the past and the present to current parenting in a group of emotionally-deprived women is made by Rutter, Quinton and Liddle (1983) in their report on the psychosocial status and parenting capacities of a group of girls who had been brought up in Care. The girls who went on to marry supportive husbands appeared to be, on the whole, good mothers to their own children, although most of these women were poorer in many aspects of parenting than a matched working-class sample. A majority of the rather 'poor' mothers either lacked husbands or cohabitees at the time of the study or had partners who were not supportive, and who often had psychosocial problems of their own.

The origins of delinquency

It would seem that the origins of severe conduct problems in boys often go back to early childhood and that many boys with severe conduct problems go on to become delinquent. Evidence for the latter claim is reviewed by Rutter and Giller (1983). Evidence for the view that many behavioural problems have an early onset is clearest in the studies of Richman, Stevenson and Graham (1982). They found that over half the boys with extreme restlessness and marked behavioural difficulties at three and four years of age were clinically assessed as having conduct or neurotic disorders (usually the former) at eight years of age. Boys who showed marked restlessness and problem behaviour at three and four years of age were more likely to come from homes where there was tension, e.g. marital friction, maternal criticism and little maternal warmth. They were also more likely to show developmental delays, probably of a constitutional kind, and their families were more likely to have experienced financial stresses and inappropriate housing.

The onset of severe conduct problems and persistent delinquency is almost certainly the outcome of the interaction of constitution and environment, although some environments seem so deficient as to produce pathology in all but the most resilient. Factors in the environment which are known to be associated with conduct disorder and/or delinquency in older boys include, firstly, parental marital discord (Porter and O'Leary, 1980; Block *et al.*, 1981; Hetherington, 1981; West and Farrington, 1973). The children in Block's study were quite small, i.e. aged between three and seven years. Persistent parental hostility to children has also been found to be highly associated with conduct problems, or a mixture of conduct and emotional problems, in boys. Quinton and Rutter (1985), studying samples of children of adult psychiatric patients in London, found that exposure to hostile parental behaviour seemed to be the main variable accounting for children's disturbance. Although it would be wrong to ignore: (a) genetic and temperamental factors, and (b) many other micro, and macro, social factors, there does seem enough evidence to assert that parental hostility and marital discord appear to be important factors in the genesis of many severe conduct problems. It follows that emphasis should be given to the provision of services aimed at modifying parental hostility and resolving marital conflicts, or helping married partners separate in a manner that causes the least additional hurt to all concerned. Where these tasks cannot be carried out successfully, and hostility and quarrelling are persistent and severe, we are bound to ask whether it is altogether acceptable that children simply be allowed to grow up in such emotionally-damaging environments, especially when these are well-known to the helping professions.

The theoretical perspective of this book is ecological. It is assumed that there will be constant interaction between the child, with all his innate and acquired characteristics, and his environment. It follows that there will be some degree of differential outcome for children who have experienced similar environments. A second assumption that goes with an ecological perspective, and one that is stressed by Bronfenbrenner (1979), is that the quality of parenting is also influenced by the wider environment with its supports and stresses.

Possible factors in the wider social environment associated with delinquency

Studies which have discovered an association between poverty and higher rates of delinquency include Wilson (1974), and West and Farrington (1973), who found a strong association between becoming delinquent and living in overcrowded conditions. Overcrowding, and the stress this causes the whole family, may be one mechanism through which social deprivation contributes to the causation of delinquency. A second factor is social class, and at least four large British studies have confirmed associations between delinquency and having parents with unskilled or semi-skilled occupations, as compared with having parents with a non-manual occupation (with sons of skilled manual fathers falling in between these two groups in their rates for becoming delinquent). These are: the nationwide sample of children at birth in the National Survey (Wadsworth, 1979), the Aberdeen General Population Survey (May, 1975), the longitudinal study of West and Farrington (1973) of boys living in inner London and Ouston's report on children in London Schools (1984). A third factor is area of residence (Baldwin, 1979). Several studies have found that certain areas of cities have higher delinquency rates than others, e.g. (Gath *et al.*, 1977) showed that certain wards within an outer London borough had much higher rates of delinquency than others. There are also very great differences in official delinquency rates between urban and rural areas (McClintock and Avison, 1968). That these differences are not simply a function of greater police vigilance in cities, or of other factors relating to the processing of crime, is shown by the much higher rates of behavioural disturbance generally found in boys in inner-city areas, as compared with rural areas. This has been found to be true in London, as compared with the Isle of Wight (Rutter *et al.*, 1975), and in Oslo, as compared with rural Norway (Lavik, 1977). A fourth social factor is that of schools. It would appear that schools exert an influence on children that is independent of social class and neighbourhood (Rutter *et al.*, 1979; Power *et al.*, 1967).

The mechanisms whereby these social factors influence delinquency is still a matter of considerable academic debate, but it has to be admitted that, to some extent, social deprivation, social class and area of residence are not totally independent of the personal characteristics of the parents. Fathers with marked criminal behaviour, alcoholism or severe personality difficulties may move down the social scale and drift into inner-city areas. Such fathers are likely to have a direct influence on their sons in the direction of making them more delinquent. Osborn and West (1979) found that two-fifths of the sons of recidivist fathers were also recidivist, a quarter being persistently so. Robins (1966) found that many of the fathers of adolescents with severe behavioural problems were themselves antisocial in personality and behaviour.

It does not follow that overcrowding, poverty and other forms of socio-economic stress have no part to play in the genesis of delinquency. It is almost certain that they raise the general level of dissatisfaction, frustration and tension in both parents and children. Anger is likely to be projected by parents on to their nearest targets: their children. Adolescents are also likely to be influenced, to some extent, by peer group behaviour, although the effectiveness of parental monitoring and control may modify the extent of peer group pressures.

In addition, there appear to be individual differences in predispositions to criminal behaviour, including levels of intelligence (West and Farrington, 1973), with less able boys being somewhat more likely to become officially delinquent. It would even appear that genetic influences may play some part, possibly through the mechanism of temperament and personality. Cadoret and Cain (1980) found that crime and alcoholism in the biological parents of adopted children predicted adolescent antisocial behaviour, although the children had been separated from them at birth. Hutchings and Mednick (1974), using the very full registers of adoption and crime available in Denmark, found that, for adopted boys, becoming delinquent was associated with both biological *and* adoptive fathers who had convictions, the worst outcome being for boys who had both a biological and an adoptive father with a history of crime.

Often, in the history of persistent delinquents, there appears to be a complex pattern of individual failure and response to that failure, in terms of anger and rejection, and these patterns occur both at home and at school. Elliott and Voss (1974) showed that, in the USA, high school drop-outs had markedly more contacts with the police than boys who did not drop out, but that, having left school, their delinquent behaviour subsided, whether or not they left school early or later.

However, it appears that the antecedents of what later become conduct problems can emerge very early in life and we have already referred to the study by Richman *et al.*, (1982) who found that most of the boys who showed extreme restlessness and marked difficulties at three or four years of age, presented with considerable behavioural difficulties at eight years of age. Kohn (1977) found that there was considerable persistence in the 'trait' of anger-defiance in the New York school-children between the ages of approximately six and ten years.

It follows that, for some children, serious difficulties that emerge in parent–child relationships at an early age may presage behavioural problems lasting over many years. Environments which are full of hostility and discord and which lack affection and a sensitive awareness of young children's needs may well contribute to life-long problems in the children – particularly if the environments do not change for the better.

In 1948, early in the lives of most of the children we have studied, Children's Departments were established throughout Britain in order to provide adequate care for children deprived of a normal home life by abandonment, or because of the illness, handicap or death of their parents, and to protect children at risk of neglect or cruelty in their own homes. The children in our study are now adults. Was the Care provided by society adequate as an upbringing for them and did children who were subject to neglect in their own homes and removed into Care appear to fare better in terms of their adult outcome than we might have expected if they had been left in their own homes? Did children who remained in inadequate homes fare worse than children removed into Care?

The lack of faith in Care

Some provision for children who lack adequate parenting is made by the state, or is under some form of state control, in most industrial societies. In Britain the official term for such provision is 'Care' and, in North America, 'foster care'. In fact, there have been two main motives for such provision: firstly, an immediate concern to protect and help children found to be suffering from loss of parents, neglect, abuse and rejection, and secondly (although often appearing earlier in the history of social welfare), an anxiety that children brought up in such environments may suffer long-term emotional damage and turn out to be antisocial adults with severe problems in living and working; that they may experience extreme difficulties in forming satisfying personal relationships. The males may be persistently delinquent and both males and females may have serious deficiencies as parents to their own children.

. In most Western countries, control over admission to Care lies largely in the hands of social workers and the courts. There are many among social workers (and to some extent also among the other helping professions) who have almost as great an anxiety about the long-term effects of living 'in Care' as about the long-term outcome for children who suffer abuse, neglect and rejection in their own homes. As Stein and Carey conclude their study of young people leaving Care, 'At its worst the state had become an added burden rather than a supportive parent.' (Stein and Carey, 1966). This 'professional' anxiety may sometimes coincide with anxieties felt by Social Services' managers and committee members about the costs of keeping children in Care, especially in residential Care. For a few years, some people in Britain have been talking of a 'crisis' in child care (Henke, 1982) and although the 'crisis' has largely been caused by a series of public-spending cuts in the late 1970s and early 1980s, coupled with an astronomical rise in the costs of residential care, there is a danger that policies which are largely dictated by economic pressures may be justified on ideological grounds, or at least that there may be some form of collusion between the needs of managers to keep down costs and the anxieties of practitioners about the assumed harmfulness of admitting children to Care. Critics of recent trends in child care policy might well argue after the manner of Scull (1984) that keeping children in their own homes at almost all costs is a further example of late-twentieth-century capitalist welfare policies, with 'economy masquerading as benevolence, and neglect as tolerance.' While we would disagree with Scull in his view that policies of community care for the mentally ill and the delinquent are based entirely on economic considerations, it would be difficult to deny that finance is often withdrawn from residential services, both for the mentally ill and for children, without there always being adequate alternatives, and this is often done under the guise of welfare.

There is still much to learn about the relative harmfulness, for children who are deprived of adequate parenting, of growing up in alternative environments, all of which are far from ideal. In what circumstances is it better for a child experiencing fairly persistent hostility, or an appreciable degree of neglect, to remain with his natural parents or to be admitted to publicly provided Care, with all its inadequacies? Once admitted, in what circumstances is it better for him to stay in Care, and risk either a series of foster placements or the greater neutrality and multiple caretaking of a residential home, to return to his natural parents or to be adopted? These questions need to be aired, but it has to be accepted firstly that, as Stein *et al.* (1978) say, the social worker 'is admonished to act in the best interests of the child, while lacking the knowledge base to do so. Decisions are required that demand greater knowledge than is actually available.' Secondly, social workers, although often criticised for failing to protect the best interests of the child, are far from being entirely free agents. Nearly all practitioners know of children living in home situations that are likely to be very damaging to children because of emotional or sexual abuse and even cruelty but, because there is a lack of evidence, it is impossible in the present legal situation and climate of opinion adequately to protect the child. In our view, child advocacy is still in its infancy. However, one assumption that has hampered the development of a proper child advocacy service is the belief that home is always the best place for a child, and that long-term separation from home is *always* bad for children (even though in most situations this is true).

The third consideration which we must build into the structure of any debate on the pros and cons of natural family v. substitute care is that, in some situations, there is no choice to make. It has to be accepted that it is absolutely inevitable that some form of substitute care should be provided by society for a small minority of children. The most obvious situation for this is when parents abandon their babies or desert their families. In such cases, society has no choice but to provide, or arrange for, some form of substitute care and to make sure that the alternative is the best possible in the circumstances.

A second kind of situation where substitute care is inevitable (at least temporarily) is where parents provide care that is so deficient or abusive as to cause their children serious physical harm or neglect.

Over and above these extreme situations, there must remain anxiety about children living in homes that are emotionally neglectful, uncaring, hostile or rejecting.

There would be general agreement that it is nearly always right to make strenuous attempts at first to find alternatives to removing children from their parents, but sometimes the alternatives do not work and there has been a strong impression in the recent past that decisions about the possible admission of children into care have been postponed again and again, while yet another effort or some new approach has been tried or a new social worker has had to make up his mind. In the meantime, some children have been severely damaged. In fact, delays in taking considered decisions about the long-term needs of children at risk were one of the mistakes which attracted particular comment in some of the enquiries into the deaths of children in Britain from physical abuse and neglect (e.g. Maria Mehmadagi, 1981). There has also been widespread public anxiety about the apparent commitment of some social workers to returning abused children to their parents, where they have sometimes experienced further abuse, in extreme cases leading to their deaths. For example, the sad case of Jasmine Beckford (Brent, 1985).

Although social workers in Britain and other countries are now likely to seek to separate children from their parents (at least temporarily) where there is severe physical abuse and neglect, the same does not always apply to 'emotional abuse', partly because emotional damage is much more difficult to establish and partly because many social workers and others would regard the admission of children to Care as a further form of emotional abuse. We need to ask whether this is a justifiable evaluation of Care and, if it is, whether it needs to be so, and whether the emotional damage produced by living in Care tends to be greater or less than the damage done to some children by living in emotionally abusive or neglectful homes.

In recent years in North America and Britain, adoption, as an alternative solution for children seriously deprived of adequate care in their own homes, has been aggressively pursued by many social workers. What has been described as 'the permanency principle' (Morris, 1984; Maluccio, Fein and Olmstead, 1986) has been increasingly influential over the past ten years in planning policy for children who need long-term substitute care.

It is argued that psychological parenting has to be permanent (Goldstein, Freud and Solnit, 1979) and it is all too obvious that children in foster care suffer many disruptions by moving from one placement to another and that those in residential homes experience both multiple care-taking and changes in placement. Retrospective studies by Meier (1965) and Murphy (1974) found that children in long-term foster care had experienced a mean average of over four placements in upbringings spent largely in Care.

Research in North America (Maas and Engler, 1959) and Britain (Rowe and Lambert, 1973) discovered that there were probably thousands of children in long-term Care whom social workers would prefer to see placed with permanent substitute families, but for whom adoption was not being pursued. In some quarters, it has been held that only adoption provides substitute care with real permanency and policies of vigorous adoption have been followed. Although there is evidence that most late adoptions work out well (Kadushin, 1970; Lahti, Green and Emlen, 1978), about a fifth of all adoptions seem to be seriously problematical and there are anecdotal descriptions of some late adoptions going very wrong, especially if made with insufficient planning, so that an arrangement that is intended to be permanent turns out not to be so, or, if permanent, turns sour for both parent and child. One important aspect of such policies is that they may embody a view of official Care as something essentially short-term so that, where children need long-term substitute care, it is assumed that this should be provided by adoptive parents or legal guardians outside the state 'system'. However, the recent implementation of provisions in the Children Act, 1975 has enabled long-term foster parents in Britain to apply for custodianship and this will offer some long-term foster parents and their children a considerable measure of permanency.

As a result of these trends, there has been a growing determination in some social work agencies in Britain and North America to attempt to take 'final' decisions as early as possible about the need for substitute care, so as to try to ensure that a child who will probably never have an adequate home life within his natural family can find an alternative substitute home and permanent parents, and avoid either 'yo-yoing' in and out of Care for several years or passing through a series of foster parents or (perhaps worst of all) being 'warehoused' in a series of residential homes.

This kind of approach is strongly resisted by other social workers and by many natural parents, who argue that social workers are too ready to seek to remove children from their natural parents and take away parental rights. They claim that, with better material and social supports, many children need not come into Care at all or that, if they do, they should only be there for short periods. Many of those who argue for a greater use of adoption, and many parents who argue for a curtailing of social work powers, would share a view of Care as an essentially short-term measure and would argue that it is harmful for children to have to grow up in Care. It is generally assumed by most child care experts that the prevention of long-term Care is an important aim in policy, and social workers have been found at fault in a recent study by Milham *et al.* (1986) for failing to maintain parent–child links when children are admitted to Care, partly on the grounds that a breaking of links leads to children feeling quite 'lost' and partly because maintaining such links is a necessary condition for children returning home.

It is necessary to ask two questions: (a) why are social workers and others reluctant to place children in Care, especially if it is likely to be long-term, and (b) what is the evidence that living long-term in Care is damaging?

Why are social workers reluctant to admit children to Care?

That most social workers are reluctant to admit children to care is not in serious doubt. Recent studies by Vernon (1985) and Packman, Randall and Jacques (1986) have confirmed that most social workers regard admission to Care as the 'last resort' and usually only admit children to Care under pressure. The reasons for this attitude are not hard to find. In the first place, separating children from their parents and placing them in what are frequently totally unfamiliar surroundings is often an extremely distressing matter for all concerned. For children, especially small children, the loss of all that is familiar and comforting is highly alarming and painful (although much of this anxiety could, and should, be prevent by a proper preparation and a gradual introduction to foster parents or a residential home – where this is feasible).

Children can be attached to even the most neglectful and rejecting parents and suffer the pain of losing them, sometimes the more severely, since admission to Care gets in the way of their obtaining the reassurance they seek; that the only people who matter (their parents) do care for them after all. Bowlby (1951) acknowledged the pain felt by 'deprived' children in this situation and saw that children, especially younger children, will often blame themselves for being put into Care.

This tendency of children to look for the causes of parental incapacity or failure in themselves is encouraged when children who are admitted to Care for reasons of family breakdown, parental illness or inadequacy are placed with children committed by the courts for reasons of being found guilty of offences or being beyond parental control.

Most parents feel sadness and worry when their children are admitted to Care (Jenkins, 1969). Sometimes the sadness is profound. However, relief and thankfulness that the child is being properly cared for are also fairly common feelings (over two-fifths of mothers and nearly three-fifths of fathers, in Jenkins' study admitted to such feelings). In addition, it would seem that a high proportion of parents whose children are troublesome and who might have gone into Care, but did not, are very far from happy with social workers' refusals to admit them. Packman, Randall and Jacques (1986), studying all cases of possible admission to Care in two English towns over a period of twelve months, found that two-fifths of all the parents whose children were *not* admitted to Care felt six months later that this decision had been the wrong one for the family.

As one would expect, anger and shame are not uncommon feelings, with anger being particularly pronounced when the method of admission is compulsory, and the reasons for admission suggest some degree of unacceptable behaviour on the part of the parents (e.g. child abuse, neglect, alcoholism and drug dependency). However deficient their own care, parents usually have a strong attachment to their children and an understandable belief that their children belong in some sense to them and that, by giving birth to them and experiencing the strains and stresses of parenthood, they have earned the right to take the important decisions about their children. Accordingly, they may bitterly resent social workers attempting to persuade or compel them to give them up and increasingly oppose social workers' applications for Care proceedings in the courts and, once a case has gone to court, whatever the outcome, they may withhold further meaningful co-operation with them. In some cases, of course, the parents themselves want, and request that their child be admitted to Care. However, they may be subject to powerful family and social pressures to avoid a step that is seen as shameful and stigmatising.

The social worker may, in fact, identify primarily with the parents rather than the child, and some degree of emotional identification will be necessary to work with them, even if the task is that of separating parents and child in the least damaging way possible. However, in most cases social workers will begin by trying to help the natural parents to become better parents, whether or not the child is temporarily separated from them. It may then become difficult for the social worker to move from a position of support and friendship to one of opposing the parents in court and having to expose their inadequacies and confidences. Confusion about who is the primary client has been apparent in some child abuse cases and was highlighted in the Beckford case (Brent, 1985). Nevertheless, sensitive social workers cannot avoid being aware of the distress they cause many parents in trying to deprive them of their children. Unless the case for removing a child is clear, social workers would be party to a moral enormity committed against the parents, particularly when the social worker comes to see that, with the same life history, he or she might well be in the same situation.

On the other hand, it would be wrong to imply that all the emotions aroused by abused and deprived children incline the social worker to oppose the use of Care. Protectiveness towards children and anger towards abusers are probably instinctive reactions to the plight of abused and seriously neglected children. Self-protection is also a powerful motive for social workers, especially in the wake of child abuse scandals in which social workers have misjudged parents. Moreover, there are now legal principles which should act as a counterbalance to assumptions that social workers are primarily concerned with families and that the interests of parents and children are essentially the same. The Guardianship of Minors Act, 1971, enunciated the principle that 'in any proceedings before any court the welfare of the child is the first and paramount consideration'. It is anomalous that this principle has, in practice, been taken to apply only to the higher courts in England and Wales and is not applied in the magistrates' courts. For children in Care, local authorities and the courts have a duty imposed by the Children's Act, 1975, in reaching decisions, 'to give first consideration to the need to safeguard and promote the welfare of the child . . . throughout childhood'. Morally, if not legally, there seems no reason why the same principle should not extend to children at risk of coming into Care.

However, there are other considerations which can powerfully suggest that there must be policies which are more just, and more effective, alternatives to bringing children into Care. The first of these is an awareness of the material deprivation and lack of adequate social supports experienced by most parents of children who come into

Care.

Social workers and experts in social administration cannot avoid noticing that children who are admitted to Care almost invariably come from the lowest socio-economic groupings, as has been confirmed in research (Packman, 1966; Mapstone, 1969). Within the lowest groupings, they tend to have poorer housing and a relative lack of household appliances (Quinton and Rutter, 1984a). A high proportion (often over half the total admissions) come from one-parent families (Hodgkin *et al.*, 1983). For some time single parents have been over-represented among parents whose children are admitted to Care (Packman, 1966). Facts such as these strongly suggest that some admissions to Care could be prevented by extra financial help, assistance with housing and provision of support for single mothers and by child-minding arrangements. Such help is often, although not always, provided in Britain by Social Services Departments and the Department of Health and Social Security, although there is a strong case for substantially increasing Child Benefit and providing a realistic income for single parents (Finer, 1974). Natural justice, and a concern for children, demand a change in social policies to ease the burdens carried by poor parents, especially those who are single, but it is not clear that such changes would, by themselves, altogether remove the need for substitute care, since they would not deal with the loss of parents or the relationship difficulties, illnesses, psychiatric disorder and other personal deficiencies in parents which are also often found to be associated with the admission of children into Care (Quinton and Rutter, 1984a; Isaacs, Minty and Morrison, 1986). It would seem that families from which children are admitted to Care are characterised by a mixture of social disadvantage, lack of support and chronic interpersonal difficulties. Quinton and Rutter (1984a, 1984b) found in a study of London mothers whose children had been admitted more than once to residential care that such mothers were characterised by the experience of disrupted childhoods, lack of marital support and material disadvantage. About half were single parents and among the other half there was a high proportion with discordant relationships with husbands/cohabitees or with partners who had been imprisoned. They were significantly worse off in all these respects than a socially disadvantaged comparison group. However, it may be that child-rearing itself can be an even more demanding activity than is sometimes acknowledged. Increasingly, it is recognised that the task of bringing up children within nuclear families, in societies which expect a measure of geographical mobility, is potentially fraught and even demoralising, as well as rewarding and fulfilling. High rates of depression or distress have been found among women with several children living at home, especially young children (Richman, 1982; Brown and Harris, 1978; Moss and Plewis, 1977). It does not appear that the stress of looking after young children is the only causal factor involved. Brown and Harris (1975, 1978) argue that having three children under fourteen at home makes women more vulnerable to the effects of 'life events' involving severe loss or the threat of loss. Other vulnerability factors discovered by Brown and Harris were the lack of a confiding relationship in a husband or partner, the lack of employment and early maternal loss. Brown and Harris (1975) discovered a class bias in depression in women. Significantly more working-class than middle-class women were found to be depressed.

Maternal depression is only one sign, or instance, of stress or of possible difficulties in the parents that can often be treated or helped by psychiatric or social work intervention. Child management problems are (within limits) open to behaviour modification techniques. The task of caring for very young children is often made much more feasible through the help of health visitors and the use of day nurseries and family centres. Other methods that appear to have some degree of success are casework with the parents (Kolvin *et al.*, 1981) and family therapy. It is not at all surprising that the predominant philosophy in relation to child Care for the past two decades has been a search for alternatives to removing children from their own homes. Tearing families apart can appear a fairly brutal and hazardous solution. Helping parents to care for and control their children seems, wherever possible, infinitely preferable. The fact that such methods often work may lead to the assumption that they should always work and that their failure implies a deficiency in technique or in therapeutic skills which can somehow be remedied. Indeed, practitioners in the field of family relationships are sometimes subject to powerful pressures, either from themselves or their agencies, which make it difficult for them to admit failure as therapists. As a result, they may work hard only to achieve a temporary patching over of 'cracks' and difficulties which does not last but which merely postpones the eventual admission of a child to substitute care. Sooner or later practitioners have to come to terms with the unpalatable truth that some parents will never find certain children acceptable and that other parents are simply unable to care for their children. Having accepted that this is the case in relation to particular children and parents, there is no way of avoiding the moral and professional responsibility of intervening before it is too late to try to obtain for a child some measure of affection, care and control that will give it a chance of proper development. The role of the social worker then becomes that of acting as an advocate for the child.

Social workers have sometimes rightly been criticised for failing to protect children when family support and rehabilitation have not worked (e.g. Brent, 1985). In Britain and North America, such failures have led to the deaths of a relatively small number of children and to the permanent disability of a rather larger group. Elmer and Gregg (1967) in a follow-up of fifty children in the USA, physically abused over several years, found only two (4 per cent) were of normal intelligence and development. Seven (fourteen per cent) had died; three of injuries caused by the original abuse but four from other causes, at least two being murdered by their mothers. Five more had been placed permanently in institutions for the mentally retarded.

Some of the children in Elmer and Gregg's study were badly abused children with multiple fractures. A more recent follow-up study in Britain (Lynch and Roberts, 1982) of a wider range of physically abused children found that nearly three-fifths of the abused children showed some developmental delay and a third showed language retardation. Almost a half were 'deviant' on the Rutter 'B' Scale (Rutter, Tizard and Whitmore, 1970), a rate over four times the norm for boys and thirteen times the norm for girls. However, none of the children who had been admitted to Care, and who had experienced several changes in placements, appeared to be well-adjusted.

This brings us back again to the most important reason why some social workers (and others) are reluctant to place children in what is likely to become long-term Care: they think that children may be more harmed than helped in the process. In Chapter 2 we shall examine some of the studies of the outcome for children who have lived long-term in Care. In this section we wish to analyse further what the anxieties are and say something about their origins. There seem to be at least two major sources of anxiety.

In the first place, there are anxieties, to some extent encouraged by Bowlby's earliest work (1946), that the actual separation of children from their parents is inevitably psychologically damaging. This is clearly not always the case. Whether these separations are damaging depends on the circumstances and the frequency, length and nature of the separations. The subject is well reviewed by Rutter (1981). However, depriving parents of their children, and children of their parents, in a fairly fundamental way is such a fraught and drastic step that it can only be justified if the remedy is known to be generally better than the condition it seeks to cure.

In fact, the second source of anxiety is a fear that substitute care will necessarily be deficient; that residential Care will be characterised (at best) by the lack of any life-long commitment by those who 'care' and, very frequently, by a multiplicity and a rapid turnover of care-takers, and that long-term foster care will be characterised by a high number of changes of placement. Maas and Engler (1959), Meier (1965), Murphy (1974) and Tristeliotis (1980) all report on the high number of placements that have been experienced by children living in long-term foster care in the USA, Canada and Britain. Between three and five placements is average. One large American study of children currently living in long-term foster Care found the number of placements experienced by children over a five-year period to be only slightly less than this. Fanshel and Shin (1978) found that, among their subjects who were still in Care at the end of five years, forty-five per cent had had three or more placements (N = 229). On the other hand, Rowe *et al.* (1984), in Britain, found that only twenty-four per cent of the 145 foster children who had been in the same placement three years or more had had three or more previous placements (and forty-three per cent had had only two). The fact that only children who had been three or more years in the same placement were included in the sample suggests that they were a relatively stable group. On the other hand, half these placements had been in jeopardy at some point in the past, so that anxieties about possible separations, and the consequences of interpersonal conflict, clearly apply even to many placements which survive.

In any case, the social worker who arranges for a child's admission to Care cannot control or predict the long-term future. It is impossible to guarantee a continuity of care for a child, in the sense that the same care-taker will look after him throughout his childhood. Even in the most ideal situations, such as in the adoption of young babies by specially selected adoptive parents, it has been shown that, in a fairly substantial number of cases, the child experiences the loss of at least one parent by divorce or death well before he reaches adolescence. Bohman (1970) followed up a cohort of early-adopted children in

Sweden and found that, in a ten year period, eleven per cent of the children had lost at least one parent through divorce and a further two and a half per cent through death. With less ideal placements, there is a much higher loss or turnover of care-takers. The main reason why children in long-term Care experience several moves of home is that placements that are intended to be long-term often break down. Several studies of foster placements in Britain (Parker, 1966; Trasler, 1960; George, 1970) have found breakdown rates of between two-fifths and one-half of all long-term placements within a five year period – or even less. There appears to be no similar study of breakdown rates in residential homes, but Wolkind (1977a) and Wolkind and Renton (1979), in a follow-up study in Britain, found that many of the boys with considerable conduct problems had anta-gonised house-parents and been moved from one home to another.

It would seem that, in deciding to place a child in Care for what is likely to be most of his childhood, social workers should at present assume that, unless he is freed for adoption, he will probably have to experience four or five placements (including an initial period of assessment and possibly a trial period at home). It may well be that current policies on the use of foster parents, together with a prepon-derance of adolescent admissions, have led to even more frequent changes of placement. Milham *et al.* (1986) found that over half of their sample of children and adolescents in Care had had three or more placements over a two-year period, and one in seven had had more than four. Packman, Randall and Jacques (1986) found that four out of five children had moved at least four times in just over six months.

Everybody would accept that this is worrying and unsatisfactory, but it is not clear just how damaging several changes of placement are. If an individual change were, in fact, from a bad placement to one which was more satisfactory, then, in spite of the pain involved, that particular change would clearly be the lesser of two evils for the child. On the other hand, perhaps some placements should never have been made in the first place, and no system of caring for children which, works on the basis of four, five or more placements whilst growing up is really acceptable.

In spite of anxieties about foster placement disruptions and breakdowns, the proportion of children in Care in England and Wales who were fostered rose from thirty-two per cent in 1974 to forty-two per cent in 1982. (Vernon, 1985).

The main, but not the only, anxiety about foster care is that it is subject to disruptions. Most disruptions are likely to be preceded by a period of anxiety, and often by arguments and unhappiness, and the fear of possible breakdown affects many of the placements which survive. Another anxiety is that children in foster care receive inadequate attention from social workers. Severe criticisms were made by the Social Work Service of the Department of Health and Social Services (1982) regarding the failure of British social workers to give children in foster care as much attention as children in residential care. They found that many children who were fostered received less attention than their situation warranted and even less attention than the regulations specified. In relation to residential care, the anxiety is not so much that placements break down, although many do, but that residential care is fundamentally deficient and is, therefore, used only as an 'undesirable last resort' (Barclay Report, 1982). Such attitudes are not confined to less experienced practitioners but are widespread and are shared by some researchers in the field. Prosser (1976), in a report from the National Children's Bureau, summarised the findings in the literature on residential child care from 1967 to 1976 and concludesd:

As a form of provision, it has been used no less, and apparently to no more effect (than in previous years) . . . staff morale seems still to be low. Clearly there is a need to develop and exploit alternative forms of Care which would be less costly in financial terms but, more important, would be less depriving to children. Therefore it is essential that the quality of residential care should be improved for those requiring temporary assessment, for any groups who can be shown to benefit best from this provision, and for children who prove beyond the capacity of alternative forms of care, i.e. as a last resort.

Some social workers and others would go even further than this. The Barclay Report (*op. cit.*) claims that, in British social work, the saying 'a bad home is better than a good institution' still has its adherents. Indeed, many would deny that there is such a thing as a 'good institution'. However, as we have already said, there is a risk that policies may sometimes be pursued essentially for economic reasons, although they are accepted under the guise of psychological health, along the lines of Scull's thesis of decarceration (1984).

The helping professions have been considerably influenced by the work of Barton (1959) and Goffman (1961) in relation to hospitals for the mentally ill, by Townsend (1962) in relation to homes for the elderly, by Morris (1969) and Oswin (1971, 1978) in relation to hospitals for the mentally retarded and by Goldfarb (1943a, 1943b,

1947), Spitz (1945, 1946) and Bowlby (1950) in relation to nurseries and hospitals for infants and young children. The 'literature of dysfunction' has swamped and largely covered what might be called the 'literature of function'. Pioneers such as Steiner (1919), Lane (1928) and Neill (1962) found in residential care a powerful instrument for therapy and the creative education of the young, but their views are not in favour with policy-makers at the present time.

Many other countries place a higher valuation on residential care than is currently found in Britain and America. Wolins (1969) has studied children living long-term in residential homes in Austria and Yugoslavia and found many to be competent and well-adjusted. Other favourable reports on residential training and care have come from Russia (Bronfenbrenner, 1974) and Israel (e.g. Wolins, 1974). In Britain and North America, those who still see potential for good in residential homes for children are now decidedly in the minority.

It is difficult not to feel that the criticisms made of residential Care are often too global and are lacking in discrimination and specificity. Kathleen Jones (1967) pointed out that 'the literature of dysfunction . . . has tended to confuse the elements in criticism, by treating the institutional situation as a whole' (Jones, 1967). It has been assumed that all types of residential care are essentially the same and that they are all unredeemably bad for the individual resident. The use of the term 'institution' has itself become suspect. Do we use it to refer to: (a) all residential settings, or (b) only those residential settings which manifest certain (undesirable) features, such as rigid divisions between staff and residents and a style of operating which has little or no consideration for the needs of the individual residents, or provides little individual care? How many bad features does a Home have to have before it is an institution? Could one speak of 'a good institution'? If not, it would seem necessary to restrict the use of the term to refer only to particular and undesirable instances of residential living or aspects of residential life. The ambiguity in the use of the term 'institution' leads some professional people working with children into refusing to consider the use of residential Care or boarding schools on the grounds that all children living in them are inevitably 'institutionalised'. That is only true in a verbal sense.

Tizard and Tizard (1974) pointed out that

any discussion of the effects of institutional upbringing in children has to take into account the age, handicaps, and length of stay of the children in residence, the type and quality of the care provided in the institution, the alternatives actually, or in principle, available for children not able to be brought up in their own homes, and above all the consequences for the child and for the family of leaving the child at home.

At the present time, a stage has been reached in social policy where, in the first place, so much effort is directed towards keeping children out of Care that it is often difficult to help them when eventually they are admitted (Barclay Report, Paragraph 4.18). In the second place, only the more difficult and disturbed children are placed in residential care, with the result that it is easy to end up with self-fulfilling prophecies.

There is an assumption, in the view of the Barclay Report we have just quoted, that in recent years younger children are less likely to be admitted to Care, but that the policy of preventing their admission sometimes only results in their admission merely being postponed, to their eventual disadvantage. Is this assumption correct?

There is good evidence for a fall in both the absolute numbers and the proportion of under-fives in Care. The proportion of children in Care who were under five remained well over half (fifty-five per cent) between 1956 and 1966, but dropped to just over a third (thirty-six per cent) in 1976. (These figures are for England and Wales, and are taken from Parker, 1980.) However, it is just possible that this argument is rendered invalid by changes in the birth rate. We calculated the proportion of children per total child population in England for the years 1972–1984. (Prior to 1972 official statistics recorded population figures for both England and Wales, but subsequently for England only.) Our findings are presented in Fig. 1. The year 1976 was, in fact, almost a peak year in this period for the proportion of the total population of under-fives in Care, being 3.8 per thousand, which was only exceeded by 3.9 per thousand in the following year. The proportion of the five to fifteen-year-olds in Care rose considerably from 1972 to 1974, possibly as a result of the Children and Young Persons' Act 1969, which transferred to local authority social workers responsibility for the care and treatment of many young offenders – usually adolescents. However, the high water mark for the five to fifteen-year-olds came in 1980 and 1981, with rates of almost 9 per thousand for that age group in Care. (Health and Personal Social Services Statistics for England, 1978, 1982 and 1986.) It is clear that, over a twelve-year period, the proportion of five to fifteen-year-olds in Care has been twice to three times that of the under-fives in the population. The median age for children in Care must have risen considerably between

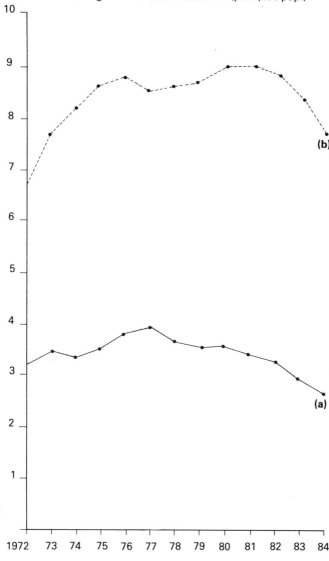

Figure 1
Proportions of the total child population in
the Care of English Authorities 1972-84 – (per 1,000 pop.)

(a) 0-4 year olds = ——————
(b) 5-15 year olds = -------------

1966 and 1976.

It needs to be stated that it is not clear that residential living always damages children and young people. The stigma which the Barclay Report (*op. cit.*) acknowledges is attached to residential Care is certainly not attached to all forms of residential living. Moss, (1975) points out that many independent schools enjoy a high status and, in the UK, their alumni occupy a wholly disproportionate share of the leading positions in politics, the professions and the Civil Service. It certainly cannot be claimed that they are stigmatised by their having lived in a form of residential care, and it is not obvious that most are damaged by their experience. Not all forms of residential care are stigmatising or manifestly damaging. However, to compare boarding school with residential care is to leave out of the equation the families from which the children come. The boy who is at boarding school usually has affectionate parents and a culturally rich life at home and knows that, if he runs into difficulties, parents can be contacted and they will help (Milham, *et al.*, 1986). The child in Care often lacks these supports and lifelines. In addition, the two groups of children will view their situation and prospects very differently. The child at boarding-school (or even a patient in hospital) can convince himself that ultimately he is there for his own benefit and that this experience will help him. The child in Care is less likely to see his placement in a positive light. Usually, he is there either because his parents could not care for him or because society put him there as a punishment.

It is possible that some of the least satisfactory aspects of living long-term in residential care come out most clearly in the retrospective impressions of young people who have grown up in residential care. Triseliotis and Russell (1984) studied in depth the experiences of forty young people who had been in Care for several years, mainly in residential care, and compared them with forty-four young people who had been adopted, all after their first two years of life. The experiences the residential group found least satisfactory were: harsh physical punishment, the rigid application of punishment or rules, the lack of individuality, lack of genealogical information, lack of information about siblings, being separated from siblings, lack of contact with the community and the relative lack of opportunities for closeness with Care staff. However, it must be stressed that these negative experiences were far from universal. Some of the young people brought up in residential care particularly appreciated their closeness to siblings and sixty per cent said they had been close, or very close, to a particular house-parent. It would seem fróm figures given by the authors that almost half were, to some degree, positive about their experience. Thirteen per cent were very positive and the same proportion very negative, with a third having mixed comments. However, just over seventy per cent felt, in retrospect, that having been brought up in a Home created problems for them, in the sense that it made them feel different and sometimes stigmatised.

None of the forty-five subjects in Stein and Carey's study of young people leaving Care found the experience of being in Care totally bad, but most seemed to have found it a mixed blessing (Stein and Carey, 1986). A third seemed to find the experience 'a good thing' and almost half found it good on the whole. (Most of the young people experienced a mixture of residential care and fostering.) The residential experiences that they found most unacceptable and unsatisfying appear to have been the ubiquity of rules, the changes of staff, the lack of knowledge about their backgrounds and, in a minority of cases, physical cruelty.

The latter two aspects of bad care are not confined to residential living, and, as we have already noted, frequent changes of placement are characteristic of much foster care. However, residential care also came in for two other criticisms: that it did not prepare young people adequately for independent living and that it rarely provided after-care or support when young people left Care. These criticisms do not usually apply to long-term foster care in Britain, since most young people who have been fostered long-term will continue to stay with foster parents after Care is officially over.

Another deficiency frequently mentioned is that young people leave Care with very poor educational qualifications. One reason for this, at least for a sizeable minority of adolescents entering Care in Britain, is that they are put into Care for failure to attend school in the first place. Although it is sometimes claimed that poor educational achievement is another indication of lack of commitment by residential care staff, some studies in fact show that children in residential care have achieved higher educational standards than their parents (Triseliotis and Russell, 1984). Indeed, the same study found that the educational standards achieved by a group of children in residential care were higher than those of a group of children brought up in long-term foster care.

In what was, at the time, a fairly definitive review of residential care, Dinnage and Pringle (1967a) concluded that the two most potentially harmful aspects of residential care were: (a) an environment which could be 'psychologically, culturally and educationally restricted . . . even depriving', and (b) the fact that 'unless special steps are taken, children may grow up without a personal sense of identity, lacking a coherent picture of both their past and their future.' Over the past fifteen years a good deal of work has been done with children living long-term in residential care through personal story books and visits to give them a sense of their past. The problems of leaving substitute care, for those who have not been adopted or fostered – long term, are still considerable. (Stein and Carey, 1986; Burgess, 1981). However, with the possible exception of residential nurseries for young children, which may inevitably be psychologically inadequate (Tizard and Hodges, 1978), it is not clear that residential care is always 'culturally and educationally restricted'. It is often claimed that the educational needs of children in Care are neglected, and no doubt this may be true in poor residential and foster homes, but it has to be accepted that most children coming into Care are already educationally and culturally deprived and a minority are admitted specifically for school non-attendance. The study by Essen, Lambert and Head (1976) concluded that the poor educational achievements of children who had been in Care were not due primarily to the Care experience. (The study is discussed in the next chapter.)

In our view, residential living, by itself and especially in large units, usually appears to be inadequate for the emotional and social development of young children. It is not so clear that it is always equally deficient for older children, especially when they have received good enough parenting in earlier years (although sadly this appears to be the exception rather than the rule for children coming into Care). Residential care may well be best: (a) for young people who are so difficult or delinquent as to be beyond the resources of even the most dedicated foster parents, (b) for children who have been so damaged and hurt by bad parenting and repeated foster breakdowns as to be unable to trust foster or adoptive parents for a long time, and (c) as a relatively short-term form of treatment to help children with poor social skills, pathologically anxious attachments to parents or other difficulties that are best dealt with in a group situation. There is also the dilemma of what to do with a large number of siblings who come into Care together. To keep them together may deprive them of the opportunity of being fostered or adopted. On the other hand, they sometimes have strong attachments to each other which foster and adoptive placements may break.

It may be that the apparent deficiencies of residential living for adolescents, as judged by the outcome of some studies, (e.g. Rutter, Quinton and Liddle, 1983), are partly: (a) the result of the size of the units (which were very large in Rutter's study, since all 150 subjects were in one or other of two homes run as group cottages), (b) the quality of care provided, and (c) the lack of any emotional and physical bases to which young people who have left residential Care can turn under stress. None of these deficiencies is completely unavoidable.

In fact, residential homes for children are highly diverse in their nature and in the quality of care they provide. The existence of different styles of residential care has been established by King, Raynes and Tizard (1971) and some indication of the different levels in the quality of Care shown by Berry (1975).

Some children who have been in residential Care have found it a very helpful experience (e.g. the children in 'Mulberry Close' in Mann's study, 1984) and it is difficult to believe that their experiences are entirely isolated.

Perhaps the clearest recorded instance of findings which show the superiority of one type of residential setting over another is Tizard's 'Brooklands experiment', in which sixteen mentally retarded children were removed from an 'austere and impoverished' mental subnormality hospital in the South of England and placed in a small country house (Brooklands), under a house-mother who gradually took over their care. In their new setting the children had far greater opportunities for outdoor activity and play. After two years there was a marked rise in the average verbal intelligence of the 'Brooklands' group. It increased by fourteen months, as compared with a six-month rise in the verbal IQ of the control group. The researchers also formed the strong opinion that the emotional stability, independence and social behaviour of the Brooklands group had improved enormously in comparison with the controls. Their stamina and physical skills had greatly improved (Tizard, 1983). Milham *et al.* (1975) found that among Approved Schools, those which promoted successful staff–pupil relationships, and offered better training facilities achieved a more favourable outcome: there was not only less offending and absconding among their residents, but after leaving their young men appeared to do better in terms of further schooling, employment and closer family relationships. Sinclair (1975) found that Probation Hostels for young men that were run on firm but very supportive lines achieved better results than others. The residents committed less crime while they lived at the hostel.

The fact that the long-term outcome for boys attending residential units for the reform or punishment of delinquency has been generally rather poor has led many researchers to the conclusion that in relation to criminality 'nothing works'. This is seen as further evidence of the uselessness of residential care. A prestigious instance of this line of argument is the study by Cornish and Clarke (1975) which compared boys placed in a therapeutic community with controls allocated (on a random basis) to a more traditional and authoritarian 'house' in the same grounds. Since there was no difference in outcome, Cornish and Clarke claim that it shows the pointlessness of using residential care for this type of problem. Our criticism of this study is that no comparison was made with boys who were treated in the community – quite apart from the fact that, since the boys in the two houses shared many facilities, the effects of the differing régimes must have been somewhat diluted.

Mortimore and Mortimore (1985) reviewed studies of the effects of 'institutions' on children and concluded that the truth about institutions is that they are more diverse than similar. They argued that with proper staff training, and the right type of internal organisation, and, where necessary, external direction and support, institutions can be benign, and not malignant, in their effects on children.

Historically speaking, a considerable amount of creative thinking has gone into the use of group methods of Care for emotionally disturbed and troublesome children (e.g. Redl and Wineman, 1957; Hobbs, 1967; Whitaker, 1979; Hoghughi, 1978). The potential for group treatment and care is well presented in Ainsworth and Fulcher (1981). The general impression is that some of the therapeutic milieus described by these authors must be helpful to some children, although there has been little systematic evaluation. Exceptions to this are the studies reviewed by Durkin and Durkin (1975) and Oliver and Knight's paper (1984) on a follow-up of children treated in a residential psychiatric unit. The majority of the children in the latter study made a great deal of progress, both in terms of symptom amelioration and improvement in scores on the Rutter 'A' scale. This improvement was generally maintained over a period of six to nine months after leaving the unit.

Finally, a common anxiety about children who grow up in Care is not that the current placement is bad in itself, but that children 'drift' along without proper consideration of their long-term needs. The administrative machinery is there (at least in Britain) in the form of statutory reviews, but these are not properly used; (Vernon and Fruin, 1986). We strongly support work towards achieving a greater degree of permanency for children in Care, provided it is done carefully and with an awareness of the range of possible placements that could achieve a measure of permanency.

Interpreting outcome studies

There are relatively few studies of the outcome for children who have been in Care, and even fewer of their long-term outcome as adults. The incides used to describe poor outcome havwe tended to be marital breakdown, alcoholism or vagrancy, convictions for offences and (in women) having illegitimate children and miscarriages. Social change has led to questioning the value and sex bias implicit in some of these criteria.

There are great temptations to think in terms of 'post hoc, ergo propter hoc'. Although many young people who have been 'in Care' at some stage of their childhood are subsequently delinquent or have considerable difficulties in their capacity to persist in 'loving and working', it does not follow that their problems are necessarily a result of their having lived 'in Care'. Children and young people could be damaged, or have their needs inadequately met, before, during or after their period in Care. If the 'damage' occurred during their period in Care, they could be adversely affected either by features of Care itself, e.g. insensitive foster (or house) parents or frequent changes of placement, or by *other* factors which occurred *during* their stay in Care but which the influence of social workers is unable totally to control, e.g. their natural parents may have remarried, disappeared or died, they may have preferred not to visit, or caused embarrassment or failed to show affection when they did, or repeatedly promised to visit and then failed to turn up.

Most children who enter Care are already considerably disadvantaged. Some are already delinquent and many are at least temporarily disturbed in their social and emotional development. It should also be remembered that children and young people may also be adversely affected by what happens to them after their discharge from Care.

Most of them return to the homes from which they were originally admitted, although, in many instances, the composition of the family will have changed considerably during their absence, as was found by Milham *et al.* (1985) in their study of children admitted to Care in five English local authorities.

In some cases the situation will have improved, but in others parents will still have considerable difficulty in providing adequate care. This was recently found to be so by Tizard and Hodges (1978) in their study of young children admitted to residential care in London. Studies of young people who leave Care with no families to go to have all found that the young people concerned find this an extremely difficult time (e.g. Stein and Carey, 1986; Brearley, 1982; Mann, 1984; Burgess, 1981).

Dinnage and Pringle (1967) claimed, in their review of the literature on residential care, that there is an association between having been in Care (among other factors) and subsequent delinquency, illegitimate pregnancies and mental illness. There is some evidence to support their claims in relation to illegitimate pregnancies and delinquency. Wolkind (1977b) found, at an ante-natal clinic in London, that were significant associations for young women between having been in Care and having subsequent illegitimate births. Ferguson (1966) found that the proportion of young men committing offences in Glasgow was much higher if they had been in Care than if they came from the working-class population generally. However, it does not follow that these undesirable aspects of outcome were caused by the experience of being in Care.

It is possible that, in many cases, admission to Care fails to make good severe deficiencies a child has already suffered prior to his admission to Care, or to modify behaviour that had been unsatisfactory for a long time before his admission. Society expects that Care will, in some measure, repair emotional damage, compensate for deficiencies and modify antisocial behaviour. It is disheartening and worrying when this fails to happen, but there is an important difference between failing to correct pre-existing impairments and distortions in development, and causing actual damage. Furthermore, in spite of the evidence available on the reversibility of adverse development (Clarke and Clarke, 1976), in practice it often appears to be very difficult, within the space of even a few years, to undo the damage done by living for many years in violent, sexually abusive or emotionally rejecting homes. This claim cannot, of course, be made in relation to children who were separated from their parents in very early infancy and who lived for most of their childhood 'in Care'. For this reason the study of adults who have grown up virtually in Care is particularly important.

What is the evidence that living long-term 'in Care' is damaging?

In order to answer this, it is necessary to review various areas of study. We shall look at these areas in the following order:

early research into residential care

follow-up studies of children who have been in residential care into adult life

follow-up studies of children who have been in foster care into adult life

follow-up studies of adopted children into adult life

the assessment of the psychological well-being of children in Care

studies of the home backgrounds of children who enter Care.

2

Overview of research

and childhood shows the man,
As morning shows the day.
(Milton)

Substitute care is not at all a homogeneous entity. Crude distinctions can be made between residential care, foster care and adoption. Child care has been greatly influenced by swings in fashion as to which forms of care are best for children. A full review of the policy issues in this area has recently been undertaken by Fuller and Stevenson (1983). In our own review, we wish to focus mainly on studies which provide evidence of the long-term outcome of different kinds of upbringing outside the natural home.

2.1 Early research into residential care

There is a long history of research on orphaned or abandoned children living in institutions, going back over sixty years. Fernald (1918), Terman and Wagner (1918) and Crissey (1937) all found that children living in institutions appeared to be retarded in intellectual development compared with normal children. Crissey (1937) found that, on the whole, the longer the stay in institutions, the poorer the IQ.

Social workers and others have been greatly influenced by the research of Goldfarb (1943, 1945, 1947), Spitz (1945, 1946) and their successors and, above all, by Bowlby (1946, 1950), who had a direct influence on the development of Child Care services in Britain (Packman, 1975). For this reason it is necessary to look at their work.

Goldfarb (1943, 1945, 1947) reported findings of serious retardation in cognitive, social and language development in children who had been brought up, until the age of three, in a residential nursery, as compared with a matched comparison group who were brought up during the same period by foster parents. However, the conditions of the nursery were appallingly bleak in relation to infants' needs for stimulation, affection and social intercourse. Spitz and Wolf (1946) describe the sadness, apathy and withdrawal found in many children aged six to twelve months living in hospital wards, after they had been separated from their mothers and no substitute was available.

Findings of this nature were substantially repeated in many studies of babies and young children living in highly unsatisfactory residential homes and hospitals. Most of the studies written in English are reviewed by Dinnage and Pringle (1967b). With the benefit of hindsight, it no longer surprises us that young children brought up in such hostile environments were severely deficient in their cognitive, emotional and social development. Many of the appalling features of institutional Care in the 1930s and 1940s are mercifully no longer to be found. Bowlby himself (1957 ed., p. 36) made a point of saying that the institutions studied by Goldfarb 'lacked the elementary essentials of mental hygiene: babies below the age of nine months were each kept in their own little cubicles. . . . Their only contacts with adults occurred when they were dressed, changed or fed by nurses'. However, most institutions are not as bad as these. Some studies have even shown that the right kind of residential care can lead to improvements in IQ scores (e.g. Reymert, 1940; Clarke and Clarke, 1954). In any case, it would be unjustifiable to generalise, from findings about the development of small orphaned children, about the use of residential care for children of all ages, and in other, and quite different, predicaments.

More recently Tizard and Hodges (1978) found that young children who had lived continuously in a large residential nursery from only a few months of age were significantly deficient in their social development at the age of eight years, but they were *not deficient* in their cognitive development. The nursery in question was characterised by a discouragement of bonding between particular children and particular staff, and by a marked lack of continuity in caretakers. It is probable that the rather unsatisfactory social development of these children was related to the nursery's policy of discouraging bonding with adults and to the very considerable discontinuities in care-taking which they had to experience. It is just possible that, in a residential home with a stable staff which encouraged bonding and reciprocal affection and trust, the social development of even young children might be satisfactory, although there must be few Homes in Western countries where these conditions exist. Indeed, outside the voluntary agencies (which usually operate on the basis of philosophical or religious beliefs about the nature of relationships) public residential care sadly seems to be increasingly characterised by the lack of a long-term commitment to the children.

2.2 Follow-up studies of children who have been in residential Care into adult life

Ideally, we should distinguish between studies of children who grew up exclusively in residential homes and children who were fostered. From the point of view of research, it is unfortunate that it is hard to find studies of children in the Western world who grew up in residential settings for the whole of their childhood. In this review of children brought up in public Care we shall look first at the adult outcome for children who lived either in residential homes or who (as was more frequent) experienced a mixture of residential living and fostering and, secondly, we shall review studies of children who were more or less exclusively fostered.

An honoured place in follow-up studies of children in Care must go to Otterström's Swedish Study.

Otterström (1956) followed up well over two thousand children living in Malmö. Her knowledge of the parental background of the children and her follow-up data are particularly thorough because of the availability of comprehensive registers on criminal behaviour, alcoholism, vagrancy and dependency on public funds. Her findings are presented with considerable rigour and deserve to be quoted at some length since they do not seem to be well-known among English-speaking students of socially deprived children.

Of her total sample, 1600 children were at some point removed from home to the care of either the Child Welfare Board or 'correctional agencies' during the period 1900–40. Just over one thousand of these were boys and 566 were girls. In addition, she included in her study 745 young offenders who were convicted by the Courts but who had not been brought into Care or sent for correctional training. At the time of her study, the eldest were forty-four years old. Otterström had in fact four sub-groups: (a) children removed from home (without having committed any crime) because conditions were thought 'to be conducive to delinquency', (b) children removed from home after committing offences, whose homes were thought to be conducive to further delinquency, (c) children or young people who were deemed to require special education or training because of 'delinquency, idleness or licentiousness', and (d) young persons convicted by the juvenile courts who were not in Groups a to c (the upper age limit for 'young people' in Sweden was eighteen years until 1926, and twenty-one from that year onwards).

Although the official terminology used by her appears somewhat redolent of a moralistic interference in the lives of the poor, Otterström demonstrates clearly that the children in Groups a and b came from the most disadvantaged homes and stayed longest in Care, but that they were significantly *less* likely to be criminal in adult life. They were also significantly *less* likely to appear on registers for vagrancy, alcoholism or financial dependence on public funds.

Skeels (1966), in a long-term follow-up study, showed how a creative use of residential living might be made through capitalising on young children's attachments to older 'sisters'. Some orphan children were removed from a poorly-run orphanage and placed judiciously in hospital wards for mentally retarded children, where bigger 'sisters' took a motherly interest in them. This experience was used to prepare the children for later adoption. The children in the experimental group were infinitely better off as adults in terms of socio-economic status and self-reliance than children who had grown up in the orphanage. They also appeared to have higher intellectual levels than their biological parents.

It is admitted that the positive outcome of Skeel's subjects cannot be said to be entirely due to their good experience in residential settings but is probably largely due to their later adoption. However, residential care was used positively as a preparation for this.

Maas (1963) has undertaken one of the few long-term follow-up studies (outside Israel) of children who were drawn from a cross-section of the population, rather than an already deprived group, and who experienced a fairly prolonged period of residential care in early life.

Maas examined, by interview and projective tests, twenty English children who had been evacuated to residential nurseries in rural areas between the ages of one and four years during World War II. At the time of interview they were aged between nineteen and twenty-six. He was particularly interested in assessing their capacity 'for feelings, for inner controls, relationships with other people, performance in key roles and intellectual functioning'. On the basis of the interview reports, James Robertson and his wife made independent ratings of each subject and projective stories were rated independently and 'blind'. Twelve of the twenty respondents showed no abnormal ratings and three more had only ten per cent abnormal ratings. Maas concluded: 'where there is evidence in individual cases of aberrancy in the adjustment of these young adults, in almost every case the data on their (natural) families seem sufficient to explain it'. On the other hand, it has to be borne in mind that these children did not remain throughout their childhood in large residential settings. Return home may well have offered them experiences which might not have been otherwise available, e.g. the security of belonging, personal interest in them and a physical and emotional base in young adult life. Most of the families from which they were evacuated, and to which they returned, were a cross-section of the population and presumably offered 'good enough parenting'.

Recently, Rutter, Quinton and Liddle (1983) have published the first details of a major follow-up study of children brought up in two large cottage homes in their adolescence. The outcome for the women, in relation to their psychosocial development and mothering skills was, in many respects, disappointing. The 'ex-care' group were significantly more likely than women in a comparison group to manifest a current psychiatric disorder, a personality disorder, to have been involved in crime, to have had one or more broken cohabitations, to have marked mental problems and to describe substantial difficulties in love/sex relationships. A significantly higher proportion showed poor parenting skills. (Nearly half, as compared with ten per cent of the comparison group, showed poor parenting skills. On the other hand, nearly a third of the ex-care group showed good parenting.)

Rutter, Quinton and Liddle (*op. cit.*) used a scale of social functioning. This was complex overall assessment based on weighted ratings: of the presence or absence of personality disorder, longstanding difficulties in past sexual or love relationships; whether or not there were current difficulties in the marriage (or the marriage was broken); whether there were problems in social relationships; whether subjects had committed crimes or suffered from psychiatric disorder, and whether they were living in hostels or other sheltered accommodation. Nearly a third of the girls who had been in Care showed evidence of poor social functioning as adults, as contrasted with none of the girls in the comparison group. To a considerable extent, problems in pre-adolescent and early teenage years 'constituted precursors of later parenting difficulties'. The sub-group of girls (N = 10) who had been in Care longest showed the highest proportion with poor parenting, although this comparison did not reach statistical significance, and the authors claim that both 'institutional rearing' and living in discordant homes were associated with high rates of poor parenting. It also emerged that sixty-four per cent of girls who became pregnant before eighteen were poor parents, as compared with thirty-two per cent of girls whose first baby was born later. Single mothers, mothers with an unsupportive spouse, or a spouse with psychosocial problems, tended to show poor levels of parenting.

Rutter *et. al.* (*op. cit.*) suggest that the backgrounds of living in: (a) institutions, with multiple changing care-takers with whom there are no close ties, and (b) unhappy, conflictual natural families *both* predispose to a poor outcome. On the basis of his data, it is possible to postulate that both of these backgrounds either work directly through effects on personality development or more indirectly through trapping a girl into early pregnancy and marriage or single parenthood. It remains open for us to ask: (a) to what extent Rutter's findings are repeatable – and the numbers in his subgroups are relatively small, (b) whether the features of residential care he studied are modifiable or necessary and inevitable, (c) whether the poor outcome of his subjects is largely the effect of living in poor public care or a result of inadequate care at home, and (d) whether residential care has different effects on girls as distinct from boys.

The findings of Rutter *et al.* (*op. cit.*) are confirmed to some extent in a longitudinal study of primiparous women conducted by Wolkind and his associates (Wolkind, 1977; Kruk and Wolkind, 1983). The women were interviewed during pregnancy at an obstetric booking clinic in a socially deprived area of London and followed up for approximately four years. There were significant associations between having been in Care for *any* period and being under twenty years of age, being unmarried, having housing difficulties and scoring highly on the Rutter Malaise Inventory. However, follow-up did not reveal an association between being single, or even being extremely young (i.e. sixteen or seventeen years of age) at conception, and having children with manifest behaviour problems when they were three and a half years of age. On the other hand, women who had been in residential Care were significantly more likely than other women to have had children with behaviour problems.

This raises again the issue of whether being in Care, especially in residential care, is damaging. There is a strong possibility that girls admitted to residential care come from homes that are particularly deprived and that many will have had behaviour problems before entering Care. Kruk and Wolkind (*op. cit.*) put forward the view that their single young women were particularly disadvantaged by their current lack of any collaborative support from their own mothers in caring for their babies. If so, this suggests that women who have been in Care may need special kinds of help when they leave, if they are to have anything approaching the same level of support as is available to other women in the community from their parental and extended families.

We have previously mentioned the study of Triseliotis and Russell (1984) which compares the outcome of a group of children in Care who were adopted with a group who remained in residential care. The two groups, each consisting of about forty subjects, were followed up into their twenties and interviewed at depth. On almost every measure of outcome, the adopted group fared better than the residential group, often significantly so. The residential group were significantly more likely to be judged to be disturbed, to drink more heavily, to attend doctors more frequently, to have problems in making friends and to express less satisfaction with current circumstances. They were also significantly more likely to have mixed or negative feelings about their Care experience (with a third expressing mixed views and thirteen per cent expressing mostly negative views). There appeared to be connections between deficiencies in upbringing and later problems, e.g. those children who moved more frequently while in Care were more likely to be referred to a psychiatrist as adults and residential subjects who expressed problems in making friendships were said to be more likely to have found it hard to get close to residential staff.

It is difficult to be certain about the direction of cause and effect in these connections and, although it is clear that the adopted group appeared to come out of the experience of substitute care better than children in residential care, at least four points have to be borne in mind: (a) the adopted group came into Care much younger than the residential group (two-thirds of the adoption group came into Care before their first birthday compared with only one in eight of the residential group, forty-five per cent of whom came into Care when five years or older, compared with only one of the adopted group), (b) the natural families of the residential group appeared from the records to be significantly more disturbed than those of the adopted group, (c) there is a marked sex difference in the two samples, with almost two-thirds of the adopted group being male, compared with only thirty-eight per cent of the residential group, and (d) it is quite possible that residential living has a different effect on girls than on boys. Certainly outcome measures have to be understood differentially in relation to the two sexes. Apart from this, the study does not compare the effects of living in residential care with those of living in inadequate natural families. Even if we were to accept that the study demonstrated the superiority of adoption to living long-term in residential care, it would still not demonstrate that living in group homes was the most detrimental alternative for children lacking adequate parents. Nevertheless, the overwhelming impression of the study is that young people who had grown up largely in residential care did less well than other children who had been admitted to Care but then adopted, whatever the reason for this difference.

The study of Stein and Carey (1986) focused largely on the difficulties experienced by young people on leaving Care – a time when, for some of them, their real troubles began. Most of their sample of over forty young people came into Care as adolescents and experienced a mixture of residential care and foster care. The aspects of residential care they objected to most were harsh punishment (which appeared to have occurred in a small minority of both foster and residential homes), the lack of privacy and freedom, and the frequent changes of placement with the need to get to know new people and routines. There was some criticism of the failure to prepare them for independent living but (possibly) more of the apparent lack of concern by Social Services Departments for them after they had left Care.

Two other studies deserve mentioning, if only because they record in detail the memories of adults who had been in Care and who appear to have had, on balance, a positive experience of Care. Kahan (1979) describes in depth the recollections of a group of ten adults who had all spent considerable periods as children in Care. Their experiences of substitute care were very mixed as to the type and quality of the placements and whether they generally succeeded or broke down. In her conclusion, Kahan says: 'they clearly felt positively about some, perhaps a majority of their experiences of the child care service . . . they were positive people, who, in the main were succeeding in general living'.

Mann (1984) records her interviews with fifteen adults (aged between approximately seventeen and thirty-two) whom she had known previously as their Child Care Officer when they were in long-term Care as children. On the whole, the children spoke affectionately and positively about their surrogate parents and care-givers but were more ambivalent about their social workers. Many found leaving residential Care a difficult time and some were very critical of the lack of help available from social workers and Social Services Departments in that period. In a period of considerable unemployment, nearly all were employed. For nearly all, their childhoods had at times, been very painful, and some had still not come to terms with parental rejection or their parents' inability to care for them.

2.3 Follow-up studies of children who have been in foster care into adult life

Theis (1924) followed up 235 children in New York who had been fostered long-term or adopted. At the time of the study they were between eighteen and forty years of age. Only a tiny minority were judged to be 'incapable'. Fostering (and adoption) appeared to have prevented the children of alcoholic and criminal parents being adversely affected by the deficiences and problems of their biological parents. However, subsequent studies by Cadoret and Cain (1980) and Hutchings and Mednick (1974) suggest that adoption does not altogether prevent the inheritance of predispositions to alcoholism and crime.

Ferguson's study (1966) was, until very recently, the most comprehensive follow-up published so far of children who had been in the Care of a local authority in Britain. Two hundred and five young people, who had been in the Care of Glasgow Children's Department, were followed up on leaving Care to the age of twenty. When in Care the majority had been fostered, often at a considerable distance from Glasgow. The employment records and criminal histories of the young men were distinctly poorer than those of working-class boys in general in Glasgow. They were more like those of boys who had attended special schools for the moderately retarded. Twenty-five per cent of the young men had committed offences between fifteen and seventeen years of age and fifteen per cent at eighteen years and over. Many of the young men had especially poor work records for the early sixties, with nearly a third having four or more jobs in two years. However, many of Ferguson's subjects were of low intelligence and he found there was an association between low intelligence and having a poor work record. Boys who had stayed with their foster parents appeared to do better than boys who returned home or who went elsewhere. In this respect, fostering in Scotland appeared to have had a very considerable advantage over fostering in Montreal (Murphy, 1974, discussed below). Ferguson found, however, that a quarter of his subjects had left their foster homes in the two years after they had left Care. Young men who had been brought up in Care changed their residences more frequently than the general population of the same age. They seemed to experience greater uncertainties and difficulties than those with a stable home background.

Meier (1965) reports on a follow-up of seventy-five children who had been in foster care in the USA. Most of the subjects seemed to be holding their own in a socio-economic sense, but the females seemed to be at a disadvantage in their reproductive and marital histories. One-third of the women (i.e. fifteen) had, between them, thirty-two miscarriages. All the women had married but the proportion who had separated and divorced was between two-and-a-half to three-and-a-half times the American rate for the period. Having a large number of placements in foster care did *not* itself seem related to poor outcome, but the quality of the most significant relationships with foster parents appeared to have consequences for good or ill.

Meier's findings are partly confirmed by Murphy (1974) who followed up 316 former foster children in Montreal, thirty being followed up in considerable depth. One of Murphy's major findings was that seven of the thirty had been married and divorced, and two more had gone through a series of cohabitations. Twenty-six of the thirty had married and had forty-two children in aggregate, although their mean age was only twenty-eight. The proportion 'married and divorced' was much higher than the Montreal norms for the period. Murphy suggested that a common feature in the former foster children was a 'precipitate desire for marriage and the home, combined with a low tolerance for the demands these can make'. Murphy rated fourteen per cent of all the males (N = 202) and twenty-six per cent of all the females (N = 114) as poorly adjusted in adult life, by which he meant that there was 'solid evidence of some mental or social disturbance'. Poor adjustment appeared to be associated with two factors, one relating to the natural home and the other to Care. Half the girls with poor adjustment had had mothers who were either unmarried or 'casually separated' and who were, for these reasons, unable to provide adequate care. Only five per cent of girls admitted to Care because of parental death were poorly adjusted as adults, as compared with sixty-five per cent of girls whose mothers were unmarried at the time of their placement. The other factor strongly associated with poor adult adjustment was 'a strong identification with the foster mother'. This is surprising, but is probably due to the fact that in Montreal it appears to have been the expectation that foster children left their foster homes as soon as payments ceased. This may well have been experienced as a considerable rejection by the foster children, some of whom must already have felt rejected by their natural parents.

Triseliotis (1980) studied a group of forty children in long-term foster care in Britain and followed them up until they were twenty or twenty-one years of age. Over two-thirds of the placements had been regarded as satisfactory, or very satisfactory, by both the parents and the 'children'. Eighty per cent of the foster children had enjoyed steady work records, albeit in unskilled or semi-skilled work. Twenty per cent had been convicted between the ages of seventeen and twenty, although most of the boys with convictions had had long histories of problems with behaviour or delinquency. The quality of the foster parent/child relationship seemed to be of more importance than whether the child had retained contact with his natural parents.

Zimmerman (1982) interviewed sixty-one young adults from a sample of 170 who had been in foster care in the USA for one or more years, and compared them as young adults with a group of young people matched for age, sex and social and ethnic background. There was little difference in the two groups, although the Care group had somewhat lower educational achievements and slightly more health problems. However, two-thirds of the ex-Care group were judged to be self-supporting, law-abiding individuals, who were caring adequately for themselves and their children. Moreover, two factors were associated with good functioning as young adults: remaining in Care until reaching adulthood and regular attendance at High School (and obtaining good grades).

Comment

The picture presented so far in sections 2.1 to 2.3 is one in which the outcome for children who have been in Care is neither altogether disastrous nor completely reassuring. Theis (1924), Triseliotis (1980) and Zimmerman (1982) present findings about long-term fostering that suggest that it can be a satisfactory form of upbringing.

If we put aside the early studies of very young children in residential care, on the grounds that the care provided was often appallingly bad, the studies tend to present a mixed outcome, and some (e.g. Otterström, 1956) present a rather optimistic picture. Only two studies present a comparison of the outcome of living for a considerable period in Care with the outcome of either living at home with very inadequate parents or returning home to very inadequate parents, i.e. Otterström (1956) and Tizard and Hodges (1978). The studies focus on different age groups and use different indices of outcome, but both of them suggest that the outcome of living 'in Care' is better than that of living with very inadequate parents. Otterström's study suggests, by her criteria, that the substitute Care available in Sweden before the Second World War was associated with a *much* better outcome.

Some of the studies (e.g. Otterström, 1956; Murphy, 1974) strongly suggest that what happens to deprived children before they enter Care may strongly influence their outcome. Others (e.g. Murphy, 1974; Rutter *et al.*, 1983) present findings which suggest that what happens to young women on leaving Care is crucial in influencing whether they become competent or poor parents.

2.4 Follow-up studies of adopted children into adult life

Since adoption in Britain has only relatively recently joined the mainstream of choices open to children in Care, it could be held that it falls outside the remit of this monograph. On the other hand, adoption could be viewed as the most radical and thorough form of substitute parenting and, as such, outcome studies of it are relevant to our assessment of the possibilities of growing up in Care. It is also true that some experts in child care have, with research to substantiate their views, been calling for some time upon social workers to make much more use of adoption in trying to find the best upbringing for children who (for one reason or another) cannot be cared for by their own parents (Maas and Engler, 1959; Rowe and Lambert, 1973; Emlen & Cascaito, 1978; Lahti *et al.*, 1978).

On the whole, studies of adoption show that the experience is satisfying for the great majority of children and parents involved, but this is a slight over-simplification. Most follow-up studies into adult life report that the majority of subjects had adjusted at least reasonably well to adult living (Theis, 1924; McWhinnie, 1967). On the other hand, about a quarter to a fifth of adopted children, or their parents, had not found the experience satisfactory. The studies mentioned so far are all mainly of adopted babies. Kadushin (1970) reports on ninety-one children adopted between five and eleven years of age. In the great majority of cases the adoptions seemed to have worked well.

In some studies it has been found that children of criminal or alcoholic parents did not inherit their natural parents' failings (Theis, 1924; Bohman, 1970) but, as has already been noted, some studies comparing the criminal histories and the 'problem drinking' of adopted boys and of their natural and adoptive fathers show that, where natural fathers had problems in drinking or had recidivist records in crime, their adopted sons appeared to have a greater than normal tendency to have similar problems (Cadoret and Cain, 1980; Hutchings and Mednick, 1974). Goodwin *et al.* (1973 and 1974) found strong evidence that the adopted sons of natural fathers with alcohol problems were significantly more likely to have similar problems themselves. This suggests that they inherited personality or temperamental characteristics which led them to abuse alcohol (and possibly other drugs), perhaps as a means of coping with stress.

One careful study of children adopted soon after birth found a slightly, but significantly, raised proportion of eleven-year-old boys with behavioural disturbances, which seemed unrelated to what was known of their natural parents or perinatal pathology. Possibly the increase in disturbed behaviour was related to the adoption situation itself (Bohman, 1970). On the other hand, a follow-up of children adopted at birth in Britain, compared with illegitimate children who might (in theory) have been adopted, revealed that the circumstances and development of adopted children was in almost every way superior (Seglow, Pringle and Wedge, 1972).

We have twice already briefly discussed the study by Triseliotis and Russell (1984). Although the vast majority (over eighty per cent) found their childhoods a satisfying or very satisfying experience, just under a fifth were more critical, and this was especially pronounced among children adopted by professional or managerial parents, where some children felt pressurised to succeed academically. Although the upward movement in terms of social class among many adopted children is generally regarded as a bonus, perhaps for a minority this has penalties in terms of parental expectations.

The Oregon project is of particular importance to social workers in showing how adoption can be used successfully for children in Care who appear to need a permanent placement and who are deemed unlikely to return home. Just over one-third of children (N = 509) aged between one and twelve were adopted either by their previous foster parents or new adoptive parents. A further one in ten children remained in foster care with a clear long-term agreement in relation to the placement. A quarter of the children returned home. Most of these arrangements appeared to be stable over a three to four year period and 'parent' satisfaction was high, including that of the adoptive and foster parents (Emlen and Cascaito, 1978; Lahti *et al.*, 1978).

Comment

In our view, adoption deserves its reputation as the best form of substitute care available to many children, but we should not overlook the fact that in a minority of cases (perhaps about a fifth) there do seem to be considerable problems. We have anxieties about policies which can aggressively pursue adoption when other forms of substitute care seem more likely to meet the needs of particular children, e.g. fostering with a view to custodianship, for a child with some links to the natural family, or small-group living either for children who have been so hurt by losses, rejections and abuse that they are unable, at least for some time, to place great trust in parental figures or for children who are so difficult that foster parents cannot cope.

Although we strongly support the greater use of adoption for deprived children with no family attachments and little or no chance of ever returning home, not all children in Care are suitable for adoption, and the fact that in an appreciable minority of cases (a fifth to a quarter) there is a rather poor outcome is itself an argument for caution.

Children who are older when received into long-term Care may already have a sense of their own identity, as belonging to a certain family, and may view any suggestion to change their name as a powerful threat to who they are. They may have attachments to their parents, their siblings and their extended families which they do not wish to lose and which adoption, as traditionally conceived, would sever. Children who have experienced repeated rejections may not for a long time be able to face the emotional closeness that is part and parcel of family life. Social workers have legal and moral responsibilities for children in Care and these can only be transferred when there is a high expectation that an adoption placement will not only last but will also really meet a particular child's needs. With the implementation of provisions in the Children Act 1975 for long-term foster parents to become custodians, fostering can also achieve permanency.

2.5 The assessment of the psychological well-being of children in Care

Numerous small-scale studies have been undertaken of the emotional and behavioural adjustment of children in Care. Abstracts of those written in English are already available in Dinnage and Pringle (1967a), Dinnage and Pringle (1967b), Prosser (1976) and Prosser (1978). Almost all studies confirm that there is a significantly higher proportion of children in Care with behavioural and emotional problems than in the population generally.

Wolkind and Rutter (1973) reporting on findings from the Isle of Wight study and an inner London Borough, found a significantly greater proportion of children who had been in Care had high levels of conduct and emotional disturbance. However, this was true whether the children had been in Care for long or short periods. Thorpe (1980) found equally high levels of disturbance in children in foster care as in residential care.

Hilda Lewis (1954) completed a psychiatric study of 500 children admitted to a reception centre in Kent between Autumn 1947 and Summer 1950, and assessed 321 to be delinquent and 181 to have a neurotic disorder. She found that there were significant associations between being described as manifesting 'unsocialised aggression' and having either a mother or a father who lacked affection, and also between being diagnosed as 'neurotic' and having a mother who was mentally ill. She did not find that there was more delinquency or incapacity for affection in children who had experienced early separations from their mothers. Children from very poor homes appeared to be more damaged than children from institutions.

Essen, Lambert and Head (1976), drawing on data from the National Child Development Study, showed that, although the reading and arithmetic scores of children who had been in Care were poorer than those of the general population, children who had been in long-stay Care (i.e. longer than six months) did better than children in short-stay Care and, in relation to reading scores, the difference was significant. Those children who were in Care early, but not at eleven, diverged most strongly from the normal population between the ages of seven and eleven. These findings suggest that the Care experience itself did not cause the poor academic progress. These are important findings, especially since the experience of Care is itself blamed for the often poor educational achievements of children who leave Care.

Lambert, Essen and Head (1977), drawing on the same data, compared findings collected at the first follow-up point at seven years with data from the second follow-up point at the age of eleven. In this way they were able to compare the adjustment of children who had been in Care before seven years, but who had also been discharged by the age of seven, with children who had not been admitted to Care by seven years of age but who were admitted by the age of eleven. (Children had been tested on the Bristol Social Adjustment Scales at both points in time). Children who had been in Care by the age of seven and returned home had the same proportion with scores indicating maladjustment as children who had not yet entered Care but who did so between the period of seven and eleven years of age. Children who had remained in Care throughout the period had only very slightly higher proportions with scores indicating maladjustment. These findings suggest that it was not Care so much as the home backgrounds that led to maladjustment. Wolkind and Rutter (1973) found, in the study already referred to, that over two-thirds of boys who had been in Care and who manifested conduct problems had been in Care for less than six months. They tended to come from larger families in which the marital relationship was likely to be either 'very poor' or 'broken'.

Wolkind (1977) and Wolkind and Renton (1979) followed up for four years ninety-two children on whom Wolkind had first made a psychiatric assessment very shortly after their admission to Care. Less than one-fifth had returned home. Ninety per cent of children with a conduct disorder were assessed as still having a conduct disorder four years later (N = 27) and nearly half of those with neurotic disorders were assessed as still having a neurotic disorder (N = 33). He suggested (1979, *op. cit.*) that a vicious circle may operate in which children with conduct problems antagonise child care staff and, as a result, are moved to other homes, thus reinforcing their sense of rejection and possibly fuelling their conduct disorder.

Rowe *et al.* (1984) studied just over a hundred children in long-term foster care in stable placements (i.e. they had all survived for at least three years). They presented findings that were, on the whole, reassuring about the happiness of the children and the current satisfaction of the foster parents. Children who had been fostered with relatives seemed to do particularly well.

Fanshel and Shin (1978) report on a follow-up study of 624 children in 'foster care' in the USA whose emotional adjustment was tested by psychologists on the basis of behavioural check-lists, teachers' reports, psychometric tests and projective tests at entry to Care. Five years later, 392 were successfully followed up. Just under sixty per cent had been aged five years or less on admission. More than half (fifty-two per cent) of the children were always rated as 'normal' and twenty five per cent, who had been rated as 'abnormal' or 'suspect', were rated as 'normal' at the end of the study. Twelve per cent moved from an earlier rating of 'normal' to a rating of 'suspect' or 'abnormal'. According to their social workers, thirty per cent of the children still in care at the end of the period had moderate or substantial difficulties. When psychologists approached the parents of children who had returned home, they found that their parents regarded approximately a third as still being 'tense' or 'nervous'. Whatever these terms mean and whatever the precise significance of the psychologists' ratings, the general tenor of the study is that a relatively high proportion of children in the USA who enter Care (i.e. about a quarter to a third) are disturbed in emotions or behaviour both on entering and leaving Care. It is not apparent from this study that those who stayed in Care were more 'damaged' than those who returned home or that the experience of Care was usually damaging in itself, although it appears from the study that possibly a quarter of the children improved and about an eighth got worse.

Packman, Randall and Jacques (1985) followed up two groups of children from two English towns: (a) all the children admitted to Care in a twelve-month period (N = 125), and (b) all the children considered for admission but not actually admitted (N = 127). Six months to a year later, the proportion of children whose behaviour was perceived by parents to have improved was much the same in both groups, although a slightly higher proportion of parents whose children had not been admitted to Care felt that the decision not to admit had been 'wrong for the family'.

Although not a study of children in Care, Bowlby's longitudinal study of sixty children admitted to a TB sanatorium before the age of four is very relevant (Bowlby *et al.*, 1956). The children spent between six months and two years in a sanatorium and were matched with school class members adjacent in age. At follow-up they were aged between almost seven and just over thirteen-and-a-half. There was no appreciable difference in intelligence or capacity for friendship between these children on leaving the sanatorium, and those in the comparison group and, although the sanatorium group were found to be somewhat more maladjusted, there was no significant difference between their scores and the scores of the comparison group.

Comment

Bowlby's failure to find a significant difference in the emotional well-being of children brought up in a sanatorium for several years of their childhood is an important, if negative, finding. It suggests that children may be damaged, not so much by separations from their parents *per se* (even long-term) or even by institutional living (provided it is not a *bad* institution), but by whether they have had the experience of real care, affection and control from some source before, during (and after) their period of growing up away from their natural parents, and perhaps also by their understanding of this experience and whether it is seen as necessary for health (as in the case of hospital or sanatorium patients) or as a real opportunity for growth and achievement (as boarding school is sometimes seen). Conversely, if it is seen by the child, his family and society as a punishment, a form of coercion, or the least costly way of looking after an unwanted child, it may be that the outcome is likely to be poor. Some hospitals and sanatoria, and most boarding schools, have positive connotations and most children in them retain links with caring families. Unfortunately, these features usually *do not apply* to many forms of public care. In addition, it could be that the more Care is seen by society and the caring professions as 'the undesirable last resort', the poorer will be the outcome for the children who experience Care and who feel stigmatised by being placed in 'undesirable last resorts'.

2.6 Studies of the home backgrounds of children who enter Care

Several studies in Britain and the USA of the home backgrounds of children admitted to Care show something of the extent of the social, emotional and cognitive deprivation experienced by children *before* their admission.

Schaffer and Schaffer (1968) studied the home backgrounds of children admitted to Care because their mothers had been confined for a subsequent childbirth and compared these with the backgrounds of children of the same social class whose mothers were admitted to the same wards for childbirth, but whose children were not admitted to Care. The children who came into Care were significantly worse off in a large number of important social aspects. They were much more disadvantaged in relation to: (a) high density of the population of their neighbourhood, (b) overcrowding in the home, (c) poor standards of cleanliness in the home, (d) several moves of house, (e) lack of support from the extended family, (f) lack of participation by the father in child care and domestic chores, (g) poor maternal standards in child rearing, and (h) a lack of emotional dependence encouraged by the mothers.

Mapstone (1969) retrospectively compared data on the 314 children in the NCDS (National Child Development Study) in Britain who had been in Care for some period in their first seven years with the remainder of the 15,000 children in the study.

Children who had been in Care, mostly for relatively short periods, were bad attenders at school. They were more than three times as likely to be judged to be poor in their social adjustment. (In fact, one third of all the children who had been in Care were judged to be poorly adjusted on the Bristol Social Adjustment Scales.) Half of them were either 'poor readers' or 'unable to read' and this was a significantly higher proportion than was true of the rest, even when matched for social class.

They were five times as likely to be born at thirty-six weeks gestation or under, twice as likely to be five-and-a-half-pounds or less at birth and seven times more likely to be illegitimate.

Quinton and Rutter (1984) found that the homes of children admitted to Care at least twice were characterised by much higher levels of both material deprivation and psychosocial stresses and deficiencies. Material deprivation was measured by the lack of basic housing amenities and normal household appliances. Emotional inadequacies and stressors were measured by disruptions in the mother's background, absence of a spouse or cohabitee, history of psychological disturbance in the parents, marital disharmony and prison record in the spouse or cohabitee.

Isaac, Minty and Morrison (1986) found that over half of a sample of mothers of children admitted to Care in two districts of Wales had seen a psychiatrist in the five years prior to their child's admission to Care and, in two thirds of the families, either the father or the mother had consulted a psychiatrist. Rates of psychiatric disturbance were higher in parents of children who remained longer in Care. For most parents, feelings of anxiety and depression had been at their worst just before the child had gone into Care.

Two other large studies confirm that the backgrounds of children who are admitted into Care come from homes that are very disadvantaged economically and socially. Packman (1966) found that, among a representative sample of children admitted to Care in Britain in 1962, there was an enormous skew towards the lower socio-economic groupings. Essen and Wedge (1982), drawing on material collected in the British National Child Development Study, found that socially disadvantaged children (i.e. children who experienced all three disadvantages of (a) large families or a single parent, (b) poor housing, and (c) low income) were seven times more likely to have been in Care by the age of eleven, and ten times more likely by the age of sixteen. Levine (1972) found low socio-economic status to be a common feature of children in Care in the USA. In other words, it is clear that most children who come into Care are already among the most disadvantaged and deprived members of our society. Some are already 'victims', to use one of Packman's terms (Packman, Randall and Jacques, 1986); i.e. they are admitted to Care because they have been abused and are likely to be abused again. But even if children are admitted because of parental illness, temporary incapacity, or death, the children admitted to Care are likely to have been severely disadvantaged in other respects too. Both they, and young people committed to Care because of their delinquency are very likely to have suffered considerable disadvantage and deprivation in a material, cultural and emotional sense. For some of them, the words 'disadvantage' and 'deprivation' will be rather bland and temperate descriptions of the emptiness and pain of their lives.

Conclusions

We have examined the reasons why social workers have been reluctant to admit children to Care. Amongst these reasons, the considerations most deserving of serious study are the anxieties that living in Care may do children more harm than good.

It is clear from our review that, although all forms of long-term substitute care are to some degree hazardous, some forms usually provide an adequate upbringing for children. The most obvious are adoption (at least as practised until recently) and foster care placements that survive. A relatively small proportion of adoptions (between about a fifth and a quarter) seem to lead to considerable difficulties and dissatisfactions, and many foster parent placements which were intended to be long-term break down.

Disruptions are not the only unsatisfactory aspect of long-term foster care. Experienced practitioners will often find that serious problems are sometimes not reported until there is a crisis, and a study of social work monitoring and support for children in foster care in Britain in the seventies indicated that some foster children were not adequately supervised (DHSS, 1982).

Unfortunately, there is very little longitudinal research on the 'outcome' of living in small family-group homes, where the number of children ranges from approximately six to twelve, and this method of care is being used less and less, partly because such homes are held to be uneconomic and partly because it is believed that residential Care has been discredited.

There does seem to be evidence that living long-term in large residential homes is a deficient upbringing for many children, especially for children of pre-school age. However, there has often been a tendency to make a global condemnation of residential Care and it has been assumed that the deficiencies that have been found are necessarily part and parcel of residential Care, whereas some of them seem entirely remediable. Some features of bad residential Care have probably gone for ever, e.g. intellectual retardation no longer appears to be a feature of young children brought up in residential nurseries, at least in Western countries (Tizard and Hodges, 1978). Critics also tend to forget the fact that there are wide variations in the quality of care provided in residential homes (Berry, 1975) and in the styles of residential living (King, Raynes and Tizard 1971) and there is some evidence, although not a great deal, that different atmospheres may be associated with different outcomes, e.g. Sinclair (1975) found that young men who lived in probation hostels where there was a mixture of firmness and affection were significantly less likely to be reconvicted, at least while they lived in the hostel. Sadly, the level of public care provided in many residential homes for deprived children often leaves much to be desired, but those who struggle to care for and help children in homes are not helped by an ideology which stresses that what they are doing is necessarily deficient and even harmful. In any case, because of the preference for foster care and because of policies aimed at preventing the admission of children into Care altogether, most children who enter residential care are already troublesome and have a history of poor care in their own homes or of foster parent breakdowns before living long-term in residential care.

There are further reasons for residential Care being a less adequate method of care and treatment for children than it could be and for it appearing to be even worse than it is. Only a minority of staff are qualified. Because of policies to combine the care of delinquent and deprived children, and because of economic stringencies, the same home has to try to help and cope with children with very different kinds of problems, and so much energy may be spent in containing adolescents who run away, threaten violence, repeatedly steal and break into property that there is little energy left for caring and therapy. Added to which, there are real dangers of contamination for some children. Boys with no record of convictions may be drawn into crime by seasoned delinquents. Children who have not run away from home may be drawn into absconding by persistent runners. Under such pressures, staff morale can break down and, as a consequence, little effective parenting is possible. A loss of morale however, can also occur in foster care and even in adoption.

It seems unjustifiable, and a serious disservice to some children, to assume that adoption is always better than foster care and that foster care is inevitably better than living in a group home. All these forms of care can be the best form of care for certain children at certain times, although outside Eastern bloc countries and Israel, residential care has been viewed as an inadequate form of long-term upbringing. Because of this, with the exception of religious organisations, there is a widespread unwillingness to make a commitment to keeping a child in the same residential home for good, even while he is in Care, let alone providing him with a base after he has left Care.

The fact that Bowlby's sanatorium children (*op. cit.*) were little more disturbed than a matched control group and that boarding schools do not seem to damage the majority of children who attend them suggests that residential living by itself is not deleterious. However, children in sanatoria and boarding schools usually also have adequate homes of their own, and are likely to view their admission to such schools, or even to hospitals, as either necessary or advantageous to their future. The predicament of children in residential care is quite different; nobody ever puts a really positive connotation on 'being in Care'.

Our overview of outcome studies of young men and women who have lived for part of their childhood in Care leaves us with the following conclusions: (a) that the outcome is mixed, but that it has to be admitted that it often appears to be generally poorer than that of the population at large, although a minority appear to do well, (b) where the outcome is poor, an attribution of blame is frequently made to the Care system alone, instead of to the family and wider social deficiencies that lead to the need for Care in the first place, to the prejudice against children in Care and the failure to support young people adequately when they leave. Most children who enter Care are already seriously deprived in some sense, and some are clearly disturbed. Many children leave Care only to return to more or less the same environment from which they came or to no home at all.

It is extremely hard to disentangle the relative contributions to outcome of: (a) the child's natural home and parenting, (b) his experience in Care, (c) his experience after leaving Care, (d) other environmental factors, (e) the child's natural endowments, and (f) his view of himself as a person who grew up in Care and whose parents, in some cases, rejected him or failed to care for him.

We have only just begun to relate the outcome of children who have lived in Care to important features of the Care experience itself, e.g. age of admission, length of admission, number of admissions, quality of experience and number of placements. Few studies compare the outcome of children who remain in Care with that of children who return to their parental homes or with children who might have been, but were not, admitted to Care. Exceptions to this last point are Tizard and Hodges (1978) and Otterström (1956).

In the first of these studies, although the eight-year-olds who remained in a residential nursery were deficient in their social development, the most deficient group were eight-year-olds who had returned home to parents with poor parenting skills.

In Rutter's study (Rutter, Quinton and Liddle, 1983) the girls who had remained longest in residential Care did badly, but were no worse off than girls who had come from very poor family backgrounds. Otterström (1956) found that the children who had been longest in Care, and who appeared to come from the worst homes, did significantly better than children who were in Care for shorter periods or who were not admitted to Care.

Packman, Randall and Jacques (1986) did not find very much difference in the apparent outcome (judged in terms of behaviour six months later) between a group of children admitted to Care and another group of children considered for admission but not, in the event, admitted. However, as we have already noticed, more parents of the non-admitted group were unhappy with the decision.

Follow-up studies so far published of children in Care over a period of years, e.g. Wolkind and Renton (1979) and Fanshel and Shin (1978), suggest that some children remain disturbed or psychologically maladjusted. Wolkind and Renton (*op. cit.*) reported that almost all the boys with a conduct disorder continued to manifest a conduct disorder four years later. Perhaps Care fails in the sense that it is often unable (at present) to provide adequate remedies for such damage. It is, of course, untrue that 'Care' is a standard or unchanging entity. The quality of Care can be improved, and often does improve when there is adequate training and support, when morale is high and when real effort and resources are put into the provision of substitute care. On the other hand, perhaps some forms of disturbance, e.g. severe conduct disorder, are difficult to rectify and, for this reason, prevention is much better than cure.

3

The study

We share the feelings of outrage concerning the appalling circumstances under which many families have to bring up their children . . . (but) associations with inadequate living conditions provide a very poor guide to levels of disadvantage in other respects.
Rutter and Madge, 1976.

This study is part of an attempt to learn more about how children who had been found by the Health, Education and Social Services a generation ago to be suffering from considerable disadvantages turned out as adults. Our subjects were three hundred children who had been brought up in an inner city area in the North of England (Northtown) and who had been born either towards the end of the Second World War or in the eight years that followed it (i.e. 1944–53). A majority had probably suffered from parenting that was inadequate in a variety of ways and for a variety of reasons. The establishment of a child guidance clinic in the early 1940s, and of a Children's Department in 1948, had produced one (probably unforeseen) consequence: that, in both these agencies, records of the children they had tried to help, and of their family backgrounds, remained for a subsequent generation to study. The records seemed more or less intact and had been maintained in a manner that was uniform in each agency.

Our original intention had been to study the childhood backgrounds of several groups of children known to be at risk of later becoming delinquent or showing other 'signs' of psychosocial stress and failure. We originally planned to compare the outcome of children 'in Care' with: (a) children seen at Child Guidance, (b) children who had appeared before the Courts, and (c) a group of children who came from the same area and social class, but who were not known to have had problems as children or to have been 'in Care'. Unfortunately, it was not possible to obtain adequate cohorts from either the courts or the general population. The court records gave no indication of dates of birth or social class, and probation records had been systematically destroyed ten years after the completion of Probation Orders. School health records had also been destroyed when children reached the age of eighteen. Although the Health Authority gave permission for some members of the general public still living in

Northtown to be included in the study, we did not feel that they would have constituted an adequate control, since Northtown has experienced considerable redevelopment and emigration in the sixties and seventies. On the other hand, in looking for the results of eleven-plus examinations (which were not available), we discovered that the Education Department in Northtown had records of chronic school non-attenders and other pupils appearing before the Courts. School non-attenders often come from socially deprived sections of society and in many ways resemble delinquent children (Tennent, 1970, 1971; Wilson, 1962). It was decided to include a cohort of school non-attenders to complement the cohorts selected from children who had been in Care for two or more years and the children who had been seen at the local Child Guidance Clinic.

Sampling

A search was made through the files of all children born between 1944 and 1953 who had been in the Care of Northtown (for however brief a period) and all cases of children who had been in Care continuously for two years or over were selected. 136 cases (3.9%) were found from approximately 3,500 files (of children who had been in Care up to 1970, when Children's Departments were merged into Social Services Departments). Boys committed straight to Approved Schools were not included, since Approved Schools were not at that time within the Child Care system. The period 1944 to 1953 was chosen for two reasons: firstly, it seemed desirable to go back in time as far as possible, so as to provide a lengthy period of adult life for study and, secondly, because, although records of children born in 1944 onwards were found fairly frequently, before that year they seemed to be increasingly rare and were, therefore, probably untypical.

Four of the 136 cases were excluded, since the files contained no reference to the social class of the parents. The remaining 132 were reduced to 100 by means of random number tables. 59 were male and 41 female. The proportion of boys to girls in the care of local authorities in England and Wales in March 1956 was fifty-six per cent to forty-four per cent (Home Office, 1956).

Matching

Child Care cases were assigned a social class on the basis of their parents' employment (as ranked in the Registrar General's Classification of Occupations). Cases where no classification could be strictly applied (because the father was dead or absent and the mother had full-time home duties) were assigned to an ad hoc Class VI, and cases where the father was chronically unemployed to an ad hoc Class VII. Child Care cases were then matched with Child Guidance cases. Child Guidance files had been stored in bundles according to year of birth and in alphabetical order. In matching children born 1944 to 1948, selection proceeded by taking the first cases that fitted, starting with an A (and working through the alphabet), and for children born 1949–53, by starting with the Zs. A latitude of one social class on either side was allowed, with Social Class III being split into non-manual and manual. A latitude of 18 months on either side of the date of birth was allowed in matching for age, and similar rules were applied in matching children known to the Education Department. This third cohort consisted not only of children whose parents were prosecuted for their children's non-attendance at school, or who were taken to Court themselves on Direction Orders, but also of children whose parents had been invited to meet a subcommittee of the Department for a final warning prior to prosecution. Matching the non-attenders proceeded by selecting all cases of the same age, sex and social class from a total of approximately 4,000 files of children born from about 1940 onwards. 244 cases were selected in this way and reduced to 100 by random number tables where there was more than one appropriate matching case.

Overlap

It is perfectly possible for the same child to be received into Care, seen at a Child Guidance Clinic and reported for school non-attendance. Registers and files of all three agencies were exhaustively checked to discover whether children known to one agency were also known to another. To a limited extent, it had been deliberate policy on the part of agencies to refer cases between one another, e.g. seven children were referred by the Child Guidance Clinic to the Children's Officer with recommendations for Care (which were implemented in five instances). Eight children in Care were referred to a Child Guidance Clinic or Child Psychiatry Department. In at least two instances, Education Welfare Officers seem to have been responsible for referrals of chronic non-attenders to a Child Guidance Clinic.

However, the extent of overlap was very much more than this and was considerably greater than we had expected.

When we excluded males who had died, emigrated or who were no longer 'known' to the National Health Service register, fifty-six of our original fifty-nine males remained. However, there were an additional thirty-four boys, from those initially identified from the Child Guidance and Education samples, who had also been admitted to Care at some period in their childhood, usually for a relatively brief time, sometimes before and sometimes after their referral to the Child Guidance Clinic or their being reported to the Education Department for school non-attendance. The existence of this overlap posed problems in relation to sampling. At first we decided to treat all the boys who had ever been in Care as one group (although, in important aspects, a heterogeneous one) but it was pointed out to us that this might be interpreted as introducing a fatal bias into the sample of boys 'in Care', since the members who were additional to the original sample could not be said to be typical of any sample of boys 'in Care'.

On the other hand, it would not be possible to ignore the fact that these boys had also been in Care, unless, of course, we excluded them totally from the analysis, and to have done this would have also affected the composition of the comparison groups.

It could be argued that the overlap is some proof of the similarity of the social and emotional backgrounds of the boys in the original Care sample and the boys in the Child Guidance and school non-attenders groups. While we feel that there is some force in this argument, it has to be remembered that more boys in the additional Care group tended to come into Care for reasons of delinquency than in the original Care group, sixty-eight per cent of them being admitted after findings of guilt or on remand, as compared with thirty per cent in the original sample. This, however, is an oversimplification, since a number of boys who were eventually committed to Care following convictions or crime had originally been admitted to Care for other reasons – almost half the delinquent boys in the original sample and over a quarter of the delinquent boys in the additional group.

There were other differences between the original and the 'additional' Care samples or groups, although these were nearly always a matter of degree: (a) the original group tended to stay much longer on average in Care, with the median for length in Care falling at eight years for the original Care sample, but at only three months for the additional group (although seven were in Care for two years or more on aggregate); (b) half the additional group were first admitted after the age of ten years and (possibly surprisingly) half were discharged by the age of twelve, whereas the median age for first admission for the original group fell just below six years and over half were not discharged until they were eighteen years old and (c) although the proportions who were committed to Care at some stage by the Courts on 'fit person orders' were roughly equal (being about two-thirds of each group), parental rights were assumed by the local authority on children initially received into voluntary Care in a quarter of cases in the original Care sample but in none of the additional Care group. However, in many respects, the boys from the two groups could be placed on continua, rather than seen as fitting into two mutually exclusive categories.

Our solution to these problems has been to present two, or even three, sets of findings in relation to each variable of the Care experience we have studied: (a) findings relating to the original Care sample, (b) findings that relate to the total Care group, and sometimes (c) findings relating to the original group minus boys admitted for delinquency.

The 'additional' group of boys in Care did not differ significantly from the original group in age or social class. Neither did the whole group of boys in Care differ significantly from the rest of the sample in either of these respects, except that there were more boys in Care who had lost, or never had, a father. (On a Mann–Whitney test the Z score was 2.17 and $p < .05$). It is to be expected that single-parent families would form a higher proportion of the families from which children were admitted to Care.

It is, in fact, our view that the additional boys in the extended Care sample are not untypical of some subgroups of boys admitted to Care. There are instances of: (a) children with personal troublesomeness, or from families with problems, who were referred to Child Guidance or reported to the Education Department and who had also previously been in Care and (b) children who, subsequent to their being seen at a Child Guidance Clinic or reported to the Education Department, were admitted to Care, usually because of the problem behaviour and the difficult home circumstances which had led to referral to a child psychiatrist or active monitoring by the Education Department in the first place. The emphasis on prevention in child care policy has probably led to an increase in the proportion of such children ultimately admitted to Care.

Hypotheses

In previous research it has been found that being in Care has been associated with higher levels of conduct disorder (Wolkind and Rutter, 1973) and having been in residential care has been associated with later delinquency (Dinnage and Pringle, 1967) but these associations hold for whatever the length of period spent in Care. In view of the lack of findings as to how far the consequences of being in Care are affected by the length and nature of Care, the main focus of this study was the outcome for children who had been in Care, recorded offences being chosen as the first index of outcome to be studied. We put forward the hypothesis that boys brought up in Care for most of their childhood would, on the whole, have a better prognosis than other boys in the sample, including boys in Care for relatively short periods. We chose recorded offences as the first index of outcome because they seemed to us to be relatively hard data and having convictions, especially repeated convictions, seemed to be an aspect of adult life that had serious consequences both for the individual concerned and for society. This is especially true when men become violent offenders.

There are, of course, other important aspects of adult living. It does not follow from the fact that individuals have no recorded convictions that they are productive or contented individuals. Wadsworth (1979) in his study of the outcome of family disruptions, as found in the National Survey of Health and Development, discovered that those boys 'discriminated' by early family disruption as likely to be delinquent, but who were not so, were more likely to have been admitted to psychiatric hospitals by the age of twenty-six. Serious mental illness was seen as an alternative outcome of early deprivation. Other criteria of outcome could be a proneness to depression or personality difficulties, or repeated marital breakdown and marked inability to parent one's own children. In this study we have only had time so far to focus on convictions as an index of outcome but, in doing so, we are following in a tradition in this field.

Since the publication of Bowlby's 'Forty-four Juvenile Thieves' (1946), the relationship between 'maternal deprivation', in some form or other, and conduct disorder and delinquency in boys has been repeatedly examined (Wooton, 1959; Andry, 1960, Naess, 1959 and 1962; Wardle, 1961; Rutter, 1971. It has to be admitted that convictions are not quite such hard data as it would at first appear. Much petty crime is never reported and a majority of reported crimes are never 'cleared up'. However, studies which have compared self-reported crime with official convictions have led to the conclusion that most boys who commit repeated crimes are eventually convicted, and this is particularly true of the more serious crimes (West and Farrington, 1977).

Crime and sex differences

Delinquency is very much commoner in boys than in girls, and the difference was even greater at the time when the subjects of this study were growing up. Consequently, we have distinguished the sexes in our analysis and presentation of findings. In fact, there was so little delinquency among the young women in our sample that, apart from one chapter of this book, all the findings and discussion will relate to males only.

The adult outcome for delinquent children

We know a good deal about the adult behaviour of delinquent children and adolescents, and we can use this knowledge in helping to assess the probable consequences of Care. It appears that about half of boys with very serious behaviour problems as children and adolescents will continue to present problems of an antisocial nature until well into adult life. This was the finding of Robins (1966) in her monumentally thorough follow-up of over 500 children and adolescents seen at the St Louis Child Guidance Clinic, and in subsequent research (1978). West and Farrington (1977), Farrington (1979) and West (1982) have discovered roughly similar findings in London in relation to recidivism in men followed up into their early twenties. Some researchers have found even higher rates of crime when following up juvenile delinquents, e.g. only twelve per cent of the 850 delinquent boys successfully followed up by the Gluecks (1934, 1940) for fifteen years had been entirely free of crime in the ensuing period and fifty-eight per cent had been arrested between the ages of twenty-four and twenty-nine.

The levels of adult criminality that can be expected from childhood populations vary according to whether the subjects chosen for study could be described as 'high' or 'low' risk. High risk groups would include boys who already manifested serious conduct problems and who lived in homes characterised by distorted relationships, over-crowding, low social class and parents with criminal convictions. Craig and Glick (1963) found that they could develop a combination of high risk factors, so that only 5.6% of a low risk group became delinquent, as compared with 82.4% of a high risk group.

Wilson (1962) found that just over two-thirds of the boys in her sample of families of truants were officially delinquent by fifteen years of age (although it has to be remembered that she counted appearances in court for school non-attendance and for being beyond parental control as delinquencies). Kvaraceus (1960) and Conger and Miller (1966) both found significant associations between early antisocial behaviour and later delinquency – a finding also confirmed by Mitchell and Rosa (1980) in Buckinghamshire, England.

The quality of the records

All Child Care files contained details as to the circumstances of the child's admission to 'Care', records of statutory reviews of the child's life 'in Care', details of every change of placement, and of any appearances in Court, both: (a) in relation to applications for making or revoking 'fit person orders' (and resolutions removing parental rights), and (b) in relation to charges of delinquency. In almost all cases there were quite detailed descriptions of the family background (except where parents had died or disappeared). There was also an assessment of the child's behaviour in a reception centre. Finally, there was a record of where the child had gone on discharge and this was usually the last note on each file.

Child Guidance records all contained notes written by the psychiatrist, psychologist and psychiatric social worker, together with lists of appointments kept and failed, and a form stating the reasons for closing the case. With one exception, all the children had received psychometric testing on the Stanford-Binet Merril Palmer or WISC Scales and there was either a social history or (occasionally) a briefer report on the social background. The same psychiatrist and psychologist had seen all but two of the cases. Education files contained outlines of family composition, at least one detailed record of attendance over a nine or eleven week period and often several, compiled at different times, with comments by an Education Welfare Officer on the probable reasons for the child's non-attendance. There were records of all court appearances, either for non-attendance or alleged delinquency, with school reports relating to such appearances. Many files also contained minutes of a Co-ordinating Committee on Neglected Children, which indicated that there had been *some* risk of such children being admitted to Care. The mean average figure for attendance at school was 48.5% of the possible number of attendances. When the proportions of actual to possible attendances were categorised into the following percentage bands: 0%–25%, 26%–50%, 51%–75% and 76%–100%, the median fell in the category 51–75% attendance.

The limitations of the data

A serious handicap in working from records is that they do not always tell the researcher the information he would like to have, and they cannot be 'interviewed' for further information. Information appeared to be collected systematically for both Child Care and Child Guidance records in relation to family structure, obvious marital and other family problems and illnesses, parental attitudes to the children and (in the Child Guidance cases) a detailed developmental history. There were other areas where questions were not systematically asked, e.g. about the criminal 'careers' or possible personality deficiencies in the parents or older siblings. A further problem is that it was not always clear whether the fact that the records did not mention something, e.g. aggressive or delinquent activity, implied that it was absent. We adopted a policy of assuming that the absence of a record about a possible problem or symptom could only be interpreted as an 'unknown', except that, in relation to child guidance cases, the fact that severe conduct problems were not recorded during assessments by all three professional members of the team strongly suggested either that they did not exist or that parents either failed to see them as a problem or were less than frank about them. Similarly in relation to children in Care for many years, if there was no mention of severe conduct problems, the assumption had to be either that there were none, or that foster or house parents chose not to mention them. In both these situations we recorded that there were no problems.

We are dependent on the assessments made by Child Care Officers, psychiatric social workers and psychiatrists, who made the original recordings (with no view to their possible use in research). Our impression is that there was a fairly high degree of objectivity in the assessments, particularly since: (a) there was a large measure of overlap between two or more professional workers at the clinic, often over a period of time, and (b) many of the Child Care reports had been made for the Children's Committee and the courts, where they might well be challenged.

Follow-up

Follow-up was done through the National Health Service Records Office, the local Criminal Records Office and the Home Office Research Unit and Criminal Records Office (CRO). Child Care and Education Department files also usually contained very thorough records of juvenile convictions. Data on adult convictions were collected for computation and added to coding sheets *subsequent to* coding the other material, in order that there would be as large an element of blindness in the study as possible.

All the data on the children's social and personal history, current state and circumstances were collected and coded together. After this had been completed, data from the local Criminal Records Office and the National CRO were collated and transferred on to the coding sheets for computation, with assessments of the seriousness-of-adult-crime being added a few weeks after. Only four of the Child Care records, none of the child guidance, and two of the Education Welfare, files contained details about adult convictions.

The National Health Service Records Office was able to confirm which subjects had died, emigrated or of whom they had lost all trace. All subjects were discounted in computation. Table 3.1 shows the extent of cohort attrition.

Table 3.1: *Cohort attrition*

Cause of loss	Male	Female
Died before 18 years	0	1
Died after 18 years	1	0
Emigrated	7	3
Emigrated and returned	0	2
Cannot be traced	3	0
Total cases lost	11 (6·6%)	6 (5·1%)
Remainder	166	117

Identifying cases

When arrested, people may use aliases and false dates of birth and addresses. It is also possible for two (or more) persons to have identical names and dates of birth. To be certain that the subjects selected as children were identical to the subjects in adult criminal records, it was necessary that they should have the same names and date of birth (allowing for common spelling variants and, at most, one discrepancy in digits) and to have come from the same area of the country. In addition, since both local and national criminal records were available, and the local records contained addresses, it was much easier to be confident about identities. Changes of name by adoption were also known, since all the adopted names of the children were already available in the children's records (the children having been fostered prior to adoption).

Measuring crime

All crimes recorded by the researcher were for indictable offences or for serious non-indictable offences such as assault or assault occasioning actual or grievous bodily harm. We also included a few fairly serious non-indictable offences committed in association with indictable offences. The commonest was for driving without a licence, in addition to the conviction of 'taking and driving away . . .' (although the latter crime itself only became indictable in 1964). Driving without insurance was not considered as a separate offence since it would have unduly inflated the number of convictions. Offences were categorised into eight subgroups: (a) Larceny without breaking and entering, (b) Breaking and entering, (c) Crimes of dishonesty (excluding the above), (d) Crimes of destructiveness to property, (e) Violence to persons, (f) Sexual crimes, (g) Taking and driving away, and (h) Other crimes.

Convictions were aggregated both generally and in the subgroups (a–h). Note was taken of the number of times a man was committed to prison (with suspended sentences being grouped separately) and also of the length of committal to prison by the Courts.

Seriousness of crime

There is no doubt that society regards some crimes, e.g. offences involving violence to the person, as being more serious than others. Criminologists widely accept this fact and several attempts have been made to produce a scale of seriousness that appears to reflect the degree of consensus in society that exists about the relative seriousness of different types of offence. Different scales have been proposed by Sellin and Wolfgang (1964), McClintock and Avison (1968) and Wadsworth (1979). Such scales can, at their 'simplest', try to rank individual offences or they may try to combine all the offences committed by the same person within one score and, lastly, they may also try to include 'offences taken into consideration', which are not counted as convictions but confessed to by the individual concerned.

Objections have been raised to seriousness scales on the grounds that: (a) there is less than complete agreement as to which crimes are more serious (Rose, 1966; Pease *et al.* 1977). This applies particularly to sexual and motoring offences. (b) it is not clear (if convictions are aggregated) whether two offences of the same nature are really twice as serious as one, or how differing crimes should be added together (Wagner and Pease, 1979), and (c) the seriousness of each crime is judged by the courts to some extent in relation to the context in which it occurred, e.g. murder of a spouse after years of provocation would be judged to be less serious than murder in the course of an armed robbery. In spite of inadequacies in this seriousness-of-crime scale, it remains true that merely counting all convictions is, in one sense, misleading. The chronic 'recidivist' with a string of petty offences may appear to be a much more serious offender than the man who is convicted of rape or a serious robbery. The latter usually receives a lengthy prison sentence which prevents further convictions for many years, his potential tally for convictions thereby being reduced.

We modified Sellin and Wolfgang's seriousness-of-crime scale (1964) by including all types of indictable or other serious crime committed by subjects in this study. We did not accept Sellin and Wolfgang's claim that there is 'a pervasive social agreement about the estimated numerical degree of seriousness of offences' but we attempted to rank crimes in a rough hierarchy from 0–7 and provided rules for the addition of convictions. The scale used is given in Appendix I. We hoped that its use might enable us to select out a group of subjects within this sample who undoubtedly had serious criminal careers as adults and about whom society would be right to be concerned. We believe that it does select out 'serious offenders' better than a simple aggregate of convictions.

Three social workers were asked to rate independently (and without practice) the criminal records of the subjects, with only the seriousness-of-crime scale as a guide. Their coefficients of agreement, using weighted Kappa Scores (Hall, 1974) and percentages of agreement, are given in Table 3.2.

Table 3.2: *Agreement of raters as to seriousness of crime*

Raters	Kappa coefficient	% total agreement	% agreement[±1]
Av.B (juvenile crime)	·878	90	98·3
Av.C (juvenile crime)	·67	82·33	92·34
Bv.C (juvenile crime)	·758	84	94
Av.B (adult crime)	·858	86	98
Av.C (adult crime)	·749	77·67	93·67
Bv.C (adult crime)	·767	76·33	94

A verdict score was used in cases of two raters agreeing and the third being 'odd man out'. In cases of complete disagreement, a mean average of scores was used. Sellin and Wolfgang (1969) present evidence for the validation of their scale in different countries. The modified version used here has not been validated, but scores on the scale correlate well with the total number of convictions. Spearman's r = .961 for adult convictions by seriousness-of-adult-crime scores and it correlated better with the aggregate of prison sentences than the total aggregate of convictions. Spearman's r for number of adult convictions by length of time sentenced to prison was .651 and for seriousness-of-adult-crime score by length of time sentenced to prison was .715 (suspended sentences were not included).

We accept that the instrument drawn up is far from being wholly acceptable – even to the authors. On the other hand, it seems to us even less acceptable solely to count the numbers of convictions, regardless of their nature. Although some progress can be made by focusing on sub-categories of crime (e.g. violent crime), such a focus, by definition, usually excludes an evaluation of an individual's total criminal career.

It is likely that most disagreement about our scale would be about whether certain types of crime should be scored a point higher or lower. The main use we make of the scale is by cutting off between points 3 and 4 and having three categories – no crime, less serious crime and definitely serious crime. Few would deny that individuals with a score of 4 or more would be regarded almost universally as having serious criminal careers. Occasionally, we use the scale as a ranking order in non-parametric tests and, although there could well be disagreement about the relative ranking of subjects at the lower ends of the scale, there is little doubt about its general drift.

With one exception, the scale is never used on its own, but always to compliment the outcome as judged by the total number of convictions, or by whether or not the subject had a conviction for a crime of violence.

Police cautioning

The system whereby the police officially caution most juvenile first offenders had not been introduced into Northtown in the childhood of any of our subjects. Counting offences and assessing seriousness is not, therefore, complicated by the issue of whether or not to include cautions in the assessment of crime. There may, of course, have been a 'system' of informal cautioning and this may have operated differentially at times. If this is so, we cannot eliminate its consequences.

Northtown

In the nineteenth century Northtown was a byword for poverty and this reputation stayed with it through to the twenties and thirties of this century. The inner city consisted of rows and rows of small terraced houses ('two-up, two-downs'), with outside toilets and a corner shop on almost every other street supplying goods 'on tick' and public houses occurring hardly any less frequently.

During the forties, fifties and sixties, when the children in our sample were growing up, the bulk of the population enjoyed a greater measure of prosperity than before and most of the adult male population were in regular employment after World War II. Our sample, however, was drawn from the poorest and largest families. Two-fifths of the families were known to be living at, or below, the National Assistance Benefit level, which was the official criterion of poverty. The average size of family was five and a half children. Chronic illness was fairly common in parents. Over two in five of all the fathers in the sample were known to be either chronically sick or handicapped, or prone to periods of 'ill-health'. Just over eight per cent of fathers had serious chest diseases. Eleven and a half per cent had been referred to psychiatrists at a time when psychiatric services were much less widespread than they are today. Well over half (fifty-five per cent) of all the fathers on whom there was accurate information were either chronically or intermittently unemployed, and that was at a time of virtually full employment. The health of the mothers was also poor. Two in five of all the mothers whose health was described were known to be chronically or intermittently in poor health. One in six of the *total* sample of mothers had been referred to psychiatrists and seven per cent of the total sample of mothers had been diagnosed as suffering from depression or other neurotic states (excluding 'personality disorders' or 'psychopathy').

It was apparent that the families from which our subjects were drawn were subject to frequent parental ill-health and unemployment, poverty, overcrowding and poor quality housing. In these respects they are similar to other samples of families whose children came into Care (Quinton and Rutter, 1984a) and to those families whose children are persistent school non-attenders (Wilson, 1962). However, within this milieu some children were even further disadvantaged. Their parents could not cope, or failed so badly to provide adequate care and control that parents and relatives requested admission to Care or the Children's Department and the Courts intervened to remove them. Did these children fare worse as adults than the rest of their 'neighbours' and contemporaries?

The social class distribution of the sample

Northtown's population as a whole was skewed towards the lower socio-economic classes, according to the '51 census. Only 11.2% of the population were in Classes I and II and 20.9% were in Class V. According to the 1% sample of the 1951 census, the proportion of men and married women in England and Wales as a whole in Social Classes I and II was 18.1% and in Social Class V was 13%. The social class distribution of the sample was even more heavily skewed to Social Class V, as Table 3.3 demonstrates. Families which were 'unclassifiable' because the father was dead or unemployed etc. are included in Class V for this table.

It is clear that the sample was not only almost entirely working class, but was skewed heavily to the lowest socio-economic groups.

Table 3.3: *Social Class distributions of England and Wales (at 1951 Census), Northtown as a whole and the sample (at 1951 Census)*

Registrar General's socio-economic grouping	England and Wales (%)	Northtown as a whole (%)	N	Sample (parents of boys only) (%)
Classes I & II	(18·1)	(11·2)	2	(1.2)
III NM			4	(2·4)
	(52·5)	(52·2)		(13.7)
III M			19	(11·4)
IV	(16·4)	(15·7)	32	(19·3)
V	(13·0)	(20·9)	109	(65·7)
Total		100	166	100

Packman (1968) found a marked skew towards the lowest socio-economic subgroupings in the parents of children 'in Care' throughout Britain. 71.3% of all the boys in our sample who were admitted to Care were from Social Class V.

4

The main findings

'Delinquent behaviour cannot be determined entirely by past events. Contemporaneous happenings . . . must influence the likelihood of appearance before the juvenile court, but such things cannot be predicted from an analysis of the individual's circumstances in earlier years.'
West, 1982.

The proportion of all males who were convicted of an offence either as juveniles or adults was seventy-one per cent (118/166). A higher proportion were convicted as adults than as children. One hundred and seven men out of 166 were convicted as adults (sixty-four per cent), and 77 out of the 166 had a conviction as juveniles (forty-six per cent). Thirty-two men (19.3%) were actually committed to prison.

The study of prevalence rates for being convicted is of fairly recent origin in Britain (Farrington, 1981). The Central Statistical Office (1986) has recently published the first of a series of cohort studies of criminal careers on men born in England and Wales in 1952, up to the age of 28. These findings are, to a limited extent, comparable with our own findings which follow up men born between 1944 and 53, up to an average age of 29. Our findings, compared as far as possible with national prevalence figures, are given in Table 4.1.

Table 4.1: *Proportions convicted in Northtown study compared with national figures (%)*

	Northtown	National
Convicted either as an adult or juvenile	71	31
Convicted as adults (> 16)	64	NK
Convicted as juveniles (< 17)	46	17
With multiple (3+) convictions as adults	40	NK
With 3+ convictions as juvenile or adult	50	10

Note (N = 166)

It will be seen from the two sets of figures that the proportion in Northtown with any convictions as juveniles or with any convictions either as an adult or juvenile was roughly two and a half times the national figures. The proportion with three or more convictions incurred either as an adult or juvenile was five times higher. The prevalence rates given above are considerably higher than those found by

Wadsworth (1979) in subjects in the National Survey of Health and Development who were followed up to the age of twenty, when almost thirteen per cent of the males had at least one conviction for an indictable offence. All Wadsworth's subjects were born in 1946. The extent of recorded crime has increased considerably in the sixties and seventies (Central Statistical Office, 1986). It has also been demonstrated in many studies (some of which have been discussed in Chapter 1) that rates of convictions vary from area to area and are greater in poor, working-class districts and are associated with family disharmony and breakdown. It is possible to discover groups in which the probability of conviction is very high, e.g. Wilson (1962) studying roughly contemporaneous juvenile offenders in families with multiple problems found that eighty-five per cent of males in 'Seatown' had been convicted by seventeen years of age. (However, she included a slightly wider range of offence in her calculations.) Undoubtedly, the Northtown figures are high and reflect the social deprivation experienced by our children. In a careful study of the prevalence of psychiatric morbidity in Blackburn, Leslie (1974) found that over one in five of 13–14-year-old boys and just over one in seven of girls of the same age were suffering from behavioural or emotional problems severe enough to be treated by a child psychiatrist. In boys, the majority of the problems would be of a behavioural nature or, at least, of a mixed conduct/emotional type. The inner city deprivation of Northtown was certainly no less than that of Blackburn. The major longitudinal study of crime in Britain (West, 1982), known as the Cambridge Study of Delinquent Development, found that a third of 411 boys living in a working-class area of London had a conviction by the age of twenty-four. West's sample is almost contemporaneous with ours, the subjects being born between 1951 and 1954.

Types of crime

Forty-one per cent of our sample were convicted of theft in adult life, twenty-four per cent of breaking and entering (or burglary) and twenty-six per cent (N = 44) of crimes involving violence or aggression to the person. This includes *two* men convicted of *indecent* assault, without other convictions for assault or violent crime, and *three* men convicted of robbery.

A quarter of the total sample were convicted of crimes of dishonesty, including handling stolen goods as adults (> 16), as distinct from having convictions for theft. Sixteen per cent were convicted of taking and driving away other vehicles and fifteen per cent of crimes of criminal damage.

Five per cent had convictions for crimes of a sexual nature (including indecent assault). Although the proportion of males in our sample with convictions or crimes against the person seems high, it is not a much greater proportion of those with convictions (for all crimes) than was found in the Cambridge Study of Delinquent Development. Eleven per cent of their subjects were found to have definitely committed crimes of violence by the age of twenty-four (West, 1982), although a much smaller proportion of their subjects (thirty-three per cent) was convicted of any crime than in this sample. There is also evidence (Cline, 1980) that males with long criminal careers commit relatively more crimes of violence in young adult life (i.e. between the ages of twenty and twenty-nine) than in other periods, and the mean age of our sample at follow-up was roughly twenty-nine.

Risk groups

It is reasonable to assume, on the basis of what we know about the outcome of boys with serious conduct problems seen at Child Guidance Clinics (Robins, 1966; Curman and Nylander, 1976), that their outcome in terms of adult convictions and other instances of socially unacceptable behaviour (e.g. alcoholism and vagrancy) would be poor. The same expectations are even more strongly held about the criminal prospects for persistent truants. There is at least one long-term follow-up study of truants and school drop-outs (among American blacks) which found a poor outcome, not only in terms of perpetrating crimes but also in terms of death through homicide (Robins, 1972). Rutter (1978), on the basis of his Isle of Wight and London studies, regards admission to Care, for whatever period, as a risk factor for juvenile delinquency. There is evidence that the long-term outcome for boys brought up in foster care (Ferguson, 1966) and in residential care (Dinnage and Pringle, 1967b) is relatively poor in terms of delinquency. It follows that boys who have lived in Care, boys seen at Child Guidance Clinics (at least for conduct problems) and boys reported for persistent non-attendance at school are all groups 'at risk' for future delinquency, but it is unclear which groups are most at risk and if boys longest in Care are no better off in their outcome than matched samples from these other two groups, this almost certainly implies a relatively poor outcome for living fairly long-term in Care.

In Table 4.2 we record the outcome in terms of: (a) number of convictions, and (b) seriousness-of-crime scores.

Table 4.2: *Risk groups and adult crime (percentages)*

Risk group	Number of convictions			Seriousness-of-crime scores			
	0	*1.2*	*3+*	*0*	*1–3*	*4+*	*(N)*
1 Original child care	32	34	34	32	46	21	(56)
2 Child guidance	33	19	48	33	39	28	(54)
3 Non-attenders	41	20	39	41	30	29	(56)

Note
$X^2 = 5·54$, 4df, $X^2 = 3·3$, 4df, p>·5 NS.
·5>p>·2 NS.

These findings suggest that the outcome for a random group of boys admitted to the public Care of a northern industrial town for at least two years was only slightly (and not significantly) better in terms of proportions with multiple (3+) convictions and serious criminal careers than samples from Child Guidance patients and chronic non-attenders at school, matched for age and social class.

However, it has to be remembered that many boys did not fit into 'pure' groups. In fact, there was a good deal of overlap between all three groups and this finding will not surprise social workers and other professionals working with children.

The picture presented in Table 4.2 changes somewhat when over-lapping cases are grouped together. Boys seen at Child Guidance but not reported for school non-attendance or admitted to Care did best, especially in terms of seriousness-of-crime scores, with only seven per cent having scores of 4 or more. However, there was no general tendency for the boys who appeared in more than one category to have a worse outcome than boys in the 'pure' categories, with the exception of boys in Care, who were also seen at Child Guidance Clinics (includ-ing those boys who fell into all three categories, i.e. they had been admitted to Care, seen at a Child Guidance Clinic and reported for chronic school non-attendance). In fact, in terms of recidivism (i.e. 3+ offences), the adult outcome for boys seen at a Child Guidance

Clinic, as well as being in Care, was significantly worse than that of boys admitted to Care but not seen at Child Guidance or reported for school non-attendance. $X^2 = 8.02$, ldf, p<.005 (N = 58). Our findings are presented in Table 4.3.

Table 4.3: *Pure and overlapping risk groups and adult crime (percentages)*

Risk groups	Number of convictions			Seriousness-of-crime scores			
	0	1.2	3+	N	0	1–3	4+
'Pure' Care	36	27	36	(33)	36	36	27
'Pure' Child Guidance Clinic	48	22	30	(27)	48	44	7
'Pure' non-attenders.	45	17	38	(42)	45	29	26
Care and Child Guidance Clinic	0	14	86	(7)	0	57	43
Care and non-attenders	28	38	34	(32)	28	47	25
Non-attenders and Child Guidance Clinic	43	29	29	(7)	43	29	29
Child Guidance Clinic and non-attenders	17	17	67	(18)	17	39	44

Those boys who were both admitted to Care and reported for school non-attendance did not have any worse an outcome than boys simply admitted to Care or boys reported for school non-attendance without admission to Care.

There is likely to have been considerable variety in the clientèles of different Child Guidance Clinics operating at that time (Timms, 1968) and the outcome of patients of a particular clinic is likely to be related to the problems brought by the patients, e.g. clinics treating boys and adolescents with severe conduct disorders are likely to have a considerable proportion who go on to have criminal careers. Such boys are likely to come from families in which relationships are distorted.

In order to understand better the complexity of the backgrounds of the boys both seen at the Child Guidance Clinic and admitted to Care, we studied their case histories in some depth. Ten of them are presented here in summary form.

The first three examples, including two from the original Care sample, show how some (at least by our limited criteria of outcome) did relatively well as adults, in spite of very difficult backgrounds.

Ten cases of boys both admitted to care and seen at a Child Guidance Clinic

1 Case 10

Benjamin A. was admitted to Care on a Direction Order at the age of eight for persistent school non-attendance – often due to his simply walking out of school. He was the third of four children to a coalman (i.e. a coal deliverer, not a miner) and a rather strange mother. His admission to Care followed ten sessions at the local Child Guidance Clinic, where the psychiatrist and social worker gave up in the face of the mother's repeated denial of the seriousness of Benjamin's problems. The family had already been helped by the NSPCC and Benjamin had been known for many years by the police for theft and wandering from home. Other problems included criminal damage to property, lighting fires and generally being unmanageable in school.

After two years in Care he was committed to an Approved School following several more convictions for theft and burglary. He continued to be sent to two further Approved Schools and finally to Borstal.

The psychiatrist described the mother as 'talking non-stop' and being 'completely irrational' and the father as apparently not in any way concerned about his son's behaviour.

In fact, Benjamin was away from home for about six years between the ages of eight and sixteen. He committed seventeen offences as a juvenile but only two as an adult, his last conviction being at twenty. His seriousness-of-crime score was 2.

2 Case 33

James B. was first admitted to Care at the age of four, at his mother's request, because of her inability to manage him. She appeared to be a woman at odds with herself, and was frequently described as 'neurotic' and 'hysterical' in the notes. The mother and father often argued and James's mother seemed able neither to accept him nor to let him go, with the consequence that he was discharged from voluntary Care on four occasions. He had eight different placements while in Care, including two placements in residential schools for the 'maladjusted'.

Throughout his early adolescence he manifested a wide range of problems, both emotional and behavioural in nature. These included theft, breaking and entering, fire-setting, wandering from home and attacking his parents and house-parents. At the age of fifteen he was seen by a psychiatrist after attacking a house-parent with a knife and was diagnosed as suffering from a personality disorder.

At sixteen he was discharged home, where his mother seemed to have calmed down considerably in her behaviour.

He had three juvenile convictions (for theft and breaking and entering). As an adult he had only one conviction. This was for dishonesty, at the age of twenty four. His seriousness-of-crime score was 1.

3 *Case 132*

Barry C. was first admitted to Care at the age of six when his mother was admitted to a psychiatric hospital following an overdose. He was readmitted and discharged six times by the age of fourteen because of his mother's confinements for subsequent children and once because of a further overdose. He was finally committed to Care at thirteen for theft but, in aggregate, his length of time in Care was only three years.

Barry's father died of asthma and bronchitis when Barry was five. His father had been described as 'fond of him', although the marriage had been poor. His mother then lived with a succession of men, by whom she had three more children.

He was referred to the Child Guidance Clinic at the age of eight with a range of *emotional* problems, e.g. he was unhappy, he had problems of initial insomnia, picked at his food and had difficulty playing with other children. Five years later he had several *conduct* problems and was committed to care at thirteen years of age. His problems included theft, defiance towards his mother and truancy. He was discharged to his mother at fourteen years of age.

In spite of this extremely unsettled background, he was convicted only once as an adult (for theft). His seriousness-of-crime score was 1.

4 *Case 111*

Bruce D. was first placed in Care at the age of three weeks because his mother felt unable to look after him. She had herself not long before come out of Approved School. He remained in Care, in one foster placement, for three years and was then discharged at his mother's request.

He was referred to the Child Guidance Clinic at the age of eight by the Education Department because he had convictions for stealing and arson and was running away from home. He was more than two years retarded in reading. At that time his mother was described as 'rejecting' and 'cruel' to him. She said she could 'not stand the child' and the school reported that at times Bruce would be left outside in the rain because his mother did not want him in the house. His step-father was also strongly ambivalent in his attitude to him and their marriage had considerable difficulties. (It was in fact his mother's third marriage.)

He was committed to Care for theft at the age of eleven and to Approved School at 16. He had at least six placements in Care (including his early fostering placement). He was finally placed at a residential school for maladjusted children and expected to return home in the holidays. However, his mother often placed him with other relatives during the holidays. He had twelve convictions as a juvenile and thirty-seven as an adult, of which seven involved 'violence' to the person. These included assault, indecent assault, assault occasioning actual bodily harm and rape. He was committed to a Special Hospital for an indefinite period at the age of twenty-eight. His seriousness-of-crime score was 6.

5 Case 154

Stuart E. was an illegitimate child first admitted to Care at his mother's request at eighteen months of age. He remained in Care until he was just over three, when his mother obtained Stuart's discharge.

At the age of eight he was referred to Child Guidance by Probation with no less than eight different kinds of conduct problem, of which the most serious were thieving from shops, persistent defiance to his parents, running away from home and truancy.

His step-father was said to have been harsh in punishing Stuart, but left when Stuart was four years of age. He was succeeded by a series of cohabitees. His mother was described as 'very ambivalent' in her attitude to Stuart and described herself as 'bad tempered'. He was committed to Care at eight years, ostensibly for a conviction for theft, and remained in Care for three and a half years. In this time he had four placements. He did not stop stealing while in Care and was committed to an Approved School. He had seven convictions as a juvenile and seventeen as an adult, including one conviction for violent crime (unlawful and malicious wounding). At twenty-one years of age, he was committed to prison for thirty months. His last conviction was when he was twenty-three, so he may have managed to avoid further criminal activity. His seriousness-of-crime score was 5.

6. Case 108

Wayne F.'s father was blind and was prone to lash out wildly when frustrated. Mr. F. had had many convictions and was committed to prison at least three times. On the third occasion this was for neglecting Wayne, when Wayne was two years of age.

Wayne's mother was subject to periods of depression involving in-patient treatment.

Wayne was first committed to Care at the age of two and stayed for five years in one foster placement, but the Children's Department allowed him home when his foster mother was admitted to hospital. Wayne was then eight years old.

At ten years of age he was referred to the Child Guidance Clinic by the Education Department with problems of stealing money from the house, destructiveness at home and extreme aggression towards his peers. He was described by the psychiatrist as excessively thin and prone to belly aches. His reading comprehension was over two years retarded in relation to his overall IQ, which was 119. The psychiatric social worker felt the mother had little affection for Wayne and the marriage was full of arguments and conflict. In fact, it broke up when Wayne was eleven.

As a boy Wayne had two convictions, both for burglary, his first offence being at fourteen years of age.

As an adult he had ten convictions, three of which involved violence to the person, one for assult occasioning grievous bodily harm and two for unlawful and malicious wounding. He was sent to prison for two years. His seriousness-of-crime score was 5.

He was not readmitted to Care after the age of eight, nor was he committed to an Approved School.

7 Case 123

James G. was the second of six siblings. He was referred to the Child Guidance Clinic by the School Medical Officer at six years of age because of 'destructive outbursts' in the home.

The psychiatric social worker described the home as 'dirty and overcrowded'. The father was chronically unemployed and said to be 'truculent' and 'hostile to authority'. The mother appeared to be neglectful and was alleged to leave the children at night. The psychiatrist described her as 'dull' and 'prone to periods of depression'. The marriage (according to the PSW and the Child Care Officer) was characterised by arguments and violence. One sibling was at a special school for moderately retarded children and another was at a school for the deaf.

James was first admitted to Care on a Fit Person Order at the age of eight, 'in the child's own interests', i.e. he was deemed to be beyond parental control. He had an IQ of 91 and was stealing, soiling and wetting. After eight months the parents asked for, and were granted, revocation of the Fit Person Order. He was placed in an Approved School at the age of nine following two convictions for theft. He remained there for two years. As an adult he was convicted of eight offences: four of burglary, one of wounding, one of arson and two of theft. His last known conviction was at the age of twenty-two. He was twice committed to prison. His seriousness-of-crime score was 5.

8 Case 129

Philip H. was the second of six children. His step-father was a labourer.

Philip was referred to the Child Guidance Clinic at the age of seven for fire-setting in his school and cruelty to other children. He was of a low average intelligence. His mother had already separated once from his father, who had a considerable alcohol problem. His mother was described by the psychiatrist as 'depressed', at least partly because of the marital situation, her husband's pathological jealousy and his violence. The house was overcrowded.

At twelve years of age Philip was committed to Care on a Fit Person Order 'in his own interests', i.e. he was beyond parental control. He was defiant and disobedient at home and school. He was threatening teachers and taking and driving away cars. He was over four years retarded in reading, in relation to his IQ. His parents had split up and his mother had remarried, apparently happily. The Children's Department attempted to place him in a boarding school but this request was refused by the Education Department. He was allowed to return home at fourteen, when his behaviour quickly deteriorated. In addition to his previous problems, he now regularly truanted as well.

He had five convictions as an adult, three for theft, one for criminal damage and one for unlawful sexual intercourse. His last conviction was at the age of twenty-four, so he may have succeeded in avoiding further crime. His seriousness-of-crime score was 3.

9 Case 166

Peter I. was first referred to the Child Guidance Clinic at the age of ten for persistent school non-attendance. He had a very high IQ but a wide range of serious problems, including enuresis and soiling, initial insomnia, hypochondriasis, temper tantrums, destructiveness at home, stealing outside the home and excessive aggression towards his peers.

His father had died when he was six and his step-father was described as punitive and cruel in his attitude to the boy. The marriage of his mother and step-father was overtly disharmonious and his mother's previous marriage was said to have been unhappy, owing to the father's addiction to gambling.

Peter was committed to Care on a Direction Order for school non-attendance at twelve and remained in Care for nine months.

He continued to truant on his return home. He was convicted twice as a juvenile: at thirteen of burglary and at fifteen of receiving stolen goods. As an adult he had two convictions, one for assault occasioning actual bodily harm and one for criminal damage.

He was well-known to the psychiatric services for his repeated overdosing. His seriousness-of-crime score was 3.

10 Case 200

Roger J. was first admitted to Care at the age of two, officially because of his bronchitis and need for convalescence. He was placed in an 'open air' home by the sea for seven months. He was illegitimate and never lived with his father. Roger's mother was described as at least 'ambivalent' towards him. She never visited him during his convalescence. She had a series of cohabitees, none of whom stayed with her. She had seven children and Roger was the third.

Roger was referred to Child Guidance at thirteen with eight different kinds of conduct problem, which included theft from the home and outside, deliberately urinating on the carpets, wandering from home (which had been going on for six years), self-injury, sex play with his younger sister and smearing faeces. He was asthmatic, pigeon-chested and described as an unhappy child. His mother was described as 'depressed', 'apathetic' and 'immature' by the psychiatrist. The house was dirty and overcrowded.

He was not known to have been in Care after the age of two.

As an adult he had twenty offences, mainly for theft and burglary, with two convictions for gross indecency, one for assault and one for assaulting a policeman. His seriousness-of-crime score was 5. He was still offending at the age of thirty.

Comment

It is clear, in all ten examples, that the boys concerned were subject to grossly inadequate parenting in childhood. Six had serious problems before their first admission to Care. In the other cases, (i.e. 4, 5, 6 and 10) the boys were admitted to Care when quite small but fairly quickly discharged back to very inadequate homes. In only one instance, Case (2), was it clear that the Care experience was seriously inadequate and even here the fault was that the boy was subject to repeated admissions and discharges, rather than that the substitute Care was in itself deficient.

The continuity of conduct disorder, juvenile delinquency and adult crime

One of the assumptions shared by many researchers and the public is that 'the environment' (however defined) in which some boys grow up may be conducive to their presenting with conduct problems or committing offences. This holds true whether severe behaviour problems are seen as 'socialised' or 'unsocialised' in their genesis. Is living in Care, with all its deficiencies and attendant hazards, more or less conducive to the presentation of these problems than living in very poor homes?

As a background to this question, it is necessary to bear in mind several studies which show a continuity between: (a) severe conduct disorders in adolescence and later delinquency and sociopathy, e.g. Robins, 1966 and 1978), and (b) early and later delinquency in males. Wolfgang (1974) and the Gluecks (1934, 1940) have presented evidence of the strong tendency to continue committing offences, often in spite of temporary changes in environment.

Our study also found considerable continuity in committing offences as a juvenile and as an adult (i.e. over the age of sixteen). Findings are presented in Table 4.4. Over half the boys who had no juvenile convictions had no convictions as adults, and nearly four-fifths of them had fewer than three convictions. At the other extreme, over three-quarters of the boys with three or more convictions as juveniles had three or more convictions in adult life.

The probability of any boy *without* a conviction as a juvenile being convicted as an adult was .46. For boys *with three or more* convictions the probability was .94.

84 Child Care and adult crime

Table 4.4: *Convictions as adult by convictions as juvenile*

Convictions as juvenile (< 17)	Convictions as adult (< 16)						Total
	0		1,2		3+		
	N	(%)	N	(%)	N	(%)	
0	48	(54)	22	(25)	19	(21)	89
1,2	9	(21)	12	(28)	22	(51)	43
3+	2	(6)	6	(18)	26	(76)	34
Total	59		40		67		166

$X2 = 40.53$, 4df, $P < \cdot0001$.

The same analysis was undertaken: (a) on the original sample of boys in Care, (b) on the original sample minus boys who came into Care because they were delinquent or had severe conduct problems, (c) on all boys coming into Care (for whatever reason), (d) on boys coming into Care for reasons of delinquency, and (e) on all boys who came into Care for any other reason. The patterns of findings remained remarkably constant, only varying when numbers were very small and therefore less reliable. A boy with *no* juvenile convictions was almost as likely to have a conviction as an adult, whether or not he was in Care, whether or not he was committed to Care because of serious conduct problems and (if he was in Care) whether or not he was in the original Care sample. Once a boy began offending repeatedly, the probability of his continuing to offend in adult life (> 16 years) was much greater than it would otherwise have been, varying between .75 to 1. The probabilities of committing offences are recorded in Table 4.5.

Although these findings suggest a rather poor outcome for boys who were 'in Care', they do not suggest that the probability of offending or having multiple offences as an adult greatly increased for boys who had been in Care. They also suggest that the outcome for boys who were admitted to Care for reasons of delinquency or severe conduct problems was likely to be worse than the rest of the sample of boys in Care.

We have already referred to a long series of studies which have demonstrated a significant association between antisocial behaviour in childhood and delinquency or sociopathy in later adolescence and adult life (Robins, 1966; West and Farrington, 1973; Kvaraceus, 1960; Conger and Miller, 1966; Mitchell and Rosa, 1980).

The boys who came into Care were mostly assessed in an

Table 4.5: *Probability of committing offences in adult life, by admission to Care for different reasons*

Care Group	Probability of adult offending with no juvenile convictions	Probability of offending with 3+ convictions as juvenile	% offending as adults	% with 3+ convictions
Original Care	(N = 56) ·46	1	68	34
Original Care for non-delinquent reasons	(N = 39) ·45	1[b]	59	31
Total Care	(N = 90) ·49	·75	73	46
Total admitted for non-delinquent reasons	(N = 49) ·49	1[c]	59	33
Total admitted for delinquent and conduct reasons	(N = 41) ·50[a]	·95	90	61

Notes
(a) Only two boys had no juvenile convictions.
(b) Only two boys had three or more juvenile convictions.
(c) Only three boys had three or more juvenile convictions.

observation centre immediately after admission. Although it is clear that some boys had severe conduct problems *before* admission to Care (often being committed to Care for offences, truancy or 'in their own interests', i.e. 'beyond control'), systematic records were not available on *all* the children's behaviour prior to admission, and, since twenty-four of the boys were first admitted by the age of three years, it is difficult to see how the normal concepts of antisocial behaviour could have made sense when applied to children of that age. For children *in Care*, aspects of conduct problems were systematically collected from records *throughout* the period in Care; for children seen at Child Guidance, at the point(s) of their contacts with the Clinic and for children who failed to attend school, from school and court reports, at periods of poor school attendance or when prosecuted for offences.

A list was drawn up of the types of behaviour we regarded as conduct problems and this appears in Appendix II. We believe there would be little disagreement that most of the kinds of behaviour which appear on the list are conduct problems, with the exception of overactivity and possibly temper tantrums and overdosing. Overactivity was defined as extreme restlessness and lack of concentration. All boys classified as such had been seen and so described by a psychiatrist (not necessarily at the local clinic). Five were described as somewhat overactive and six as very overactive (including one who was definitely brain-damaged). Fifteen boys over the age of five were described as being prone to excessive tempers. Only two subjects overdosed as children, i.e. at under seventeen years of age.

We followed Robins' method (Robins, 1966) of awarding one point for each type of conduct problem and did not attempt to weight this according to the severity or pervasiveness of the problem. The method is based entirely on descriptions of behaviour, without any attempt at diagnosis or formulation.

Correlations between adult criminality and childhood variables

Given numerical data, the best statistical tests of the relationship of childhood factors to adult crime are tests of correlation. Since the data do not follow Gaussian distribution curves and the seriousness-of-crime scores do not contain equal intervals, a non-parametric test of correlation (Spearman's) was used.

Four childhood factors were taken as independent variables: juvenile convictions, seriousness-of-juvenile-crime scores, numbers of antisocial symptoms and length of time in Care. The dependent variables were the number of adult convictions and the seriousness-of-adult-crime scores.

The findings are presented in Tables 4.6 and 4.7, and in subsequent discussion, and demonstrate that length of time in Care was *negatively* correlated with adult criminality, in all instances significantly so.

Table 4.6: *Spearman's correlation of number of juvenile convictions, seriousness-of-juvenile-crime, number of (juvenile) antisocial symptoms and length of time in Care by number of adult convictions*

Independent variables	r	Sign level	N
1 Number of juvenile convictions	·51	·001	166
2 Seriousness of juvenile crime	·49	·001	166
3 Total number of antisocial behaviours	·41	·001	166
4 Length in Care (original sample)	−·31	·01	56
5 Length in Care (total care sample)	−·28	·01	89[a]

Note
(a) One case, length in Care unknown.

Table 4.7: *Spearman's test for number of juvenile convictions, seriousness of juvenile crime, number of antisocial symptoms and length of time in Care by seriousness-of-crime scores*

Independent variables	r	Sign level	N
1 Number of juvenile convictions	·50	·001	166
2 Seriousness of juvenile crime	·46	·001	166
3 Total number of antisocial behaviours	·40	·001	166
4 Length in Care (original sample)	−·25	·05	56
5 Length in Care (total care sample)	−·25	·01	89

In other words, there are significant positive correlations between the extent of conduct problems, juvenile convictions and seriousness of juvenile convictions as boys, with both numbers of convictions and seriousness of crime over the age of sixteen. On the other hand, there are significant *negative* correlations between length of time in Care and adult criminality. These correlations hold good both for numbers of convictions and seriousness-of-crime scores. They were found to apply both to the *original* sample of boys in Care and to the *total* group, which included all boys who were ever known to have been in Care. They are therefore not simply a function of the larger sample possibly being 'contaminated' by the addition of boys who were in Care for only brief periods and possibly for reasons of delinquency or conduct problems. These findings strongly suggest that the Care experience itself was *not* usually a causal factor in the adult crime found in boys who had been in Care, but possibly protected them to some extent from criminogenic environments.

However, neither the original sample nor the total group of boys in Care were homogeneous in the sense that they consisted of boys who came into Care at roughly similar ages and for similar reasons. Both samples contained a subset of boys who came into Care because they were already delinquent or beyond the control of their parents. Seventeen of the original sample came into Care for these reasons. They had a significantly poorer outcome than the other boys in the original sample, at least in terms of being convicted v. not being convicted in adult life. Only two out of seventeen (twelve per cent) were free from adult convictions, as compared with sixteen out of thirty-nine (forty-one per cent) of the other boys ($X^2 = 5·55$, 1df, p<.05). However, the proportions who were recidivist, or who had scores of 4+ on the seriousness-of-crime scale, were *not* very different.

When boys admitted to the original sample for reasons of delinquency were excluded, and Spearman's correlation test was used, we still found that there was a significant negative association between the length of time spent in Care and adult convictions (Spearman's r = −.28, p<.05, N = 39). For length of Care by seriousness-of-crime scores, Spearman's r = −.25, p = .066 (NS). It still seemed to be the case that the longer a boy was in Care, the *better* was his outcome.

A tabular presentation of our results would help clarify the interrelationship between length in Care, belonging to the additional care group and not having been in Care. Starting with the original Care sample, we divided this group at the median for their length of Care, which fell at precisely eight years. We further divided these groups according to whether they had remained continuously in Care or were discharged more than once, on the assumption that boys with several admissions and discharges would have had a different experience from boys with only *one* admission.

Findings are presented in Table 4.8.

It will be seen that boys continuously in Care for more than eight years did *best*, in relation to having the smallest proportion with 3+ convictions, and also in relation to having *much the smallest* proportion with seriousness-of-crime scores of 4 or more.

Although the group continuously in Care for the longest periods had the best outcome of all the subgroups in the original Care sample, this result was not significant. Comparing boys in Care continuously over the median for length with all other boys in the original Care sample did not lead to a significant difference. (X^2 = 2.66, 1df, p>.05). However, the boys with the longest and 'purest' Care experience (Group 1a in Table 4.8) did have a significantly better outcome than boys in the additional Care group (Group 2 in Table 4.8), both in relation to proportions with three or more convictions (X^2 = 9.29, 1df, p<.005) and in relation to the proportions with seriousness-of-crime scores of 4 or more (X^2 = 7.47, 1df, p<.01). This again strongly suggests that the Care experience itself was not usually the factor accounting for the poor outcome (at least in terms of crime) for boys who had been in Care. If we take these findings, together with the findings given in Tables 4.6 and 4.7 (of negative correlations between length in Care and the number and seriousness of adult convictions), the implications are that boys longest in Care are likely to be least delinquent as adults.

We then divided the *total* group of boys in Care at the median for

Table 4.8: Periods of time in Care, (a) by adult convictions and (b) by seriousness-of-crime scores (%)

Period in Care	Adult convictions				Seriousness-of-crime-scores		
	0	1,2	3+	(N)	0	1–3	4+
1. *Original Sample*							
(a) Boys continuously in Care over eight years	47	32	21	(19)	47	47	5
(b) Boys in Care over eight years with interruptions	25	50	25	(8)	25	50	25
(c) Boys continuously in Care less than eight years	17	33	50	(18)	17	56	28
(d) Boys in Care less than eight years with interruptions	40	30	30	(10)	40	30	30
2. *Other boys in Care (not original sample)*	18	18	65	(34)	18	35	47
3. *Boys not known to have been in Care*	46	34	20	(76)	46	34	20
(*Total*)				(165)			

Note
One case of length in Care unknown.

their length in Care, which fell at five years and ten months, and then at the four quartiles, the first falling at eleven months and the third at nine years and five months. Boys in Care over the third quartile were significantly less criminal as adults than other boys in Care. Less than a quarter (i.e. twenty-three per cent) of boys in Care over the third quartile had three or more offences as adults, compared with over half (fifty-two per cent) of the rest of the sample ($X^2 = 5.83$, ldf, p<.02). Only two (nine per cent) had scores of 4 or more for seriousness, compared with thirty-nine per cent of the rest of the boys in Care ($X^2 = 5.47$, ldf, p<.02). Findings are presented more fully in Table 4.9 and in Figs 2 and 3.

The findings just presented strongly suggest that Care is *not* in itself usually a criminogenic factor but, paradoxically, it could still be true that, on the whole, the outcome for boys who had been in Care is worse than that for boys who had not been in Care. In order to see if

Figure 2
Adult convictions by length in Care

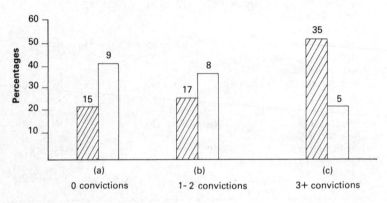

x² (a+b)v(c)=5·83, 1df, p<·02

Figure 3
Seriousness of adult crime scores by length
in Care

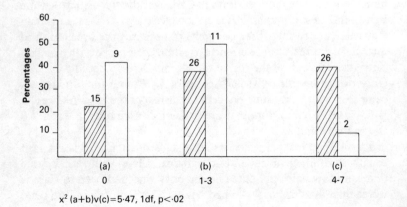

x² (a+b)v(c)=5·47, 1df, p<·02

Table 4.9: *Quarter of total Care group in Care for the longest period of time and rest of boys in Care by adult convictions and seriousness-of-crime scores (%)*

	Adult convictions			(N)	Seriousness-of-crime scores		
	0	*1,2*	*3+*		*0*	*1–3*	*4–7*
Quartiles for length in Care							
Over third quartile	41	36	23	(22)	41	50	9
Under	22	25	52	(67)	22	39	39

$$X^2 = 6.03, 2df, p < .05 \qquad X^2 = 7.25, 2df, p < .05$$

there are any grounds for the widespread professional view that boys who have been in Care tend to be particularly criminal as adults, we simply compared boys in the total Care group with the rest of the boys. On a simple distinction between the proportions with and without a conviction over the age of sixteen, boys who had ever been in Care tended to be *significantly more* criminal. Seventy-three per cent of all boys who had ever been in Care (66/90) had a conviction as adults, as compared with fifty-four per cent of the remaining boys (43/76) (the comparison group were themselves more likely to have convictions than the average population). (For Care group v. comparison group, $X^2 = 5.13$, 1df, p<.05.)

However, significant adverse findings did not persist when comparisons were made for 'recidivism' (3+ convictions) and for high seriousness-of-crime scores. Forty-four per cent of the boys who had been in Care were 'recidivists', compared with the thirty-four per cent of boys not known to have been in Care ($X^2 = 1.8$, 1df, p>.1(NS)).

On seriousness-of-crime scores, thirty-one per cent of boys who had ever been in Care had scores of 4 or more, but only twenty per cent of boys not known to have been in Care ($X^2 = 2.98$, 1df, p>.05 (NS)).

Since the outcome of the quarter of boys longest in Care was relatively good, it seems important to examine what we know of their experience in some detail and compare it with the rest of the group of boys who were 'in Care'. Table 4.10 describes, in barest outline, the nature of their Care experience and outcome. Their experience of Care was all quite considerable, only one boy being in Care for less than ten years and a majority staying for over twelve years. The two boys with by far the worst outcome had both been in Care as babies,

Table 4.10: Outline of the Care experiences and outcome for the quarter of boys longest in Care

Case no.	Age on admission	Age on first subsequent admissions	Length in Care	number of times discharged	Age last discharged and destination	Type of Care	Number of placements	Reason for admission	Adult convictions seriousness-of-crime score	Comments
4	3	—	14 years 6 months	1	18 fp	fp	5	neg	2/3	A
6	3	—	14 years 6 months	1	18 fp	fp	2	neg	1/1	
9	1	—	17 years 6 months	1	18 fp	fp & lgh	4	neg	1/2	B
15	2	—	15 years 10 months	1	18 fp	fp	6	neg	0/0	
16	1	16	17 years	2	18 lo	fgh	7	mo ill	0/0	C
23	3	—	14 years 4 months	1	18 lo	fgh	12	no ho	3/3	
24	0	—	17 years 8 months	1	18 fp	fp	2	mo ill	5/3	D
42	1	—	16 years 10 months	1	18 lo	fgh & fp	8	mo dead	0/0	
46	0	—	17 years 3 months	1	18 lo	fp	4	ab	5/3	E
48	1	—	16 years 4 months	1	18 af	fp	11	mo mi	1/1	
58	3	5,7	10 years 5 months	2	18 re	lgh	12	neg	25/6	F
62	0	—	17 years 4 months	1	18 fp	fp	5	ab	0/0	
64	2	—	15 years 5 months	1	18 fp	fp	3	no ho	0/0	
72	3	—	12 years 2 months	1	15 sister	fgh & lgh	8	no ho	1/1	G
96	0	—	17 years	1	18 fp	fp	6	no ho	0/0	
111	0	8	10 years	2	15 as	lgh & fp	7	beyond control	37/6	H
36	5	—	12 years 7 months	1	18 lo	lgh	6	pa's dead	0/0	
41	7	—	10 years 8 months	1	18 pa	fgh	4	no ho	1/1	
51	6	.	11 years 5 months	1	18 pa	lgh	11	mo des	1/1	I
77	5	5	10 years 9 months	2	16 pa	fp	3	neg	1/1	
76	8	—	9 years 9 months	1	18 fp	fp	3	mo mh	0/0	
91	5	7	10 years 5 months	2	17 pa	fp & fgh	8	neg	2/3	

Abbreviations

1 *Type of Care*
   This refers to the predominant type, i.e. the type of Care which accounts for two-thirds of the boys' time in Care.

   fp   foster parents
   fgh   family-group home
   lgh   large-group home

2 *Destination (on discharge)*
   fp   foster parents
   lo   lodgings
   af   armed forces
   re   remand home
   as   approved school
   pa   mother or father

3 *Reason for admission*
   neg   neglect
   mo ill   mother chronically ill
   ab   abandoned
   mo mi   mother mentally ill
   no ho   family homeless
   mo dead   death of mother
   pas dead death of both parents
   mo des   mother deserts family
   mo mh   mother mentally handicapped

Comments

A The only offences were committed in a psychotic state. The subject was then committed to a secure hospital.
B The longest foster placement lasted eleven years but broke down in adolescence, allegedly due to the subject's difficult behaviour.
C The mother had TB and was confined to a sanatorium where she died.
D The mother was severely epileptic and mentally retarded and was admitted long-term to an epileptic colony.
E An apparently successful foster placement broke down after eleven years.
F The father had a long prison record.
G The mother had several prison sentences – for soliciting.
H The mother was described as suffering from severe personality problems and had a series of cohabitees. The father had several spells in prison.
I This subject had several convictions as a juvenile.

then discharged home and then readmitted at seven and eight years of age, one because of his parents' gross neglect (for which they were both sent to prison) and the other because, at the age of eight, he was deemed to be beyond his parents' control.

Half were fostered for at least two-thirds of their stay in Care and the other half had either a mixture of foster placements and residential homes or lived in small or large group homes. Apart from the two cases already referred to, the outcome for boys growing up in residential homes, or a mixture of fostering and group living was no worse than for the boys who were fostered whilst growing up in Care. Only three other boys had three or more offences as adults (two with five).

We can speculate on the reasons for having a poor outcome, and it is noteworthy that in one instance (Case 23) the boy had twelve placements whilst in Care, and in another (Case 46) a long term foster placement broke down in adolescence and the boy left Care to go into lodgings. In one other instance (Case 4), the subject had two offences for wounding and no other convictions. He was diagnosed as schizophrenic and deluded at the time of the offence. His mother was also schizophrenic.

Comparison of the experiences and outcome of boys admitted to Care, divided at the four quartiles for length in Care.

Brief details are presented in Table 4.11, in terms of means and percentages of the experience of boys in Care and their outcome. Attention is focused particularly on age of admission, length in Care and reason for admission. In this table "major" reasons for admission, as given in the notes, are divided into: (a) delinquency, remand and difficult behaviour, (b) school non-attendance, and (c) family 'inadequacy' (including neglect, moral danger, parental illness and death, and homelessness).

When the quarter of boys longest in Care are compared with the other quarters, it is apparent that the proportion of boys admitted because of delinquency and serious conduct problems rises sharply from only five per cent to forty-five per cent as we move from the quarter longest in Care to the next quarter for length, and remains at a high level. The scatter of adult convictions for the boys longest in Care is also remarkably wide – ranging, in fact, from 0 to 37, so that although most of the boys longest in Care did fairly well (by our limited criteria) a few did rather poorly and two did extremely poorly.

Table 4.11: *Characteristics of total care sample by length in Care*

Quarters for length	Age first seen Mean	Age first admitted Mean (SD)	Reason for major admission (%) (a) delinquency/ (b) family inadequacy (c) non-attendance at school.		
			(a)	(b)	(c)
1 Under 11 months	8 years 3 m	10 years 4 m	59	29	12
2 11 months 5 years 10 months	7 years 9 m	9 years 3 m	69	13	18
3 5 years 10 months 9 years 5 months	6 years 8 m	7 years 6 m	45	45	9
4 9½ years and over	2 years 6 m	2 years 8 m	5	95	0

Proportion discharged twice or more (%) Mean	Number of anti-social problems Mean	Juvenile convictions Mean	Adult convictions Mean (SD)	Seriousness-of-crime score	Proportion additional to original sample (%)	N
5	3·0	4·1	4·9 (5·8)	2·8	100	22
43	3·3	3·3	5·4 (2·0)	2·6	39	23
41	2·0	1·2	5·3 (6·3)	2·4	5	22
23	1·5	0·6	3·9 (9·1)	1·6	5	22

The scatter of results for the other quarters was not as great. The boys in Care for the shortest period, who were also largely the last to come into Care, had about the same proportion admitted for reasons of delinquency (fifty-nine per cent) as the rest of the boys (fifty-seven per cent) (excluding the quarter in Care longest). They were hardly any more criminal as adults than subjects in the second and third quarter. They do not simply represent a group of delinquent adolescents who were only briefly admitted to Care as a stepping stone to committal to Approved School, even though this was true of six of the boys in the shortest quarter. Nearly a third of them were admitted because of family inadequacy.

Reasons for entering Care and outcome

It would be in keeping with all our findings so far presented, especially Table 4.11, and with what we know of conduct disorder and delinquency generally, if boys who entered Care because of conduct problems tended to continue to present with conduct problems after leaving Care. What is of greater interest is the criminal outcome of boys entering Care for *other reasons*. Ferguson's study (1966) suggests that a fairly high proportion of such boys are convicted as adults.

We categorised the main official reasons for all the boys admitted to Care and, where boys were admitted more than once, we selected the reason for their longest admission. We eventually selected four categories, based largely on the principle of whether the reason related to: (a) delinquency and other serious conduct disorder, (b) school non-attendance, (c) home conditions that might be thought to be conducive to delinquency, and (d) other causes.

Category (a) consisted of twenty-nine boys committed to Care for offences, six placed in Care on remand and six committed because they were, in effect, beyond parental control (N = 41).

Category (b) consisted of boys committed to Care on 'Direction Orders' because of chronic non-attendance at school. It was clear in many cases that the families were generally neglectful to their children (N = 9).

Category (c) consisted of boys who came into Care from homes which might have been thought to be damaging because of a serious lack of care or because of attitudes and behaviour on the part of the parents which might have been thought to be conducive to delinquency, i.e. nine boys were committed to Care because of parental neglect and four because they were in moral danger (N = 13).

Category (d) consisted of boys admitted to Care because the parents were unable to continue to look after them, for a variety of reasons connected with parental inability to care: illness (5), death (9), mental handicap (2), homelessness (3) or the desertion of the mother (8) (N = 27). The outcome for boys from the above-mentioned groups is given in Table 4.12.

Table 4.12: *Adult convictions and seriousness-of-crime scores according to reason for admission (original sample, percentages)*

Reason for admission	(a) Adult convictions				(b) Seriousness-of-crime scores		
	0	1,2	3+	(N)	0	1–3	4–7
(a) Delinquency being beyond control	9	29	61	(41)	9	49	42
(b) School non-attendance	56	22	22	(9)	56	33	11
(c) Damaging home conditions	31	46	23	(13)	31	46	23
(d) Parental failure	41	18	41	(27)	41	33	26

$X^2 = 16 \cdot 64$, 6d.f., p < ·02 $X^2 = 13 \cdot 5$, 6d.f., p < ·05

Over ninety per cent of boys who had been admitted to Care for reasons of delinquency, remand or being beyond control had convictions as adults (i.e. >16 years) and three out of every five had three or more convictions. They had a poorer outcome than any of the other groups.

The number of young men in the fourth group (whose parents had died, been ill or were in other ways unable to cope) who had three or more convictions as adults was also disappointingly high (forty-one per cent), although exactly the same proportion was entirely free of adult convictions. Several of the boys who were admitted to Care because of parental illness or death had been subject to very inadequate care for years prior to their admission and, in at least one case, to very harsh treatment.

Packman, Randall and Jacques (1986) have suggested that children entering Care can be divided roughly into three groups, whom they call villains, victims and volunteered. The villains are children

admitted (often on Court Orders) for delinquency or difficult
behaviour, the victims are essentially abused and neglected children
and the volunteered are those whose parents request that they be put
in Care. The groups are not mutually exclusive and there is a good deal
of overlap. It will be seen that our categories (a) and (b) are roughly
equivalent to Packman's villains, except that the children admitted
for school non-attendance did not consist altogether of the popular
stereotype of antisocial truants, but contained a fair number of children who were in effect withdrawn from school, or never sent, by their
parents. In fact, they tended to disprove the general view propounded
by Healey and Bronner (1926) sixty years ago that truancy is the
kindergarten of crime. The school non-attendance of many of our
boys seemed to be a form of parental neglect, and occasionally a
symptom of the family's non-integration with society at large. The
history of the education files was less certain than that of the other files
and it could be that there was an over-representation of families in
which several children had poor-school-attendance problems. None
of the boys admitted to Care for reasons of school non-attendance
appeared to be cases of school refusal, although three cases of school
refusal were 'diagnosed' at the clinic and one of the cases included in
the education sample appeared to be a 'school refuser'. None of these
boys ever had any convictions.

Our category (c) corresponds roughly with Packman's victims and
our category (d) with the volunteered. However, there were no
"physically or sexually abused" children among our victims, since
such problems were not recognised at that time. We should also like to
stress the overlap between our categories. Many in our last group
(which seems to correspond roughly to Packman's volunteered) were
clearly victims in some sense, and many had become villains as well.
Some of our victims, who had been exposed to long periods of neglect,
were also villains by the time they were received or committed to
long-term Care. To a limited extent, we share the thinking behind the
Children and Young Persons' Act (1969), which was framed on the
assumption that, on the whole, depraved children were deprived
children. However, we should prefer to see the connection phrased
along the lines that many severely deprived children later turn out to
be 'depraved' young people.

The outcome for the boys in our sample who had been subject to
neglect or 'moral danger' was relatively good. They were nearly all
admitted as young children and tended to stay for relatively long

periods (see Table 4.13), although some were initially discharged after relatively short periods and then readmitted 'for good'.

We started from the assumption that a proportion of boys growing up in atmospheres of criticism and hostility, frequent marital rows and general neglect will become antisocial in their behaviour and officially delinquent (the evidence for this view is presented in chapters 1, 9 and 10). However, we wished to see if removal into Care, prior to official action to commit seriously delinquent or antisocial children, in any way diminished the proportions who later became seriously criminal. (We did not assume that social workers admitting children to Care had the prevention of later delinquency as an objective in any except a handful of cases. They acted to protect the child and the family.) Consequently we divided all the boys into two groups, with one group of delinquents and boys with serious conduct disorders, i.e. thirty-five boys committed because of convictions or on remand, plus six boys committed because they were beyond parental control (N = 41), and the remainder of the boys admitted for other reasons, including boys committed because of chronic school non-attendance (N = 49).

On Wilcoxon rank sum tests, the two groups differed significantly in relation to the total number of adult convictions and the serious-ness-of-adult-crime scores, with the boys committed to Care for conduct problems having the worse outcome. (For adult convictions, the W score was 2173 and the X score -2.53, P<.02. For seriousness-of-crime scores, the W score for the two groups was 2177 and the X score -2.57, P<.02.)

We then compared these two groups with the boys who were not known to have been committed to Care at all on a Kruskal–Wallis l-way Anova test. Boys committed to Care because of delinquency or being beyond control had significantly more convictions on average than either boys not known to have been committed to Care or those admitted for reasons other than delinquency and being beyond control ($X^2 = 12.1$, 2d.f. p<.002). Boys admitted for reasons *other than* delinquency and being beyond control were then compared with boys not known to have been admitted to Care. There was no significant difference in outcome. When comparisons were made in relation to convictions and results were corrected for ties, the Z score was $-.62$ and P>.5. Findings in relation to seriousness-of-crime scores were very similar to this. As one would expect, however, boys committed to Care for reasons of delinquency and being beyond control had a mean ranking score for both adult convictions and seriousness of crime that was significantly worse than boys not known to have been admitted to Care (P<.001 in both cases).

In other words, when one tried to compare the *total number* of convictions and the *total seriousness* of crime committed by males in each group as adults, boys who had been in Care for reasons unconnected with delinquency and being beyond parental control committed on average no more crime than the other boys in our sample who were not known to have been in Care. Boys committed to Care for reasons of delinquency and being beyond control committed much more crime as adults than either of the other two groups.

Reasons for admission to Care and length of time in Care

The findings presented in Table 4.12 comparing adult convictions with the reason for admission to Care gave no indication of the length of time boys spent in Care or their age on first admission. We found that there were associations between reasons for admission and length of time in Care, and also between the reasons for admission and their *age* on first admission.

When we compared boys divided at the four quartiles for length in Care, there were very significant differences in the length of time spent in Care by boys admitted for different reasons. This is implicit in Table 4.11 but is made clearer in Table 4.13.

Table 4.13: *Comparison of periods of time spent in Care and reasons for admission (%)*

| Reasons for admission | Length in Care (in quartiles) | | | | |
	1 (up to 11 mths)	*2* 11 mths–5 yrs 10 mths)	*3* 5 yrs 10 mths –9 yrs 5 mths	*4* (Over 9½ yrs)	*(N)*
Parental failure	15	7	31	46	(27)
'Damaging' home	8	8	15	69	(13)
School non-attendance	33	44	22	0	(9)
Delinquency	32	40	25	3	(40)
	(N = 22)	(N = 23)	(N = 22)	(N = 22)	

$X^2 = 38\cdot99$, 9d.f., p< ·00001
One case missing.

Over three-quarters of the boys in our sample admitted for parental failure or home conditions that were thought to be damaging to the child (neglect or moral danger) were in Care for approximately six years or more. Over three-quarters of the boys admitted for delinquency, conduct problems and school non-attendance were in Care for shorter periods.

An alternative analysis

Another way of presenting our findings is to compare childhood anti-social behaviour and juvenile convictions of our sample with their adult convictions and seriousness-of-crime scores, breaking the sample down into four groups: (a) the original care sample, (b) the additional group of boys admitted to Care, (c) the child guidance sample (minus boys admitted to Care), and (d) the school non-attenders' sample (minus boys admitted to Care).

Table 4.14 presents findings on the mean and SDs for the four groups for the variables just referred to, together with an analysis of variance.

In other words, the 'additional' group of boys admitted to Care were significantly more anti-social and delinquent than all other subgroups.

Their mean scores for their total of *juvenile* convictions were almost four times the mean number for the original sample of boys who were in Care, but the gap closed to some extent for adult convictions. This closure calls for some explanation. However, the analysis strongly suggests that the poor outcome for boys in Care is strongly influenced by boys who have problems as children *additional* to their being in Care.

Comparison groups

What our sample lacks, as a control, is a group of apparently problem-free children coming from the same type of environment as the original care sample. However, there was a sub-group of boys in our comparison group who could probably be assumed to be relatively free of conduct problems, at least at the point of their referral to the Child Guidance Clinic.

It is clear from Robin's major follow-up (1966) that children seen at Child Guidance with mainly neurotic problems had no worse an

Table 4.14: *Analysis of variance – antisocial problems and crime*

	(a) Antisocial problems				(b) Juvenile convictions				(c) Adult convictions				(d) Seriousness-of-crime scores				
	Mean	SD	F ratio	Probability	Mean	SD	F ratio	Probability	Mean	SD	F ratio	Probability	Mean	SD	F ratio	Probability	N
1 Original 'in Care' group	2·5	2·3			1·0	2·5			3·9	5·7			2·0	1·9			56
2 Additional group	4·2	2·3			4·3	4·0			6·6	7·8			3·0	2·0			34
			15·6	·00001			9·7	·00001			2·5	·08			5·0	·002	
3 Child guidance	1·6	1·5			1·3	4·2			2·9	5·9		(NS)	1·3	1·6			34
4 School non-attenders	1·5	0·8			1·0	1·7			3·8	5·9			1·8	2·0			42

Note
For all tests N = 166, df between groups = 3, and within groups = 162.

Between groups	(a) 167.9	(b) 285·1
Within groups	(a) 582·8	(b) 1587·8

(c) 265·9	(d) 53·2
(c) 6385	(d) 576·8

outcome in terms of crime and sociopathy generally than those of a group of children in the community matched for social class, who (according to school records) did not appear to have severe problems. There were nine boys who, at the point of their initial assessment (in social worker's, psychologist's and psychiatrist's reports), had *no* antisocial behaviour recorded about them and had at least one neurotic/emotional symptom. This subgroup was used as a comparison for boys longest in Care.

The boys who had been longest in Care, with only one admission and discharge (N = 17), had a somewhat worse outcome but not *significantly* so.

It seemed reasonable to reduce the quarter of boys longest in Care by withdrawing boys who had been in and out of Care more than once, since their experience of Care was less 'pure' than those who had remained in Care. Findings are given in Table 4.15.

Table 4.15: *Outcome for boys continuously longest in Care compared with boys without conduct problems and not in Care*

Sample	(a) Number of convictions (%)				(b) Seriousness-of-crime scores (%)		
	0	1,2	3	(N)	0	1,2	3
No conduct problems	78	11	11	(9)	78	22	0
Continuously longest in Care	47	35	18	(17)	47	53	0

Numbers are too small for X^2 tests. On Fisher's Exact Test for convictions v. no convictions, p = .138 (NS). In other words, although the outcome for boys in long-term care was worse, it was not significantly so. The boys chosen for comparison with the long-term Care subsample were possibly abnormally free of conduct problems in their social setting at the time they were assessed, when their average age was eight.

The proportion of boys in the quarter longest in Care with a conviction (fifty-three per cent) remains high – nearly twice the national figure for a roughly contemporaneous period. The prevalence for offending in Northtown is likely to have been much higher than the national rate, since it was an area of conspicuous social deprivation. The relatively superior outcome for the quarter of boys longest in Care appears strongest when we compare those boys continuously in Care over the third quartile for length: (a) with boys in Care for shorter periods, and (b) with boys not known to have been in Care at all. Eighteen per cent of the boys longest in Care without a break had three or more convictions as adults, compared with seventy-one per cent of *all* other boys in Care and thirty-four per cent of boys not known to have been in Care. None of the boys continuously in Care over the third quartile had scores of 4 or more for seriousness of crime, compared with twenty per cent of boys not known to have been in Care and just over half of boys in Care for shorter periods (fifty-two per cent).

5

Age on admission to Care

'Give me a child until he is seven, and he is mine for life.'
Saying attributed to the Jesuits.

Social workers and other professional people concerned with children tend to be greatly exercised over admitting young children to Care. It is generally agreed that young children find it difficult to conceive, or retain, the idea of constancy or permanence over time and therefore find separations from home and parents particularly threatening and distressing. The age from six months to four years is thought to be a particularly vulnerable period. It could be that children who are separated from their homes at that age are especially at risk of incurring developmental delays and other psychiatric disturbance which may last throughout childhood, e.g. Douglas (1975) found associations between, on the one hand, both: (a) hospital admissions lasting longer than a week, and (b) repeated admissions between six months and three and a half years, and, on the other, troublesome behaviour at school at thirteen and fifteen years and low reading ability at fifteen years. When early admissions had also been followed by at least one admission after five years, there was an association between long and repeated admissions and later delinquency and job instability. On the other hand too great a reluctance to separate young children and their parents may well lead to a failure to protect them from neglect and abuse. Social workers in the past have also wished to avoid young children suffering the deficiencies of 'institutional' care, although changes in the practice of social work over the past thirty years have led to a very much greater use of fostering for young children. The assumption that residential care causes delinquency in boys is, however, questionable. Wolkind (1974) found that antisocial disorder in a group of ninety-two children aged five to twelve years who had all been in residential care for at least six months was associated with aspects of the child's *biological home*, and *not* with aspects of Care. It was associated with coming from a large family and having an absent father – whether the absence was permanent or intermittent.

Disinhibition, on the other hand, was associated with admission to Care before the age of two years. There remains, however, an anxiety that the more distant relationships of residential living, or 'contamination' by living with boys who are already delinquent, can lead to a greater delinquency in older boys.

Our focus at the moment is on early removal from home and admission to Care. In a study of 121 foster children of varying ages, most of whom had been in their foster homes for many years (the mean average being six), Thorpe (1980) found that significantly *more* children admitted to Care before their fifth birthday had scores on the Rutter 'A' and 'B' Scales suggesting psychiatric disturbance than those admitted láter. However, children placed in their foster home *before* the age of two were significantly *less* disturbed than children placed between the ages of two and four. It is not clear from Thorpe's account how many of her subjects had experienced residential placements. There was a relatively high rate of disturbance in the whole group of children studied by Thorpe. Thirty-nine per cent, or almost two-fifths, had scores on the Rutter Scales suggesting psychiatric disturbance. Since similar rates of disturbance have been found in children in residential Care (Yule and Raynes, 1972; Wolkind, 1971), Thorpe's study provides no evidence that long-term fostering leads, over a period of a few years, to generally greater adjustment and emotional and behavioural 'well being' than residential Care.

This whole area seems to be of crucial importance, and yet difficult to unravel. In some sense, the foundations of human relationships seem to be laid in the earliest years (Bowlby, 1969, 1973, 1980; Sroufe, Fox and Pancake, 1983). However, there is still debate as to whether this is so because the earliest years (0–4) are particularly sensitive, or because, for many children, what comes after these years, in terms of experience of environment, is often of a piece with what went before, (Clarke and Clarke, 1976). However, the years 5–7 also seem to be of particular importance. Many cultures seem to define childhood as ending at about the eighth year of life, and it is probably no accident that the English legal system regarded the age of responsibility as starting at eight until the passing of the Children and Young Persons' Act (1969). It could be that what children learn, for good or bad, before that age is harder to unlearn after it.

A corollary of the reluctance to admit young children into Care is that the homes from which they come must be particularly damaging or deficient before they are removed. Indeed, the more alternatives are found to the admission of young children to Care, the more this is likely to be true. At the time when the subjects of this study were growing up, the alternatives – other than family casework – were limited.

Age on admission to Care could be connected with later delinquency in two other ways. Firstly, once children in our study had reached the age of eight and committed offences, they could be prosecuted as having reached the 'age of responsibility' and, as a result, could be committed to Care. Now it is well-known that the best predictor of later delinquency is early delinquency (e.g. Kvaraceus, 1960) and, although there is a general assumption, based on persistent findings of associations, that discordant and neglectful home surroundings tend to produce delinquency, social factors so far appear to have much less predictive power than actual delinquent or antisocial behaviour. Since serious conduct disorder and delinquency are fairly persistent traits (Robins, 1966; Wolfgang, 1974), boys who are delinquent at eight might well be expected to continue to be delinquent and, as we have already found, did continue to be so. Secondly, boys who came into Care early in life, and who stayed in Care, necessarily had a longer experience of Care than boys who were either admitted for brief periods or first admitted later in childhood. The 'early admitted group' more often came into Care primarily for reasons of family breakdown, maternal neglect or inadequacy, rather than because of child behaviour, whereas boys who were admitted later (i.e. at eight years and older) came into care for a variety of reasons including delinquency, breakdown in parenting and a mixture of anti-social behaviour and home circumstances.

If living in Care were itself damaging, then the outcome for boys who were admitted earliest and who remained longest should be the poorest. Equally, if living in Care is less deficient as an upbringing than factors in poor natural homes and environments, or if living continuously in Care is less harmful than repeated admissions and discharges, then the outcome for the group of boys longest in Care should be better than for both: (a) boys living in discordant and neglectful homes, and (b) boys admitted to, and discharged from, Care on more than one occasion.

We began by comparing the outcome for the boys in the *original* sample according to their age on admission to Care. Boys were divided, according to age of first admission (for whatever length of time), into four age bands: 0–3 years, 4–7 years, 8–11 years and 12–15 years. The outcome for boys admitted between the ages of 8 and 11 was almost identical to that of boys aged 12–15, and these two age groups were combined. There was no significant difference in outcome, although, in relation to multiple convictions, boys admitted between four and seven years of age had a slightly better outcome than boys admitted earlier or later, as is shown in Table 5.1.

Table 5.1: *Age on first admission by adult convictions and seriousness-of-crime scores (original Care sample)*

	(a) Number of convictions (%)				(b) Seriousness-of-crime scores (%)		
Age on first admission	0	1,2	3	(N)	0	1,2	3
0–3	37	32	32	(19)	37	47	16
4–7	42	42	17	(12)	42	42	17
8–15	24	32	44	(25)	24	48	28
Total				(56)			

We then compared the outcome for boys in the *total* Care group and found significant differences in relation to 'recidivism' in boys admitted before and after their eighth birthdays. ($X^2 = 4.02$, ldf, p<.05). Findings for boys with, and without, 3+ offences as adults are given in Table 5.2.

Table 5.2: *Comparison of recidivism by age of first admission to Care*

	Number of convictions as adults		
Age on admission	0,1,2	3+	Total
	N (%)	N (%)	
0–3	13 (54)	11 (46)	24
4–7	13 (87)	2 (13)	15
8–15	22 (43)	29 (57)	51
Total	48	42	90

$X^2 = 8.83$, 2d.f., p < ·02

The findings favour boys first admitted aged 4–7. It would appear that boys first admitted before their fourth birthday had a poorer outcome than boys admitted aged 4–7, even though the comparison is not statistically significant (Fisher's Exact Test, p>.05, N = 39).

The findings so far presented do not take into consideration the fact that several of the boys first admitted before the age of four did not remain continuously in Care, and a few only remained for relatively short periods. In order to try to disentangle the possible consequences of early v. late admission, short v. long-term Care and single v. multiple admissions, we looked for a sample of boys who: (a) were admitted to Care before their fourth birthday, (b) remained in Care for a long time, i.e. over the third quartile for the total sample (i.e. nine and a half years or more), (c) had only one admission, (d) belonged to the original sample, and (e) were not admitted for conduct problems. Thirteen boys fell into this category. There were also six other boys from the original sample who were first admitted by the age of three but who either had *more than* one admission or who were in Care for shorter periods.

If the Care experience is the really damaging factor, then the group of boys largely brought up continuously in Care should have the worst outcome. On a two-by-two contingency table, the sector representing the group who lived *longest* in Care and who had a *poor outcome* should be relatively large. In fact, the reverse was found. This was clearest in relation to seriousness-of-crime scores. Of the thirteen boys living continuously in Care for nine and a half years or more and admitted by the age of three years, *none* had scores of 4 or more, whereas *half* of the others had, as is shown in Table 5.3.

Table 5.3: *Boys admitted 0–3 years of age (original sample), length of Care and continuity by seriousness of crime*

| Length in Care | Seriousness-of-crime scores | | Total |
| | 0–3 | 4–7 | |
	N	N	N
Continuously in Care over third quartile	13	0	13
All others	3	3	6
Total	16	3	19

Fisher's Exact Test, p = ·021.

When three or more convictions was taken as a criterion of 'recidivism', three of the boys longest in Care (twenty-three per cent) were recidivist, compared with half of the others (Fisher's Exact Test, p = .25, NS).

When the total Care group was used, the tendency for the boys longest in Care to do best came out even more clearly. Of the twenty-four boys admitted by the age of three years, seven had scores of 4+ on the seriousness scale for adult crime. *None* were in the group of boys who were admitted *earliest* and remained *longest*. The seven constituted sixty-four per cent of the boys who were admitted by three years of age but who either stayed for shorter periods or who did not remain *continuously* in Care (Fisher's Exact Test, p = .0009).

Eleven boys out of the twenty-four had three or more convictions. Three of these were among the boys continuously in Care for the longest period, so that twenty-three per cent of boys continuously in Care for the longest period were 'recidivist', as compared with seventy-three per cent of the rest of the boys first admitted before their fourth birthday (Fisher's Exact Test, p = .021).

It could be argued that the additional Care cases (N = 34) were a biased sample. Certainly the fact that they were drawn from populations of non-attenders and Child Guidance patients implies either that they probably had personal problems of some kind or that they were not conforming to social rules (about school attendance) at some point in their childhood. However, we have noticed that not *all* the additional group were late admissions to Care, neither was it *only* the late admissions who had serious problems of delinquency. Table 5.4 presents findings for the age of first admission by adult convictions and seriousness-of-crime scores for the additional group of boys in Care.

Table 5.4: *Age on first admission for additional care sub-group by (a) adult convictions and (b) seriousness-of-crime scores (%)*

Age on first admission	(a) Adult convictions				(b) Seriousness-of-crime scores		
	0	1,2	3+	(N)	0	1–3	4+
0–3 years	0	0	100	(5)	0	20	80
4–7 years	0	100	0	(3)	0	100	0
8–15 years	23	12	65	(26)	23	31	46

Note

For recidivism v. non recidivism boys admitted 0–3 years v. 4–7 years, Fisher's Exact Test, p = ·002.

For scores 0–3 v. 4–7 on seriousness, boys admitted 0–3 years v. 4–7 years, Fisher's exact test, p = .007.

The findings just tabulated might, by themselves, suggest that it was slightly better for social workers to wait until boys were past the age of eight before admitting them to Care! This assumes, of course, that they had that choice, which is probably not the case. However, it is clear from findings already presented that those boys who came into Care early, and who *remained*, did relatively well. None of the boys in

Table 5.4 admitted before eight years remained in Care continuously for over two years on their first admission. The likeliest explanation is that they came from homes which were failing to meet their needs and that their return to these homes and environments was one factor accounting for their later delinquency. The reason why boys admitted before *four* had a significantly worse outcome than boys admitted before *eight* could be either that the mothering received by the earliest admitted group was particularly poor or that disruptions were particularly damaging for the youngest group.

A further test was used on *all* boys in Care first admitted before the age of eight (when boys began to be admitted because of behaviour difficulties and delinquency) who came from homes in which at least *one* 'adversity factor' had been noted (N = 47). (Adversity factors are discussed in chapter 9.)

On Spearman's ranking correlation test there was a negative correlation between length in Care and the number of adult convictions (Spearman's r = −.354, p<.01) and for seriousness-of-crime scores (Spearman's r = −.268, p<.05). This strongly suggests that, in comparison with poor natural homes, living in Care was less conducive to later delinquency.

Although it has already been shown that there was (as expected) a significant difference between the outcome for boys admitted with conduct problems and other boys, we have not yet compared the outcome for boys admitted at eight years and later, depending on whether they were admitted for delinquency/behavioural problems or for other reasons.

In one sense boys admitted to Care at eight years and over for non-delinquent reasons did significantly better as adults. Less than half had a conviction (9/19) in comparison with ninety per cent of boys admitted for reasons of delinquency or serious conduct problems (3/41). ($X^2 = 10.63$, 1df, p<.01). In another sense, there was not so much difference: almost a third of boys admitted for non-delinquent reasons had scores of 4 or more for seriousness of crime and, when one compared the average number of convictions and seriousness-of-crime scores for boys in the two groups, their outcome was very similar. The mean number of adult convictions for boys admitted for delinquency or difficult behaviour was 5.6 (SD, 6.4). For boys admitted at eight years and above for non-delinquent reasons, the mean was 5.3 (SD, 7.2). Although there was slightly more difference in the mean average for seriousness-of-crime scores (with the delinquent-admitted group scoring almost 3 and the non-delinquent groups just over 2, there was no significant difference on Mann–Whitney tests between the two groups for either the number of adult convictions or seriousness-of-crime scores.

One way of interpreting these facts is the view that if boys remain in very inadequate environments until eight years of age, their deprivation will tend to manifest itself in later criminal activity, whatever the official reason for their admission to Care. Not all the families from which boys came were equally deficient, and some boys would have had more resilience than others, but, in general, it is possible that the older the child on admission to Care, the greater the likelihood of a poor outcome.

6

Varieties of Care

'Institutions came to be seen as "bad", and child care authorities vied with each other to be at the top of the fostering league.'
Triseliotis and Russell, 1984.

One obvious division of types of Care is into fostering, small group homes and large-group homes. Fostering itself could be divided into fostering with (approved) 'strangers' and fostering by relatives or other friends of the child. There is no agreed upper limit on the size of a small-group home, but with more than twelve children it becomes impossible to regard the group as resembling a natural family in size, and this was the maximum number recommended by the Curtis Committee (1946).

There is a widespread assumption, which was written into the 1948 Children Act, that fostering is the best form of child care. Evidence of the strength of this view in the 1940s and 1950s is to be found in Heywood (1959) and Packman (1975). Its truth has been questioned, e.g. by Eisenberg (1962) and Wolins (1969). Two recent studies, one of young children by Tizard and Hodges (1978) and the other, a retrospective study by Rutter, Quinton and Liddle (1983) of adolescent girls, suggest that there can still be deficiencies in long-term residential care. On the other hand, it could be argued that what seems to be needed in child-care provision is a range of different types of care and treatment, some of which seek to replicate family situations and some of which try to provide a more emotionally neutral, but still committed, environment (cf Davis, 1981).

Two further points need to be made in relation to foster care: (a) it is subject to disruptions, with about half of placements intended to be long-term breaking down within a five-year period or less (Parker, 1966; Trasler, 1960), and (b) many children in residential care, who have experienced foster breakdowns, often feel dislike and resentment towards fostering. Such was the view of a large number of children interviewed in Homes in Britain in the mid-seventies (Page and Clarke, 1977).

It could still be true that fostering is better for most children, and

Triseliotis and Russell (1974) made a very thorough attempt to study whether adoption provided a better environment for children to grow up in than residential care. Their findings are in line with the general view (which we support) that adoption tends to be the best form of substitute care for many children who lack natural caring parents of their own, especially for children whose parents have given them up, or who show no interest in them, or behave in ways that are quite destructive to them. Long-term fostering, however, is not the same as adoption. Frequently, for both foster parents and children, the level of emotional security is not as great as in adoption, and this was even more true in the period in which our subjects grew up, since legislative changes have subsequently increased the rights of foster parents in Britain. We have to ask, in relation to our own study, did boys who were fostered do better than boys who were brought up largely in residential Care? Answering this question for boys in our sample was difficult for four reasons: (a) many of the boys admitted to Care experienced a mixture of types of placement and this is characteristic of children in long-term foster care (Meier, 1966; Triseliotis, 1980), (b) there were very unequal chances of experiencing different types of placement, depending on age on admission, behaviour and (sometimes) parental attitude, (c) the average length of time in Care varied considerably between boys who were fostered and boys who lived mostly in large residential homes, and (d) boys in both foster and residential homes were subject to changes of placement.

The solution we used to try to overcome the first of these problems was to aggregate the lengths of each type of placement and allocate children to a 'predominant' type of placement. If two-thirds of their length of time in Care was spent in any of the following kinds of Care, that was held to be their 'predominant' type of Care. In order to include all boys in Care, two of the categories used had to be composite in nature. 'Predominant' types of Care were as follows: 1, fostering (with either approved or de facto foster parents), 2, a mixture of fostering and group living (small or large), with the greater part in residential Care, 3, small-group and large-group homes, but with a greater period spent in small group homes, and 4, large-group homes.

Was good enough parenting due to length of care or fostering

One of the paradoxical findings so far presented in this monograph has been that, although the outcome for boys in Care was generally poor, boys in Care for the longest periods were significantly less likely to have multiple convictions as adults. It is, of course, possible that this outcome has nothing to do primarily with the length of time boys spent in Care but with other factors, such as the type of Care, i.e. fostering v. residential Care. The subgroup of boys who did particularly well were the quarter of the total sample longest in Care. Half of this group were fostered for most of their period in Care – a higher proportion than that found in any of the other 'quarters'. However, half were not mainly fostered but were brought up either in residential care or in a mixture of residential care and foster placements.

The outcome for the 'half' that was fostered was not significantly better than that of the half that was not. Forty-five per cent of the fostered 'half' had no convictions as adults and eighteen per cent had three or more. Of the residential or 'mixed' half of boys, thirty-six per cent had no convictions and twenty-seven per cent had three or more convictions as adults. The difference was not significant. However, this analysis focuses only on boys who were in Care for the longest periods (over nine and a half years). It is important in that a greater part of their childhood was spent 'in Care'. If there are specific long-term effects of being fostered or living in small-group homes, then these boys should show it.

However important the subgroup of boys who remained longest in Care, they are not a representative sample of children in 'long-term' Care. To obtain a picture of the outcome of such a sample we need to go back to our original cohort of boys (N = 56) who were two or more years in Care. Table 6.1 summarises our findings.

Table 6.1: *Adult crime by types of care (original care sample – percentages)*

Types of Care	(a) Number of convictions				(b) Seriousness-of-crime scores		
	0	1,2	3+	(N)	0	1–3	4+
Fostering	46	21	33	(24)	46	37	17
Mixed	18	50	32	(22)	18	64	18
Large-group homes	30	30	40	(10)	30	30	40
Total				(56)			

$X^2 = 5\cdot8$, 4d.f., $p < \cdot2$ $\qquad\qquad\qquad\qquad$ $X^2 = 7\cdot1$, 4d.f., $p < \cdot1$

It is clear that boys who were mainly fostered were significantly less likely to have convictions than boys in the mixed category (mainly boys in small-group homes). (X^2 for convictions v. no convictions = 5.23, 1df, p<.05.) Since their length of stay in Care was about equal and was longer than for boys in large-group homes, this comparison seems appropriate. It is also clear that, in terms of serious crime, boys in large-group homes did poorly, although numbers are small.

However, it will be remembered that Table 6.1 contains seventeen boys who were committed to Care for reasons of delinquency or being beyond parental control. When these boys were removed from the analysis, we were still left with the impression that the fostered group did slightly better than the other groups and that the group brought up in large residential homes did worst, although differences were not significant, as shown in Table 6.2.

Table 6.2: *Adult crime by types of care. Original care sample – minus admissions for delinquency and being beyond control (%)*

	(a) Number of convictions				(b) Seriousness-of-crime scores		
Types of Care	0	1,2	3+	(N)	0	1–3	4+
Fostering	52	21	26	(19)	52	32	16
Mixed	29	43	29	(14)	29	57	14
Large-group homes	33	17	50	(6)	33	17	50
Total				(39)			

$X^2 = 3 \cdot 799$, 4d.f.; $5 > p > \cdot 4$ $X^2 = 6 \cdot 499$, 4d.f., $\cdot 2 > p > \cdot 1$

It also appears that between a sixth and a quarter of boys who were mainly fostered did rather poorly, depending on our criteria of outcome.

Another way of expressing our findings is to compare the outcome for boys experiencing different types of Care according to whether or not they were admitted: (a) for reasons of delinquency or serious conduct problems, or (b) for other reasons. Our findings appear in Table 6.3.

It appears that, with the exception of large-group homes, the outcome for boys who entered Care for reasons of delinquency and serious conduct problems tended to be worse than that for boys entering Care for other reasons, whether or not the type of Care experienced was mainly fostering or a mixture of fostering and

Table 6.3: *Adult convictions by type of care and reason for admission (%)*

Type of Care	Reason for admission	Adult convictions			
		0	1,2	3+	(N)
Fostering	Non-delinquent	53	21	26	(19)
	Delinquency	20	20	60	(5)
Mixed	Non-delinquent	29	43	29	(14)
	Delinquency	0	63	37	(8)
Large-group	Non-delinquent	33	17	50	(6)
home	Delinquency	25	50	25	(4)
Total					(56)

small-group homes, although, because of small numbers, the differences are not significant within each type of Care. However, for the tiny group of boys in large residential homes (N = 10), the outcome was poor whether or not they entered Care because of delinquency or for other reasons. Only the group of boys who were fostered and who entered Care for reasons other than delinquency or serious conduct problems had a relatively good outcome and, even here, just over a quarter had 3+ convictions as adults.

When we compare the above analyses with the total sample of boys in Care, the picture does not alter dramatically, except that the outcome for boys who had an experience of living mainly in small-group homes or a mixture of fostering and group homes deteriorated when compared with the figures given in Table 6.3. Percentages for convictions for the total Care group are given in Table 6.4.

The increase in the proportions of boys in the mixed type of Care with three or more offences was due to the fact that four 'extra' boys included here were all recidivists as adults.

Since generalisations are frequently made about the outcome of living in Care and the advantages of this or that type of Care, we believed it could be helpful to relate both the outcome and the type of Care to other factors which do not depend upon the Care experience itself and which are often beyond the total control of the professionals involved. These are: the age of a boy on admission, the length of time he spends in Care and the reasons for admission. Confining our analysis to the *total* group of boys in Care, we discovered very considerable differences in the length of time spent in Care by boys in different types of Care. In fact, there was a difference of nearly eight and a half years between the mean length of time spent in Care by boys who were mainly fostered and boys in large-group homes. Average

Table 6.4: *Predominant type of care by number of adult convictions (total care sample) (%)*

Predominant type of Care	*Adult convictions*			
	0	*1,2*	*3+*	*(N)*
1 Fostering	44	20	36	(25)
2 Mixture of fostering and group living	11·5	46	42·5	(26)
3 Mainly small group homes, with some experience of larger homes				
4 Large-group homes	24	21	55	(38)
Total				(89)

$X^2 = 10·92$, 4d.f., p < ·05

lengths and standard deviations for the periods spent in Care for boys experiencing different forms of Care are given in Table 6.5.

In view of the enormous difference between the average length of time spent living in large-group homes and other types of Care, comparisons of outcome seemed inappropriate, but it seemed fair to compare the outcome for boys who were mainly fostered with boys who mainly experienced either small-group living or a mixture of fostering and residential care. We found no significant differences in the proportions who became 'recidivists' (i.e. who had 3+ convictions), but there were significant differences in terms of the proportions who had no convictions as adults, as compared with those who had a conviction ($X^2 = 5.21$, ldf, p<.02). Boys who were fostered did

Table 6.5: *Mean lengths of time in Care by type of Care (total Care sample)*

Type of Care	Mean length	SD	N
1 Fostering	10 years 5 months	4 years 10 months	25
2 Fostering and group living			
3 Small-group homes with some experience of larger homes	8 years 4 months	4 years 8 months	26
4 Large-group homes	2 years 0 months	3 years 2 months	38
Total Group	6 years 4 months	5 years 6 months	89

better in this respect than boys who lived in small-group homes or who had a very mixed experience of types of Care.

It has to be remembered that, in the period of time we are studying, fostering was the preferred, even almost the obligatory, first 'option' for children in Care and that children were boarded out unless they were judged to be too old or too difficult or had already been fostered (usually on several occasions) and their placements had broken down. In these circumstances, they were admitted to residential care and they tended to remain there only if they were thought to be unsuitable for further foster placements.

Some indication of the 'raw material' for fostering and for small-group and large-group homes is available by comparing the predominant 'type' of Care with the official reasons for admission. Nearly two-thirds (sixty-four per cent) of the boys who were fostered were admitted because of parental neglect or their parents' death, illness or handicap. These reasons accounted for only just over a quarter of boys living mainly in large residential homes and nearly two-fifths of boys living in small-group homes or experiencing fostering and group living equally. These differences are apparent in Table 6.6.

Table 6.6: *Reasons for entering Care by predominant type of Care* (%)

Predominant type of Care	Illness, death of parent, etc. (Column %)	Moral danger, neglect (Column %)	School non-attendance (Column %)	Delinquency remand, beyond control (Column %)	
Fostering	42	46	33	12	
Mixed	31	39	11	30	
Large-group home	27	15	56	57	
(N)	(26)	(13)	(9)	(40)	(89)

$X^2 = 14{\cdot}52$, 6d.f., $p < {\cdot}05$
One case missing.

Other factors

The type of Care experienced was also found to be significantly associated (as we had anticipated) with the age of the boy on admission to Care. Using the original four categories of type of Care (ie 1 fostering, 2 mixed, 3 small-group, and 4 large-group), there was a ranking correlation co-efficient of .341 (p<.001) between age on admission and the type of Care experienced. Using the same test (Kendal's T), there were found to be significant correlations between the number of juvenile convictions and the predominant type of Care experienced (T = .334, p<.001) and also between the number of kinds of antisocial disorder recorded of the child and the predominant type of Care experienced (T = .256, p<.001). In other words, although when we looked at the total sample of boys in Care the outcome for boys who were fostered was distinctly better in relation to the proportion altogether free from convictions, the boys who were fostered were different from boys who lived mainly in residential care in several important respects: on the whole they entered Care earlier and largely for different reasons and they were less disordered in conduct and less delinquent as juveniles than boys in residential care.

Conclusion on the outcome for boys in different types of Care

The findings presented in this chapter have consistently suggested that boys who were fostered did slightly better than boys in residential care, at least in the sense that a higher proportion were totally free of convictions as adults (approximately one-third had three or more convictions). On the other hand, we are not comparing like with like, in that the older the boy on admission and the more problems he had, the less likely he was to be fostered in the first place, or (if he was) to remain in foster care. Most of the boys with serious conduct problems or convictions experienced mainly residential care. Only five boys from the original sample who were admitted for reasons of delinquency continued to live mainly in foster care. Their outcome was poor. However, numbers here are very small and the expectations of the foster parents and the Children's Department a generation ago were undoubtedly different from those of contemporary 'specialist' foster parents and social workers when delinquent boys are placed with foster parents, often on a contract basis (Shaw and Hipgrave, 1983). The outcome for the boys in our study who grew up in large-group homes was poor, although numbers again are very small and need to be treated with caution.

There are several other complicating factors, such as the number of placements experienced by these boys, the amount of family contact and their 'destination' on discharge, all of which affect an evaluation of the outcome of different types of care.

7

Changes of placement & parental contact

'There's nothing in this world constant but inconstancy.'
Swift.

One of the most widespread reasons for anxiety about the quality of public Care provided for children deprived of a normal home life has been that children in long-term Care experience a considerable amount of discontinuity in parenting, partly because of multiple care-takers and staff rotas in residential Care, but also because of changes of placement in both foster and residential care.

Moving from one Home to another, or from one set of foster parents to another, almost invariably arouses anxiety and not infrequently the pain of loss or self-blame. Some of the anxiety and pain can be considerably diminished by proper introductions and the way in which the transition is managed. It is sometimes true that once a child has got over leaving one home and settling into another, he may really begin to thrive. He may indeed feel relief at having left what had become for him a seemingly awful and impossible predicament. That fact does not justify placing children in what are likely to be impossible situations. We have already referred (in Chapters 1 and 2) to several studies which have found that children in long-term Care experience an excessive number of changes of placement. (Meier, 1965; Murphy, 1974; Parker, 1966; Trasler, 1960; Triseliotis, 1980). There is some evidence that, in recent years, the pace of changes in placement might be increasing. Milham *et al.* (1986) and Packman, Randall and Jacques (1986) both found high rates of changes of placement for newly admitted adolescents and children in England and Wales. Milham *et al.* (*op. cit.*) found that over half their subjects had had three or more placements in a two-year period, and fourteen per cent had had more than four. Packman, Randall and Jacques (1986) found that four out of five children had moved at least twice and a quarter had moved at least four times in the space of a few months.

Attachment theory might lead us to suppose that a childhood

characterised by frequent changes in placement could well lead to faulty conscience development, since there might be either failure to make adequate attachment bonds or a frequent breaking of bonds that had been made. It might lead to a child thinking of himself as an out-and-out failure or to viewing the adult world as essentially untrustworthy. If this were so, we might expect boys with an above average number of placements to be more criminal as adults. It is also likely that boys with conduct problems antagonise foster parents and residential social workers and are likely to be more quickly moved from one home to another. On the other hand, it could be that residential living encourages a more neutral atmosphere and allows for greater tolerance of conduct problems, so that the 'turnover rate' for boys with conduct problems may be slower in residential homes than in foster homes. However, it is clear that breakdowns do occur in residential homes and Wolkind (1977a) found, when he studied a group of boys in residential Care, that there was a significant association between being relatively less deviant in conduct and staying two years or more in the same Children's Home.

Although children often find the experience of moving anxiety – provoking and distressing, and young people who have left Care comment unfavourably about it (e.g. Stein and Carey, 1986), there is so far little hard evidence of its long-term consequences. However, Triseliotis and Russell (1984) found an association between frequent moves and later psychiatric treatment. It is unclear what exactly this association means or which way the causality works.

The range of the number of placements for the total sample of boys in our study who were in Care was one to thirteen, with the median falling at two and the mean at 4.5. To have divided at two placements would not have produced a group of boys whose experience was clearly of several placements. We divided at the mean average, i.e. between four and five. In addition, there were almost a priori grounds for such a cut-off point, given that nearly all the children in our study had to have at least two placements if they stayed any length of time in Care since, unless they were already in de facto foster placements on admission, their first placement was always in an assessment centre and was inevitably temporary. Three, or possibly four, placements might seem just acceptable in terms of good child care, especially when one considers that if parents discharged children and they then returned to Care, this was counted as one change in placement.

There was no evidence that a large number of placements was

associated with an increase in adult offending.

Outcome for type of Care and number of placements for the original sample is presented in Table 7.1

Table 7.1: *Adult offending and seriousness-of-crime scores by number and type of placement (original sample) (%)*

Number of placements and type of Care	(a) Number of convictions				(b) Seriousness-of-crime scores		
	0	*1,2*	*3+*	*(N)*	*0*	*1–3*	*4*
Fostering (1–4)	41	18	41	(17)	41	41	18
(5–8)	57	29	14	(7)	57	29	14
Mixed (1–4)	12·5	37·5	50	(8)	12·5	62·5	25
(5–8)	21	57	21	(14)	21	64	14
Large (1–4)	17	50	33	(6)	17	50	33
Homes (5–8)	50	0	50	(4)	50	0	50

The above table includes seventeen boys admitted because of delinquency or being beyond parental control. When these were removed, much the same picture emerged for boys in the original sample admitted to Care for reasons other than delinquency and conduct problems as is shown in Table 7.2.

Table 7.2: *Adult offending by number and type of placements (original sample minus admissions for delinquency)*

	Number of convictions			
Type and number of placements	*0* (%)	*1,2* (%)	*3+* (%)	*(N)*
Fostering (1–4)	50	17	33	(12)
(5–8)	57	29	14	(7)
Mixed (1–4)	20	40	40	(5)
(5–8)	33	44	22	(9)
Large (1–4)	25	25	50	(4)
group (5–8)	50	0	50	(2)
Total				(39)

Findings in relation to seriousness-of-crime scores are roughly similar.

It is noteworthy that in all types of care except large-group homes (where numbers, in any case, are small), boys with less than the mean number of placements (4.5) did slightly, but not significantly, *worse* than boys with more than the mean number.

We wished to see if there was any association between the sheer number of placements, as a measure of disruption, and outcome in terms of numbers of convictions and seriousness of crime. To do this, we ignored the type of care experienced. There was no association between having a greater than (mean) average number of placements and having three or more convictions, or scores of 4+ for seriousness. Findings for the original sample are given in percentages in Table 7.3.

Table 7.3: *Number of placements by number of adult convictions and seriousness-of-crime scores (original sample – percentages)*

Number of placements	(a) Adult convictions				(b) Seriousness-of-crime scores		
	0	1,2	3	(N)	0	1–3	4+
1–4	29	29	42	(31)	29	48	23
5–13	36	40	24	(25)	36	44	20
Total				(56)			

$X^2 = 2 \cdot 01$, 2 d.f., $\cdot 5 > p > \cdot 3$ $X^2 = 0 \cdot 31$, 2 d.f., $p > \cdot 5$

It is clear that there is little difference in outcome, but that boys with a larger than average number of placements did slightly better. However, this comparison does not take into account the length of time boys stayed in Care. We focused firstly on boys in Care for more than the median length for the original sample (eight years five months). Twenty-eight boys fell into this category, of whom ten (thirty-six per cent) had had between one and four placements and the rest had had more. Forty per cent of the boys with up to four placements had no convictions as adults and thirty-nine per cent of the boys with five or more placements. Slightly more of the boys with *fewer* placements had three or more convictions (thirty per cent v. twenty-two per cent). For seriousness of crime, slightly more of the boys with *more* placements (i.e. seventeen per cent v ten per cent) had seriousness scores of 4 or more. For boys in Care *up to* the median in length, outcome in terms of seriousness of crime was very much the same for boys with up to and over four placements. There was a slightly higher proportion of boys with fewer placements who were recidivist (forty-eight per cent v. twenty-nine per cent) but this did not approach statistical significance.

Finally, we examined the outcome for the total sample of boys in Care, as is shown in Table 7.4, revealing that boys with fewer placements were more criminal as adults.

We checked this result with non-parametric test of correlation.

Table 7.4: *Comparison of number of adult convictions according to number of placements in Care (total sample)*

Number of placements	Number of adult convictions			
	0 N (%)	1–2 N (%)	3 or more N (%)	Total
1–4	14 (23)	14 (22)	33 (55)	61
5–13	10 (36)	11 (39)	7 (25)	28
Total	24	25	40	89

$X^2 = 6.60$, 2d.f., $p < .05$

Kendal's T for the number of placements by the number of adult convictions was $-.124$, $p<.05$, $N = 89$ (for seriousness-of-crime scores $T = -.110$, $p>.05$, NS).

Part of the reason for this is that boys entering Care later, for reasons of delinquency and conduct problems, tended to have fewer placements (seventy-seven per cent had between one and four compared with sixty-one per cent admitted for other reasons). The placements also tended to be shorter. For boys entering Care for reasons of delinquency and conduct problems, the average length of a placement was just one year (with a standard deviation of a year), for all other boys entering Care, the average was two and a half years (with a standard deviation of almost three years).

In addition, the longer a boy stayed in Care, the more likely he was to have several placements, partly because foster families are subject to all the natural hazards that affect nuclear families (e.g. illness, death and marital disharmony), and more besides, and partly because residential homes may close as staff move on, morale breaks down, the property becomes unsuitable or there is a change in child-care policy.

It is possible that one good placement makes up for a lot of poor or unhappy ones. It is also likely (but not inevitable) that foster care placements which lasted over many years were, on the whole, a help to boys in Care. We measured the length of the longest foster placement of boys whose predominant experience of Care was either fostering or fostering and group living ($N = 35$) and compared the length of this placement with the number and seriousness of adult convictions. It was reassuring to find a significant negative correlation. For length of longest placement by number of adult convictions, Kendal's $T = -.201$, $p<.05$, $N = 35$, and for seriousness-of-crime scores, $T = -.219$, $p<.05$, $N = 35$. In other words, the longer the longest foster placement, the less the criminality of the individual concerned (after sixteen years of age). However, since many of the longest fosterings resulted in the child remaining with the foster parents after official discharge from Care, these foster children experienced the very considerable 'bonus' of careful supervision and emotional support in their nineteenth and subsequent years, which were not available to many other boys who had been in Care.

We wished to see if there was an association between foster breakdown or disruption and later crime. The strength of fostering lies in its resemblance to natural families, with the creation of strong bonds and a great deal of emotional closeness. It seemed to us that breakdown of long-term fostering relationships might be more damaging than other breakdowns. We focused on the longest foster placement each boy experienced (although it is possible that shorter placements were sometimes more significant for children, and their breakdown or disruption more upsetting).

We wished to see if there was an association between the experience of fostering and the outcome in terms of adult crime. We found that we could group together 'experiences' into four kinds: (a) where the placement apparently went well and no serious difficulties were reported, (b) where there were serious problems and placements appeared to be in some jeopardy but did not actually break down, (c) where the boy's behaviour allegedly led to a breakdown in fostering, and (d) where illness, death or other problems in the foster family, or unease by children's officers about the level of parenting skills, led to the placement being terminated.

There were no significant differences in outcome, but this may be due to small numbers. Three out of the four boys in the first category (no problems, and no breakdown) had no convictions as adults, whereas this was true (a) of only a third of boys who were moved allegedly because of their difficult behaviour, and (b) of only just over a quarter of boys who had to change placements because of difficulties in the foster family or inadequate foster care.

Since we wished to study boys who had had a reasonably long experience of foster care, we confined our study to boys whose longest foster placement was two years or more (N = 33). Rather to our surprise, by far the commonest reasons for 'breakdown' or 'disruption' were difficulties in the foster family, followed by the Department's anxieties about inadequate foster care.

Among the commonest difficulties leading to breakdown were the death or serious illness of foster parents (six cases). In two cases the reason was the break-up of the foster parents' marriage, in one case the arrival of a further natural child and, in another, problems in the foster parents' own children. However, there were also less 'acceptable' reasons for breakdown: in two cases the Children's Department placed further children with the result that the foster mothers could not cope, there was one case of indecent assault by a foster father and one case in which the foster father was convicted of receiving stolen goods. Fifty-six per cent of all boys in 'long term' placements which did not break down were free of convictions as adults, compared with just under thirty per cent of boys in placements which did break down. (Fisher's Exact Test for convictions v. no convictions, p = .123 NS). Proportions with three or more convictions ranged from a quarter in placements which did not break down to just over a third in placements which did.

Contact with parents

Lack of contact with natural parents has been alleged to be a damaging factor in Care. Weinstein (1960), Holman (1973), Jenkins (1969), Thorpe (1980) and Milham *et al.* (1986) all present findings which show associations between lack of regular parental contact and various measures or signs of maladjustment in the child. It would not follow that lack of regular contact is the only, or even the main, cause of maladjustment or disturbance, although research into the related field of loss of parents by marital separation or divorce (Wallerstein and Kelly, 1980) suggests that failure to visit by the non-custodial parent is a source of distress and disturbance. Nor does it always follow that it is best for the child to keep on trying to revive flagging parental interest, although we would strongly support Milham *et al.* (*op. cit.*) in arguing that more thought and effort needs to be put into maintaining links with parents when children come into Care.

Pringle and Bossio (1960) found that most children in Care seemed better adjusted if they had regular contact with parents or other adult figures who 'came in' from outside the Care situation. On the other hand, Holman (1973) and Wolkind (1977a) found that irregular visits seemed to produce more disturbance than no visiting at all. George (1970) found that regular visiting appeared to make no difference and Thorpe (1980) and Bowley (1951) describe instances of visits by disturbed or rejecting parents which led to children becoming disturbed in behaviour or feeling very distressed.

Visits by parents or other relatives and the frequency of the child's stays at home appear to have been fairly regularly noted in most of our files. There was also note of letters received from natural parents and other relatives. Children were divided by the criterion of whether or not, for the greater part of their stay in Care, they had received four or more visits a year (or gone home four or more times or had four or more letters from parents or other relatives). There was some fluctuation in the amount of parental contact for some children who were in Care for several years, with relatively more contact for the first few months or just prior to discharge, but in most cases, i.e. in all but one of the original sample and in all but sixteen of the total sample, it was clear from the records whether the children had had regular contact with their parents or not.

There were significant associations between having *regular* contact and being *more* criminal in adult life. Findings are shown in Table 7.5.

Table 7.5: *Parental contact and adult crime (original sample)* (%)

Amount of parental contact	Number of convictions				Seriousness-of-crime scores		
	0	1,2	3+	(N)	0	1–3	4+
More than four letters, visits a year.	13	39	48	(23)	13	57	30
Fewer than four letters, visits a year.	47	31	22	(32)	47	41	12
Total				(55)			

$X^2 = 7 \cdot 67$, 2d.f., p $< \cdot 05$ $X^2 = 7 \cdot 55$, 2d.f., p $< \cdot 05$
One case missing – no evidence.

It is apparent that more than half the boys in the sample (fifty-eight per cent) had less than this somewhat minimal level of contact, and this is in keeping with other studies of children in long-term Care, e.g. Walton and Heywood (1971), in a study of 367 children in the Care of local authorities in the North-West, found that more than half received fewer than two visits a year. Triseliotis (1980), in a study of forty children fostered continuously in the same placement, found that seventy three per cent had had no contact with parents for over two years.

There did not appear to be any organised scheme of visiting by lay 'uncles' and 'aunts' for boys in our sample who lacked parental contact. When we examined the *total* sample of boys in Care, our findings were very similar to those already given for the original sample of boys in Care, as the figures in Table 7.6 show.

Table 7.6: *Number of adult convictions of boys in care divided according to the level of parental contact during care total sample*

Amount of parental contact	Number of adult convictions			Total
	0 N (%)	1–2 N (%)	3 or more N (%)	
Four or more visits or letters a year	7 (18)	13 (32)	20 (50)	40
Fewer than four visits/ letters a year	15 (44)	10 (29)	9 (27)	34
Total	22	23	29	74

Note
15 cases unclear.
$X^2 = 7.033$, 2d.f., p < ·05

Lack of parental visiting is likely to be related either to length of Care or to the reasons for admission, or both. Only the parent with strong bonds with his child will be likely to continue regular visits to a child in Care over several years, and some of the reasons why children were admitted to Care (death or desertion of a parent, severe handicap or illness in a parent and parental neglect) themselves suggest why children were not regularly visited. On the other hand, if a boy is committed to Care because of his delinquency or conduct problems, this does not in itself usually lead to severance of parental contact.

Strong associations were, in fact, found between length of time in Care and the regularity of parental contact. Sixty-three per cent of the total sample of boys in Care up to the median length (5 years and 10 months) appeared to have at least four letters or visits annually and many had considerably more (N = 40), compared with fifteen per cent of children in Care over the median for length (N = 34) ($X^2 = 15.5$, ldf, p <.0001). Significant associations were also found between being admitted for reasons of delinquency, conduct and truancy, as compared with other reasons. Only eight per cent of the 'former' group had fewer than four visits or letters per year (total N = 36), as compared with nearly two-thirds (sixty-three per cent) of boys in the latter group (total N = 38) ($X^2 = 21.7$, ldf, p<.001.).

It becomes apparent that boys admitted to Care for reasons of delinquency, truancy or being beyond parental control largely continued to retain contact with parents whilst in Care. It could be that contact with parents was not a criminogenic factor, either in its presence or its absence, but tended to be associated with other factors (e.g. conduct disorder or delinquency) which were themselves causally related to adult crime, although it is probably true that some boys who were fostered long-term or who lived in stable small-group homes for many years would have come to accept their care-takers as having a quasi-parental role.

Comments

The findings presented in this chapter strongly suggest that having several changes of home and care-taker in childhood was not conducive to greater delinquency in adult life. Undoubtedly, changes in placement can be extremely painful or upsetting for children, especially small children. It could well be that many changes were followed by periods of disturbed emotions or conduct. If that were so, either the consequences did not continue into adult life or, if they did, they were reflected in ways other than in official crime. That other adverse outcomes may be a kind of alternative to crime is shown in Wadsworth's study (1979), which showed that certain psychosomatic illnesses (e.g. ulcerative colitis and referral to a psychiatrist) were found more frequently among males with deprived childhoods who did not become criminal.

When these findings are combined with our findings about the adverse consequences for children of experiencing very inadequate parenting in their natural homes (Chapter 9), they strongly suggest that social workers, lawyers and magistrates should question the force of the frequently-used objection to admission to Care: that it will involve several changes of placement and that this will inevitably damage a child. Of course, this is no excuse for children having to experience a large number of placements and we have (personally) heard of children in Care who have had several more changes of placement than even the maximum found for boys in our study. Also, recent studies suggest (as we have already noted) that changes in placement are becoming even more frequent for children in Care (Milham *et al.*, 1986; Packman, Randall and Jacques, 1986).

Our findings in relation to parental visiting are in line with common-sense expectations and social workers' experience: the longer boys stay in Care, the less, on the whole, parents visit. Many social workers would wish to express this the other way round: the less parents visit, the longer their children stay in Care. Our data do not provide evidence to show whether this was the case or not, except that in some cases it was clearly impossible for parents to visit – they had died or were in a hospital, sanatorium or prison. However, our data suggest that, judged by the very limited criterion of adult crime, children were able to grow up in Care without contact from their natural parents and they did not, as a consequence, become recidivist or commit serious crimes. Many did form strong bonds with substitute parents. The relationship between rehabilitation and parental contact is that the latter is a necessary, but not a sufficient, condition for the former.

8

Age and destination on discharge from Care

'It's not being in Care – what matters is when you've got to leave it . . . it frightens me . . . thinking: "where am I gonna be next year? I'm not gonna be here. Where am I gonna be?".

Quotation from boy in Care after eighteen years; Stein and Carey, 1986.

All the boys in our sample who had remained in Care until seventeen years of age legally ceased to be the responsibility of the local authority on their eighteenth birthday. It seems not only possible but very likely that the social environment of young men between the age of fifteen and twenty, including their home and peer group, will considerably influence their behaviour and thus the probability of their becoming involved in crime. Gibbens (1963) found that thirty-one per cent of their sample of Borstal lads only committed their first offence after the age of seventeen years and that a further 42.7% had committed only one previous juvenile offence. The child who has remained in Care up to the age of eighteen may then find himself with no home of his own and very little by way of emotional supports. The boy who is committed to Care for reasons of delinquency may well return to his own home and a neighbourhood which was originally at least part of the cause of his delinquency. However, his family may have changed considerably – sometimes for the worse.

We compared the outcome for the boys in our sample with their age on discharge, first for the original sample and then for the total sample. For the original sample there was an almost significant difference, in relation to having a conviction, between the proportions discharged by the age of fifteen and those discharged later. Our findings are presented in Table 8.1.

A cut-off point was made at fifteen years of age because most boys who had been committed to Care for reasons of delinquency, truancy or being beyond parental control were allowed home at fifteen (when compulsory school attendance was over and they were able to start earning their own living). Although the outcome of the boys discharged later was better, over a fifth had seriousness-of-crime scores of 4 or more, which means that a minority did decidedly poorly.

When we compared the outcome for age on discharge for the whole

Table 8.1: *Adult crime by age on discharge – original sample*

Age on discharge	Number of adult convictions				Seriousness-of-crime scores		
	0	*1,2*	*3+*	*(N)*	*0*	*1–3*	*4+*
Up to 15 years	9	45·5	45·5	(11)	9	73	18
After 15 years	38	31	31	(45)	38	40	22
Total				(56)			

Note
For convictions v. no convictions – Fisher's Exact Test, p = ·065.

Care sample, we again found that boys who were *older* than fifteen on discharge were significantly less likely to commit offences. Thirty-five per cent were altogether free, compared with only fifteen per cent of boys discharged by the age of fifteen ($X^2 = 3.96$, ldf, p<.05).

In relation to multiple convictions (three or more offences) there was a difference which was almost significant which favoured boys discharged later. Forty-five per cent of boys discharged after the age of fifteen had three or more offences as adults, as compared with over half (fifty-six per cent) of boys discharged at fifteen years of age or younger. The result approached statistical significance ($X^2 = 3.82$, ldf, p>.05, NS).

There are at least two possible explanations for these findings, but these are not altogether mutually exclusive. Firstly, we have noted that many boys who were allowed home at fifteen were boys who entered Care because of some form of conduct disorder or delinquency (convictions or being beyond parental control). Conduct disorder and recidivism are often very persistent traits and it is likely that a high proportion of boys still had conduct problems on leaving Care and went on being convicted. Secondly, boys with delinquency and conduct problems (as we have already noted) returned to the environments from which they came and which had possibly partly caused, or failed to prevent, their delinquency in the first place.

We think there is probably some truth in both these explanations. It was certainly true that there were differences in outcome for the boys according to their destinations on discharge. The last record on most of the Child Care files was the address to which the child had been discharged. Table 8.2 shows the proportions of adolescent boys from the original Care sample who returned to their natural homes, stayed with foster parents, went into 'corrective establishments', i.e. Approved Schools, Detention Centres and Remand Homes in other authorities, or went to other 'settings', such as hostels, lodgings, farming, forestry or residential employment. Discharge to grand-parents, siblings and other relatives was included as part of discharge home – even though the relatives' home may have been very different from the parental home. Six young men went into the armed forces or merchant navy and, for purposes of assessing criminal careers, present separate problems. They are omitted from analysis in Table 8.2.

Table 8.2: *Adult crime by destination on discharge from Care*
Original sample – %

Destination on discharge	Number of convictions				Seriousness-of-crime scores		
	0	1,2	3+	(N)	0	1–3	4+
Natural/ relatives' home	15	50	35	(20)	15	65	20
Foster parents	50	22	28	(18)	50	28	22
Correctional agency	0	33	67	(3)	0	33	67
Other	33	22	44	(9)	33	56	11
Total				(49)			

$X^2 = 8.75$, 6d.f., $.3 > p > .2$ $\qquad\qquad$ $X^2 = 11.05$, 6d.f., $p < .1$
For convictions v. no convictions, natural parents v. foster parents, $X^2 = 3.87$, 1df., $p < .05$

A similar picture emerged when the *total* sample of boys in Care was compared for the outcome of boys going to different forms of living arrangements on leaving Care in respect of convictions v. no convictions, as appears in Table 8.3.

It is to be expected that boys who were discharged from Care to correctional agencies (usually Approved Schools but, in one case, Borstal) would have a poorer outcome as adults. In both the original and the total Care samples, a significantly higher proportion of boys who stayed with foster parents were altogether free from adult convictions, as compared with boys returning to their own homes or relatives (for the total sample $X^2 = 6.43$, 1df, p<.02). However, it is noticeable that the proportion of boys 'discharged' to foster parents (in Table 8.2) who had seriousness-of-crime scores of 4 or more was slightly higher than that of boys who returned home. It is also noteworthy that, although a *high* proportion (sixty-six per cent) of boys who

Table 8.3: *Adult criminality by 'destination' on discharge from Care*
  (percentage)

Destination on discharge	Percentage convicted as adults	Total number
Natural/relatives home	83	(41)
Foster parent	47	(19)
Correctional agency	92	(14)
Other (except armed forces etc)	67	(9)
Total		(83)

Note
$X^2 = 11 \cdot 72$, 3d.f., $p < \cdot 01$ (the small actual numbers involved in the bottom line do not greatly affect the X^2 value).

went into hostels, lodgings etc. had convictions, a very *low* proportion (eleven per cent) were considered to have really serious criminal careers (i.e. seriousness-of-crime scores of 4+). However, numbers in this last group are small (N = 9).

Are we observing the long-term consequences of growing up in different types of Care, of living arrangements on leaving Care, of both or of something else? Some caution is certainly needed in interpreting these findings. Firstly, it is clear from some files that at least a few boys did not remain long in any of the settings to which they were discharged. Secondly, there were extremely unequal chances of being discharged home, to foster parents or elsewhere, depending on the length of time spent in Care. The longer a boy was in Care, the less likely he was to return home (sometimes because there was no home to go to). Boys who stayed with foster parents usually had the benefit of a home base and concerned adults and friends to turn to, especially in times of need. However, it was clear from some records that at least a few foster children, both male and female, left their foster homes shortly after their official discharge from Care. The reasons are not clear from the notes.

When the total group of boys was divided at the median for length in Care, it was found that length of time in Care and destination on discharge were very significantly associated, as appears in Table 8.4. $X^2 = 26.35$, 2 df, p<.001 (including boys discharged to armed forces and merchant navy). The difference is almost entirely accounted for by the proportions of children staying with either foster parents or natural families on discharge.

Was the superior outcome of the quarter of boys longest in Care to

Table 8.4: *Comparison of length of time in Care and destination on discharge*

Length of time in Care	Natural family N (%)	Foster parents N (%)	Other N (%)	Total
Up to the median	29 (67)	0 (0)	16 (33)	45
Over the median	12 (27)	19 (43)	13 (30)	44
Total	41	19	29	89

$X^2 = 26\cdot35$, 2d.f., p < ·001

some extent due to their living arrangements in discharge? Only twenty-three per cent of the quarter of the boys longest in Care returned to relatives or their natural families, as compared with over three-fifths of other boys. Nearly thirty per cent of the boys longest in Care moved to lodgings, the armed forces, the merchant navy or work that offered living in, e.g. forestry or the hotel business. This was true of less than five per cent of the rest of the sample. From boys longest in Care, fewer than one in ten moved out of Care into Approved Schools, Remand Homes or Borstals (N = 2). By contrast, one in five of the rest of the sample moved out of Care into remand or corrective institutions of some kind. Nearly two-fifths of the quarter of boys longest in Care remained with foster parents on discharge, as compared with fewer than one in six of the rest of the sample. These differences may well account for some of the variation in outcome in terms of adult crime, although boys in the long-stay group would appear to be advantaged in some ways and disadvantaged in others, e.g. we would assume that living in foster care was an advantage, but that moving into various forms of residential settings might be a disadvantage.

Thirdly, an association was found between 'destinations' on discharge and the level of juvenile delinquency, which suggested that their level of delinquency and conduct disorder as *juveniles* was in some ways (and for different reasons) related to their 'destinations' on discharge. Our findings are shown in Table 8.5.

When the total number of antisocial symptoms recorded in childhood was compared with destinations on discharge, with 0 and 1 antisocial behaviours being compared with the rest, the results were almost identical with the above ($X^2 = 10.23$, 3 df, p<.02, N = 83).

These findings suggest, as one might expect, that where a boy lives on leaving Care and his subsequent criminal career are both influenced at least indirectly, and sometimes directly, by his behaviour in

Table 8.5: *Juvenile convictions by destinations on discharge*

Destination	Percentage convicted as juvenile	(N)
Natural parents/ relatives' home.	58·5	(41)
Foster parent	31·6	(19)
Correctional agency	84·6	(14)
Other	44·4	(9)
Total		(83)

$X^2 = 10·18$, 3d.f., $p < ·02$ (see comments on Table 8.3).

adolescence, including his officially recorded convictions. There was, however, evidence that where he went to live on discharge might affect not only the level of his offending, but also society's response to it.

Twenty-six young men who had been in Care were 'sentenced' to prison. A disturbing finding was that four of the nine young men who were discharged to lodgings, farms, forestry and residential work were sentenced to prison. In comparison with boys discharged to other destinations, this was relatively high, only being surpassed by the boys discharged to a corectional agency. Findings are presented in Table 8.6 of proportions (from the total Care sample) sentenced to prison and their seriousness-of-crime scores.

It appears worrying that only one of the four young men in the

Table 8.6: *Sentencing to prison by destination on discharge and seriousness score*

Destination	Sentenced to prison No N (%)	Yes N (%)	Seriousness-of-crime score 4+	Total
Natural/relatives' home	30 (73)	11 (27)	(29)	41
Foster parent	16 (84)	3 (16)	(22)	19
Correctional agency	6 (43)	8 (57)	(69)	14
Other (except armed forces etc)	5 (55·5)	4 (44·4)	(11·1)	9
Total	57	26		83

Note
$X^2 = 7·57$, 3d.f., $p < ·055$ (see comments on Table 8.3).

bottom group who were sentenced to prison had a seriousness-of-crime score of 4 or more. By contrast, the proportions of men in the other three groups judged to have a seriousness-of-crime score of 4+ was, in each case, slightly higher than the percentage sentenced to prison.

Although numbers are small, this raises the question of whether young men in the bottom group suffered more severe penalties, or threats of penalties (i.e. suspended sentences), either because they lacked families and allies to speak on their behalf, or obtain legal representation in Court, or because the Courts might more frequently use, or threaten to use, a custodial sentence on a young man with possibly no fixed address and no relatives. The criminal records of the four were examined in more detail.

Two were in fact committed to prison, one for non-payment of a fine (of £25) incurred for theft, his only offence, and the other on two occasions; after being given three suspended prison sentences for crimes of violence and then going on to commit further crimes of violence.

The other two young men received only suspended sentences and, since they apparently kept clear of crime, they were not actually committed to prison. The numbers involved are small, so that not too much weight should be placed on the finding. It is also the case that there has been a rapid increase in the extent to which legal services can now be obtained free of charge in Britain since the period in which our subjects were growing up. On the other hand, it could still be the case that magistrates, judges and the police take a slightly harsher line towards young men who have been in Care, because of the use of Care as a punishment for crime.

Our findings give limited support to the case eloquently made by Stein and Carey (1986) and Burgess (1981) that young people leaving Care not only require good preparation but are entitled to continued help and support from the community. If the community is to act as parent, then it cannot simply cut off its responsibilities when young people cross the threshold of adult life.

Discussion

The whole area of what happens to the approximately fourteen thousand young people discharged annually from Care in Britain between the ages of sixteen and eighteen has until recently received all too little attention. What happens to young people *after* leaving Care is almost certainly just as important as what happens to them while they are *in* Care. One reason why the long-term outcome for many – but by no means all – young people who have been brought up in Care is relatively poor is that, on leaving Care, many young people run into problems with accommodation, lack of money, loneliness and having nobody and nowhere to fall back on. Stein and Carey (1986) discovered a great deal of loneliness, poverty, problems with accommodation and unemployment among a group of about forty young people who had left Care. The original sample of eighty dropped to almost half, probably because of the rootlessness of the young people involved. Mulvey (1977) points to the need for preparation for independent living while young people are still in Care, including experiencing shopping, cooking and budgeting. Such training seems extremely important, but the grimmest facts that emerged from his study of a small group of young people discharged from Care in the Greater London Area were their stark material poverty, and their lack of friends and caring 'parental' figures. Only one boy had any utensils of his own, and only one girl owned her own bedding (out of a total of sixteen subjects). Of the eight young people who had been ill enough in the two and a half years since discharge to require a period in bed, two had had to manage on their own, and two had been admitted to hospital. Four of the eight said they would have to look after themselves if they became ill again. Eleven of the sixteen had suffered from depression or anxiety, in one case to the extent of overdosing.

Although it seems right to encourage all young people to be fairly self-supportive, a policy of expecting most sixteen to eighteen-year-olds to manage entirely on their own seems quite unrealistic and unfeeling. How many natural parents would feel it in their own children's best interests to push them from the 'nest' at sixteen, or even eighteen, years of age? Some local authorities are now trying at least to provide accommodation and a befriending service to young people leaving Care. It is apparent from the follow-up study by Rutter, Quinton and Liddle (1983) of girls who had been in residential Care, that the liaisons and supports they found in the years after leaving Care, and all that they experienced, then, were extremely important for them. It is not difficult to see how young men and women with inadequate accommodation, little money and no friends or parental advice, are tempted to steal or become involved in other dishonest or illegal practices.

9

Possible family and other social influences

'I was much too far out all my life
And not waving but drowning.'
Stevie Smith.

When social workers and others are considering whether or not to remove a child from home and place him in what is likely to be long-term Care, they are acting as brokers between evils. It follows that, in studying the possible consequences of living long-term in Care, it is not sufficient simply to assess the factors associated with living in Care. It is necessary to try to calculate the consequences of leaving a child in his own family.

Associations have repeatedly been found in research between delinquency in boys and: (a) living in distorted relationships, and (b) lax parental supervision. Distorted relationships include both skewed parent/child relationships and hostility and schism between spouses. Hewitt and Jenkins (1946), Lewis (1954) and McCord and McCord (1959) all found associations between a lack of adequate parental affection and care (or downright rejection) and delinquency in boys, particularly of an 'unsocialised aggressive' type. Glueck and Glueck (1940), McCord and McCord (1959), Craig and Glick (1963), Power *et al.* (1974) and West and Farrington (1973) found associations between overt marital disharmony and delinquency. Rutter (1971) found an association between separation due to marital disharmony and conduct disorder in boys, and West and Farrington (1973) between lax parental supervision and delinquency. Gladstone (1973) found vandalism in boys to be associated with poor parental supervision.

There are still anxieties, however, about the effects of separations, especially those occurring in the 'sensitive' period (between six months and four years), and their possible association with later crime. Bowlby (1947) found an association between early separation and stealing, and Wadsworth (1979) between separations before five years of age and later delinquency in young men. Others, e.g. Naess (1959, 1962), have failed to replicate these findings. (It could be that there is a causal association between later delinquency and *some* of the home factors that lead to separations, e.g. parental neglect, lack of control and protection, a lack of care and severe marital discord.)

We felt that we could, on the whole, trust the Child-Guidance and Child-Care records for at least a crude assessment of: (a) parenting capacities, (b) parental attitudes to the child, and (c) whether the marriage was overtly under considerable strain. Child-Care workers, psychiatrists, psychologists and psychiatric social workers all seem to have routinely asked about certain kinds of separation as well, e.g. if the parents had left home for lengthy periods or if the children had lived away from home for an appreciable time for any reason. Not all records were trustworthy and we did not assume that the mere absence of any mention of some feature (e.g. separations) implied that there had been none.

Socio-economic factors

We compared the outcome for males in our study in relation to a number of socio-economic conditions affecting them as children. We found surprisingly few significant associations, there were, for example, no significant associations between growing up in poverty (defined as living at or below the National Assistance Benefit level) and later crime, nor between growing up in what was clearly structurally poor housing and later crime, nor between overcrowding and later crime.

There were significant associations in the expected direction between social class and having convictions (as compared with no convictions) in adult life, and in relation to having higher seriousness-of-crime scores (4+), when the social classes were divided: (a) between classes III Non-manual and 3 Manual, and (b) when comparing Classes I, II and III with Classes IV and V (all these associations were significant at the .05 level).

It is possible that the sample was so homogeneous in a socio-economic sense that there was an inadequate number of relatively affluent families to form an adequate contrast group to the vast majority of families who appeared to live either not much above the poverty line, or even below it.

Similar considerations *may* explain the lack of an association between later crime and boys living in structurally poor housing and overcrowding. In an inner-city area where a lot of housing was poor and many families were on the verge of being technically overcrowded, differential consequences may be much less apparent. An alternative explanation is that some of our records failed to indicate the size or state of housing, although the size of the house could often be fairly safely inferred from the address. Child-Guidance records frequently failed to describe income. The exact family income, however, was usually indicated somewhere in Child-Care records and Education Welfare files, because of the need to assess parental contributions for children in Care or to provide magistrates with evidence relating to possible fines. Even where records were complete, they often only described a family's income and housing conditions at one or two points in time and the family's fortunes may subsequently have altered considerably – for better or worse.

Loss of a parent by death

We found no association between loss of a parent by death before the age of eleven and subsequent convictions in 'adult life' (> 16). 62.5 per cent of men (N = 16) who had lost their mothers by death by the age of eleven had a conviction as adults. 62.5 per cent of males (N = 104) who did not appear to have lost their mothers by the age of eleven also had a conviction as adults. Fifty-two per cent of boys who were known to have lost their fathers by death by the age of eleven had a conviction as adults, compared with sixty-two per cent of boys who did not appear to have lost their fathers.

Other separations from, or lack of, a parent

Child-Guidance and Child-Care records could not be relied on to have noted every separation for purposes of short hospital admission of parent or child, or brief absences of one parent or another for family or personal reasons, but most appeared to have made a systematic attempt to record 'major' separations for such reasons as a parent deserting the family or being admitted for a long time to a mental hospital or TB sanatorium, or admission of the child to Care or the child being sent to live with relatives.

For mother/child separations, three categories were used: (a) permanent (except by death) or long-term (i.e. five years or more), (b) temporary and repeated, and (c) no major separation recorded. (We defined 'repeated' as meaning more than one and 'temporary' as less than five years.)

For fathers the same categories were used, but (a) temporary separations included fathers working away from home, and (b) a fourth category was needed where the child was illegitimate and had never been adopted or accepted by any 'father'.

Comparisons of outcome by varying types of separation from mothers are summarised in Table 9.1.

Table 9.1: *Types of separation from mother and adult offences*

Type of separation	Whether convicted as an adult		
	No N (%)	*Yes N (%)*	*N*
Permanent or long-term (not by death)	12 (37·5)	20 (62·5)	32
Temporary and repeated	5 (16·1)	26 (83·9)	31
Apparently no major separation	25 (41·7)	35 (58·4)	60
Total	42	81	123

Notes

X^2 (Yates) = 6·144, 2df, p < ·05 (mother dead, only one temporary separation or records unclear, 44).

X^2 for temporary v. permanent separations = 2·36, ·1 > p > ·05.

Findings for 'seriousness of crime' were significant when boys with repeated and temporary separations were compared with boys with permanent separations ($X^2 = 4.13$, 1df, p<.05). Forty-two per cent of boys with repeated but temporary separations had scores of 4 or more, as compared with 15.5 per cent of boys permanently separated.

Boys who had experienced temporary and repeated separations from their fathers did rather better than boys who had experienced permanent separations, at least in the proportions who were non-recidivist and the proportions scoring less than 4 points in the seriousness-of-crime scale, but the results were well outside the levels of statistical significance. Boys who were illegitimate had the worst outcome and had a significantly lower proportion *without* adult convictions than boys who had not experienced a major separation from their fathers by eleven years of age (2/14 compared with 22/40, X^2 (Yates) = 5.411, 1df, p<.05). This is in keeping with the generally poor outcome for illegitimate boys found in many other studies. In Britain, illegitimate boys are twice as likely to suffer from perinatal mortality (Butler and Alberman, 1969). They are also twice as likely to become delinquent in adolescence (West and Farrington, 1973) and are twice as likely to be regarded as maladjusted at seven years of age (Crellin *et al.*, 1971).

Distorted Relationships

Parental rejection
An attempt was made to assess the quality of the parents' predominant attitude to the child (both father's and mother's separately), as judged by assessments and descriptions in the records. One of us (BM) categorised 'attitudes' into one or other of the following categories: (a) rejecting or hostile (or at least seriously ambivalent), (b) neglectful, (c) overprotective, (d) apparently unconcerned, (e) affectionate but, because of personal handicaps, unable to provide adequate care, (f) normally caring, (g) insufficient evidence, and (h) not applicable. To be considered as 'rejecting', 'hostile' or seriously ambivalent', a parent had to have shown repeated and inappropriate harshness, or to have spoken about the child in an extremely negative way, so as to have given the interviewer (usually a psychiatrist or social worker) the impression that they disliked the child *and* could find nothing positive to say about him. Eleven fathers and twenty-five mothers fell into this category. One or two of these mothers had also expressed persistent feelings of nausea when near the child. (No attempt was made to assess whether this 'attitude' had been present since birth or had been formed over time. In many cases we cannot say whether the attitude persisted throughout the child's minority.)

Parents were categorised as *neglectful*: (a) if they had been convicted of neglect, (b) if their child had been committed to Care because of parental neglect, (c) if the records unequivocally described the parent(s) as neglecting their children in relation to their physical care. Several instances of this occurred when a Co-ordinating Committee in Child Neglect had resolved in its minutes that a child was being neglected. To be 'overprotective', parents had to show two out of the three characteristics specified by Levy (1943); infantilising, over-closeness and over-control. To be 'unconcerned', parents had either (a) to desert the family and not to make any contact with the children, or (b) to leave the children in Care and not show any interest or make contact. In addition, *fathers* were so categorised if the mother had indicated that they showed no interest at all in the child *and* never did anything with them. It follows that unconcern in fathers may include cases of less serious inadequacy than in mothers.

Our evaluation rests heavily on the recorded evidence and evaluations of the social workers, psychologists and psychiatrists involved, but the records almost always provided evidence from at least two professionals to support our choice of category. In almost half the cases, we felt it wisest (in view of the evidence) not to attempt to fit the attitude into any categorisation.

These evaluations of parental attitude (or style) were made when children first presented at one or other of the agencies used in the study. The average age of the children at this time was six years and eleven months with a SD of four years and six months. Clearly, in the vast majority of cases, they antedate officially recorded delinquency. The same comments are true of the assessment of the quality of the marriage, except that where children were removed from home permanently before the age of three years, we believed that it would be unfair to regard them as being exposed to marital disharmony long-term, and such children were not included in computations for the outcome of living in homes with parental marriages of different qualities.

When a comparison was made of the outcome of sons in the sample who had 'rejecting' fathers with those whose fathers were apparently caring, there was a significant association between having a 'rejecting' father and having a conviction as an adult. Sons of 'rejecting' fathers were also significantly more likely to have multiple convictions and were more likely to have scores of 4 or more on the seriousness-of-crime scale. Table 9.2 shows findings in respect of convictions.

Table 9.2: *Father's attitude by adult convictions*

| Attitude | Whether convicted | | |
	No N (%)	Yes N (%)	Total
Apparently caring	12 (50)	12 (50)	24
'Rejecting'	1 (9)	10 (91)	11
Total	13	22	· 35

Fisher's Exact Test, p < ·05

When the same comparison was made for mothers' attitudes and adult convictions in sons, findings did not reach the accepted level of statistical significance but, when a comparison was made of those with three or more convictions as against those with either no conviction or one or two convictions, there was a difference approaching significance which favoured sons of caring mothers ($X^2 = 3.739$, ldf, p>.05, N = 52).

At least two questions arise: (a) how did the sons of parents who could not be described as either 'rejecting' or 'normally caring' turn out? and (b) what was the outcome for boys who had one parent who was 'normally caring' and the other either 'rejecting' or 'neglectful', or in some way unable to provide adequate care?

Of the fathers who were described as neither 'rejecting' nor 'normally caring', forty-three were described as 'apparently unconcerned', eight as 'neglectful' and seven as 'affectionate but, because of personal handicaps, unable to provide adequate care'. One was judged to be 'overprotective'. The outcome for boys with fathers with these differing, but deficient, 'attitudes' was very similar. When contrasted with the outcome for boys whose fathers appeared to be 'normally caring', the boys with caring fathers were less likely to have a conviction as an adult ($X^2 = 3.798$, ldf, p>.05, N = 68). (The difference approaches significance.)

If *one parent* were described as 'normally caring', even though the other were described as rejecting or (in some other way) unable to provide adequate care, did this act as a protection for the child against adult criminality? This appeared to be the case, since boys from such homes had an outcome that was much closer to that of boys from homes where *both* parents appeared to be normally caring than to that of boys from homes where *neither* seemed to provide adequate care. Findings are reported in Table 9.3.

Table 9.3: *Combined attitudes of fathers and mothers and adult crime*

	Number of adult convictions			
Parental attitudes	0 N (%)	1,2 N (%)	3+ N (%)	Total
1 Neither able to provide adequate care – including rejecting attitudes and only one parent	15 (24)	17 (27)	30 (48)	62
2 One parent caring, the other unable to provide adequate care	9 (41)	6 (27)	7 (32)	22
3 Both caring	5 (45·5)	3 (27)	3 (27)	11
Total	29	26	40	95

$X^2 = 4\cdot1$, 4d.f., $\cdot5 > p > \cdot2$

When (2) and (3) are combined v. (1) on no convictions v. convictions, X^2 (Yates) = 5.96, ldf, p<.02.

When seriousness-of-crime scores were used as the dependent variable, twenty-one boys (thirty-four per cent) from homes of Category (1) parenting had scores of 4 or more, compared with three (fourteen per cent) of boys from Category (2) type parenting and only one (nine per cent) from Category 3. When 2 and 3 were combined against 1, $X^2 = 4.19$, 1df, p<.05.

In other words, it seemed that the presence of one caring parent largely nullified the effects of the other parent, but that, where neither parent was able to provide adequate care, the long-term outcome, at least as judged by official crime, tended to be poor.

Adult convictions in the sons of parents with marital tensions
The same method that had been adopted for comparing the associations of different parental attitudes and adult crimes in sons was adopted for comparing possible associations between the quality of the parents' marriage and adult crimes in sons. Marriages were rated on a 6-point scale:

1 – No quarrels reported and appears to be a satisfying marriage.
2 – Temporary quarrels reported, normal level of disagreement, mild–moderate problems.
3 – Considerable difficulties.
4 – Almost entirely acrimonious/unsatisfying to both.
5 – Mother only dissatisfied.
6 – Father only dissatisfied.

(There were only three cases in Categories 5 and 6 combined).

For comparisons, Categories 1 and 2 were combined, as were Categories 3, 4, 5 and 6. (All cases, N = 24, in which the child was known to have been removed from the parents' home for good before the age of three years were omitted.)

There was a significant association between growing up (for some period of time) in what was reported as being an atmosphere of marital conflict and having a conviction as an adult. Only 16/72 boys growing up in such an atmosphere had no conviction in adult life, compared with 12/26 boys whose parents appeared to have had a relatively harmonious marriage ($X^2 = 4.25$, 1df, p<.05, N = 98).

When multiple convictions (3+) were included in the comparison, forty-nine per cent of boys whose parents had had a disharmonious marriage had three or more convictions in adult life, as compared with thirty-one per cent of boys whose marriages seemed harmonious ($X^2 = 5.47$, 2 df, p>.05, N = 98), but boys whose parents' marriage was disharmonious were significantly more likely to have seriousness-of-crime scores of 4 or more and were significantly more likely to be sentenced to prison, as is apparent in Tables 9.4 and 9.5.

Table 9.4: *Seriousness-of-crime score by quality of parents' marriage*

	Seriousness-of-crime scores			
Quality of marriage	*0 (%)*	*1–3 (%)*	*4+ (%)*	*N*
Apparently harmonious	12 (46)	11 (42)	3 (12)	26
Serious difficulties				
or worse	16 (22)	30 (42)	26 (36)	72
Total	28	41	29	98

$X^2 = 7 \cdot 73$, 2d.f., p < ·05

In sixty-eight cases, either the parents were not living together or no description of the marriage was available, or the child had left before the age of three.

In Table 9.5 we record the outcome in terms of being sentenced to prison (whether or not the sentence was suspended). Less than one-tenth of sons of apparently harmonious marriages were ever sentenced to prison, compared with a third of sons of parents with a disharmonious marriage ($X^2 = 5.19$, ldf, p<.05). Nearly a fifth of sons with disharmonious marriages were sentenced to prison at least three times (which inevitably involved actual committal to prison at least once).

Table 9.5: *Sentencing to prison by quality of parental marriage (%)*

	Number of times sentenced to prison			
Quality of marriage	*0*	*1,2*	*3+*	*(N)*
Apparently harmonious	92	8	0	(24)
Serious difficulties				
or worse	67	14	19	(72)
Total				(98)

$X^2 = 7 \cdot 032$, 2d.f., p < ·05

The question of the probable causative factors involved in the relationship between marital difficulties and delinquency has been discussed again recently by McCord (1982), using data from the Cambridge Somerville Study on Juvenile Delinquency. She found evidence: (a) that paternal absence was not itself criminogenic, (b) that being reared in an atmosphere of conflict was criminogenic, and (c) that it appeared that where a difficult parental relationship ended and boys remained with affectionate mothers, their rates for delinquency were lower. Our own data strongly support the second of these hypotheses. They neither confirm nor refute either the first hypothesis (of paternal absence) or the third (that marital separation is preferable for sons, provided the mothers were affectionate). The sons of parents in our study who separated from their spouses, and who did not remarry had a poor outcome, but they may be a very biased sample. Findings for the marital quality and status of parents' marriages by outcome are given in Table 9.6.

Table 9.6: *Marital status and quality of marriage in parents by criminal outcome in sons (%)*

Parents' marital quality and status	Number of adult convictions				Seriousness- of-crime scores		
	0	1,2	3+	(N)	0	1–3	4–7
1 Intact marriages, few problems	50	25	25	(12)	50	33	17
2 Intact marriages, serious problems	17	26	56	(23)	17	40	43
3 Separation, no remarriage	10	10	80	(10)	10	30	60
4 Separation and remarriage	7	43	50	(14)	7	64	29

It is apparent that the only group with a relatively good outcome are the boys who grew up in a home where the parents had a fairly good marriage and who had not separated by the time they were first seen by the Education and Child-Care services. It has to be remembered that the median age at which this occurred was eight, so these assessments usually antedate any official delinquency. On the other hand, there could well have been considerable changes in both the status and quality of the marriages of our subjects' parents during their childhood. Since divorce and remarriage were uncommon in the period when our subjects were growing up, it is possible that, among the working classes, only the more deviant and unusual separated or divorced, or divorced and remarried.

The outcome for boys whose parents' marriage was intact and relatively harmonious was significantly better than the rest of the sample in relation to having convictions v. having no convictions at all ($X^2 = 6.04$, 1df, p<.02). It was also: (a) significantly better than that

of boys whose (custodial) parents had separated and remarried
(Fisher's Exact Test, p = .02), and (b) 'almost' significantly better
than that of boys whose parents had separated and whose mothers had
not remarried (Fisher's Exact Test = .058).

Multiple psychosocial disadvantages

Many children grow up in homes in which they not only suffer
parental hostility, but their parents may: (a) have unhappy marriages,
(b) they may suffer from personality disorders, and (c) they may
repeatedly leave their children (or cause them to leave home) for one
reason or another. A 'parenting deficiency score' was calculated by
ascribing one point for each of the following deficiencies and aggregat-
ing the total number of points accumulated: (a) having a mother
described as rejecting or highly ambivalent, (b) having a father so
described, (c) having parents who appeared to exercise inadequate
control, (d) having parents whose marriage was disharmonious (as
measured above), (e) having a mother described as apparently suffering from persistent difficulties in personality and social relationships,
and (f) having a father so described. Points were added to the score if
either of the following conditions applied: (g) boys had been separated
from their mothers for what might be described as a 'major separation'
on more than one occasion by the age of eleven years, and (h) boys had
lost their fathers completely (*except by death*) by the age of eleven
years, or had never had a father.

The scale is admittedly deficient. It cannot safely be assumed that
all these factors might be equally associated with poor outcome. It
fails to make provision for family strengths and the records sometimes
failed to give adequate evidence as to whether some children might
have experienced a particular deficiency or not.

An assessment of 'apparently suffering from persistent difficulties
in personality and social relationships' was made on the basis of
records in relation to fifteen fathers and sixteen mothers. Such an
assessment excludes parents who had been diagnosed by a psychiatrist
as suffering from other forms of mental illness or disorder. Five of the
fathers had been diagnosed by a psychiatrist as 'psychopathic' and
three more as suffering from a 'personality disorder'. Seven more had
been described in the records as behaving in ways that suggested
persistent and marked difficulties in personality and had all been
through three broken marriages or cohabitations. None of the

mothers had been diagnosed as 'psychopathic' by a psychiatrist, but four had been diagnosed as suffering from a 'personality disorder' and twelve more persistently appeared to have shown marked difficulties in personality and to have been through at least three unsuccessful cohabitations/marriages.

Our findings in Table 9.7 indicated that there was a clear association between an increase in parenting deficiencies and higher levels of adult crime in sons.

Table 9.7: *Parenting deficiency score by (a) adult convictions and (b) seriousness-of-crime scores (%)*

Deficiency score	Number of convictions				Seriousness of crime scores		
	0	*1,2*	*3+*	*(N)*	*0*	*1–3*	*4+*
0	60	13	27	(30)	60	27	13
1,2	40	21	39	(57)	40	37	23
3,4	23	32	46	(57)	23	46	32
5+	23	27	50	(22)	23	41	36

$X^2 = 14\cdot45, 6df, p < \cdot05$ $\qquad\qquad$ $X^2 = 14\cdot63, 6df, p < \cdot05$

We compared the outcome for all boys who had been in Care over the third quartile with boys who came from homes with three or more deficiencies and who: (a) were not admitted to Care (N = 19), and (b) were admitted, but stayed for less than the third quartile for length (nine years and six months, N = 55). The outcome for boys longest in Care was noticeably better than either of the other groups: (a) in respect of the proportions without any criminal conviction in adult life, since two-fifths of the boys longest in Care had no adult convictions, compared with rates of only twenty per cent for both the other two groups, (b) in respect of the proportions with three or more offences, since fewer than a quarter of the boys longest in Care had three or more convictions, as compared with just over half of other boys in Care, and just under half of boys from very deficient homes who did not go into Care, (c) in respect of boys who went on to have 'serious criminal careers' (i.e. they had scores of 4 or more for seriousness-of-crime). Only nine per cent of boys longest in Care had such scores, compared with two fifths of boys in Care for shorter periods and just over a quarter of boys not in Care. The differences between boys longest in Care and boys from poor homes who were in Care for shorter periods were significant at the .02 and .05 levels. The differences with boys from poor homes who were not admitted to Care did not reach statistical significance, possibly owing to small numbers.

In other words, there are clear indications of there being associations between having several convictions in adult life and growing up within homes in which parenting is deficient or distorted in a *multiplicity* of ways. The greater the number of deficiencies and distortions, the poorer the outcome in terms of adult crime. In making decisions whether or not to admit boys to Care, it is necessary to consider the probable consequences of leaving them in their natural families, as well as the probable consequences of their living in Care (including the possibility that once boys have very serious conduct problems, neither admissions to Care nor treatment in the community may dramatically change their behaviour).

The relative predictive power of behaviour and adverse social factors

A regression analysis was carried out using the number of juvenile convictions and most of the possible psychosocial and socio-economic factors as independent variables, with the *number* of adult convictions as the dependent variable. Juvenile convictions accounted for twenty-two per cent of the variance and 'major' temporary separations from the mother by the age of eleven for another six per cent. Convictions in the father, permanent separations from the mother and separations from, or lack of, a father together amounted to a further five per cent.

What distinguishes males who were altogether free from convictions from males who had at least one conviction?

Another way of enquiring what the study reveals about the background of these boys is to ask how males who succeeded in avoiding a conviction (either as adults or juveniles) were different from other males in the sample.

They tended to be of slightly higher social class, bearing in mind the fact that the vast majority of the sample came from the working classes. Forty-two per cent came from families in which the father worked in an occupation placed in the Registrar General's socio-economic groupings I–IV, as compared with only twenty-two per cent of males who had a conviction ($X^2 = 7.34$, 1df, p<.01, N = 166). This difference was *not* due to males with a conviction coming predomin-antly from families in which the father was either dead or chronically unemployed; there was no difference in these respects. However, males without any conviction had a greater proportion of fathers who were chronically sick or handicapped, or prone to disability or illness (mental illness was not included here). Sixty-two per cent of males who had no conviction had fathers with chronic health problems, as compared with thirty-six per cent of males who had convictions ($X^2 = 9.1$, ldf, p<.01, N = 97, not known: N = 69). The non-offenders also had a slightly higher proportion of *mothers* with chronic ill-health, but this difference did not approach statistical significance.

The outstanding differences that were apprent in this study were that males with convictions came from families characterised by distorted and disrupted relationships. Males *without a conviction* were *ten* times more likely to have a father described as 'normally affec-tionate', as contrasted with a father described as 'rejecting', 'hostile' or 'ambivalent' (Fisher's Exact Test, p<.01), and *twice* as likely to have a 'normally affectionate' mother. The marital relationship was *four* times more likely to be described as either 'happy', 'good' or 'with no more quarrels than is normal' ($X^2 = 9.1$, ldf p<.01, N = 98). No significant differences were found in the proportions of boys with or without eventual convictions who were found to be living in intact families at five, ten or fifteen years of age, i.e. with both natural parents. On the other hand, males with convictions were, on the data available, known to have been more likely to have experienced more than one 'major' but 'temporary' separation from their natural mothers before their sixteenth birthday ('temporary' was defined as 'less than five years'). To a certain extent, this was due to boys going into Care for *less* than the median period of time for length in Care. Almost one-third of boys with convictions were in Care for less than five years and ten months (the median length), compared with only eight per cent of boys without convictions ($X^2 = 5.49$, ldf, p<.02, N = 165). Slightly higher proportions of boys without convictions had either not been in Care at all (fifty-eight per cent v. forty-one per cent) or had been in Care over the third quartile for length of time (seven-teen per cent v. eleven per cent).

On the basis of IQ tests done at the Child Guidance Clinic or at assessment centres, boys with IQs of 100 and above were somewhat less likely to have convictions: 13/22 (fifty-nine per cent) compared with 31/77 (forty per cent) of boys with a conviction at some point in their lives. Twenty-three per cent of boys without a conviction had IQ scores of 115 or above, compared with sixteen per cent of boys with convictions. (For sixty-seven boys we had no record of psychometric-testing and figures refer only to boys who were given an IQ score or grading by a psychologist.)

We found no great difference between boys with or without convictions in respect of overcrowding, poverty, ordinal position in the family or total number of siblings and half siblings. It is possible that our sample was too homogeneous in relation to socio-economic factors to produce enough contrast in relation to the variables just mentioned, with the consequence that our lack of significant findings in this area is simply a function of the nature of our samples.

The major longitudinal study of delinquency in Britain, known as the Cambridge Study (West, 1982), does find evidence of associations between most of the socio-economic factors just referred to and being delinquent. It also found (*op. cit.*) that persistent recidivism was much more likely to be associated with poor or harsh parental care and overt marital disharmony. In this respect, our findings are in agreement with the Cambridge Study. Two points seemed to stand out in our study: (a) among a population, most of whom experienced relative social and economic deprivation, the boys who went on to become recidivists, or who had serious criminal careers, tended to come from homes in which there were distorted relationships (for boys who were admitted to Care by the age of three, assessments were made on relationships within the *foster* home where the boy spent the longest period), and (b) boys who grew up mainly in Care were less likely to be 'recidivist' or to have serious criminal careers.

10

Crimes of violence

'The aggressiveness of . . . delinquents . . . convicted for violence reflected the fact that they were particularly persistent delinquents from particularly bad backgrounds. . . .'
West, 1982.

One of the drawbacks of the seriousness-of-crime scale is that it does not indicate the nature of the crimes committed. We have already stated that crimes of violence often accounted for a considerable proportion of the higher scores on the scale.

It is self-evident that crimes such as assault leading to grievous bodily harm, wounding, robbery, rape and murder involve the infliction of serious wrongs on others and that any light thrown on the backgrounds of men who commit violent crimes could be of some importance. Farrington (1978) found that the factor which was most clearly related to later violent delinquency was 'harsh parental attitude and discipline at the age of 8.14 per cent of those receiving a harsh parental attitude and discipline became violent delinquents, as compared with 3.6 per cent of the remainder. (X^2 = 12.3 1df p<.001)'. Of the other family environment factors, Farrington continues, 'criminal parents and separations both significantly predicted violent delinquency, and poor parental supervision and marital disharmony at 14 would have been significantly related to it, if the numbers had permitted valid X^2 tests'.

Forty-four out of 166 men in our sample (twenty-six per cent) had convictions for crimes involving assault (or violence) to the person or the threat of it (as in robbery). Most of the men who had a conviction for violence also had multiple convictions for other offences as adults. Only three men had the one conviction (i.e. for violence and no other crimes). For men with convictions for violence, the mean average for the total number of their convictions (for all types of indictable and serious crime) was 9.8, and the standard deviation 8.38. As previously noted (Chapter 4) the proportion of men with crimes of violence is high, but in Chapter 4 we also pointed out that it is no higher a proportion of those convicted than was found in the Cambridge Study in Delinquent Development, i.e. about one-third (West, 1982). Just over a third of our subjects who had a conviction for 'violence' had two or more convictions for crimes of violence. To count as a crime of violence, a conviction had to be for 'robbery', 'assault', 'assault leading to actual or grievous bodily harm', 'assaulting a policeman', 'wounding', 'manslaughter' or 'murder'. In addition, three men were included who had been convicted of sexual crimes which involved an element of aggression. The crimes were indecent assault on a female, indecent assault on a boy and rape. (In the last case, the individual had already been convicted of other crimes of violence.)

The types of violent crime committed and the number of convictions for each type are shown in Table 10.1. The totals add up to more than the total number of individuals concerned, since more than a third had convictions for more than one crime of violence.

Table 10.1: *Number of men convicted for different types of violent crime*

Total convicted of assault occasioning actual or grievous bodily harm	26
Total convicted of wounding with intent	10
Total convicted of assault or indecent assault	10
Total convicted of assaulting a policeman	9
Total convicted of robbery	3
Total convicted of rape	1
Total convicted of murder	1
Total convicted of a crime of violence	44
Total convicted of more than one crime of violence	18

Assaulting the police may be thought of as different from other crimes of violence, in that frightened or inarticulate people, or men under the influence of alcohol, may resist arrest. Of the nine men convicted of assaulting the police, five, in fact, also had convictions for other types of violent crime.

The man convicted of murder had several juvenile convictions (not for violent crime) but committed murder at the age of eighteen as part of a brawl involving several youths and was committed to prison for many years. Consequently, he had only two convictions as an adult.

Precursors of adult crimes of violence

Behaviour

Antisocial behaviour in childhood was the factor most strongly associated with adult crimes of violence. This was particularly true of *convictions* before the age of seventeen. Having several convictions as a juvenile was strongly associated both with having convictions as an adult and with having convictions for crimes of violence. Findings are presented in Table 10.2.

Table 10.2 *Adult convictions for violence by number of juvenile convictions*

Number of juvenile convictions	Adult convictions			
	None N (%)	For violence N (%)	For other crimes N (%)	Total
0	48 (53·9)	14 (15·7)	27 (30·3)	89
1,2	9 (20·9)	13 (30·2)	21 (48·8)	43
3+	2 (5·9)	17 (50·0)	15 (44·1)	34
Total	59	44	63	166

$X^2 = 33·71, 4df, p < ·00001$

There is an unmistakable trend for boys with a greater number of juvenile convictions to commit crimes of violence as adults. Half the boys with three or more juvenile convictions committed at least one crime of violence as an adult, compared with less than one-sixth of boys who had no convictions as a juvenile.

Table 10.3 shows further that there was a significant association between manifesting many different types of conduct disorder as a boy and later being convicted of crimes of violence.

Table 10.3 *Adult convictions by number of different types of conduct disorder shown as a child*

Number of types of conduct disorder in childhood	Adult convictions			
	None N (%)	For violence N (%)	For other crime N (%)	Total
0	18 (72)	3 (12)	4 (16)	25
1,2	32 (43·3)	16 (21·6)	26 (35·1)	74
3,4	6 (14·3)	14 (33·3)	22 (52·4)	42
5+	3 (12)	11 (44)	11 (44)	25
Total	59	44	63	166

Note
$X^3 = 31·97, 6df, p < ·001$

There is a strong trend for the total proportion of boys with an adult conviction to increase as the aggregate of types of antisocial childhood disorder increases, and the same principle applies to convictions for violent crime. More than two out of every five boys manifesting five or more different kinds of conduct problem were later convicted of crimes of violence.

We tried to explore whether any particular *types* of conduct problem were associated with later convictions for violence, since aggressiveness appears in longitudinal studies to be a fairly persistent trait (Lefkowitz *et al.*, 1977; Olweus, 1979).

However, numbers with definite information were too small for X^2 tests. When we examined abnormally aggressive behaviour shown *outside* the family (or both *within and outside* the family) before the age of ten years, only one out of twenty-two boys manifesting a problem of aggressive behaviour at that age was free from adult convictions, and eight (thirty-six per cent) had a conviction for violent crime. One aspect of childhood behaviour *was* significantly associated with adult crimes of violence. This was running away from home. Boys were judged to be running away from home if: (a) they ran/wandered from the own home repeatedly, or (b) they had run off and stayed away for at least one whole night without parental permission. Comparisons were confined to the age group ten to twelve years of age. 9/13 runners committed crimes of violence as adults, compared with 8/29 apparent non-runners (X^2 = 4.85, ldf, p<.05).

Admission to Care
We have already shown that the proportion of boys who had been in Care and who committed violent crimes in adult life was 30/90, or thirty-three per cent, and of boys who were not known to be in Care, 15/76 or 19.7%. When comparisons were made of boys with at least three offences for violent crime in adult life, 10/90 (11.1%) of boys who had been in Care had three offences for violent crime as adults, compared with 1/76 (1.3%) of boys who were not known to have been in Care (X^2 = 6.42, ldf, p<.02). These findings may only indicate the extent to which many of the boys admitted to Care were *already* significantly more delinquent on admission. We tried to explore this possibility in two ways. Firstly, boys were matched for the *level* of juvenile convictions on entry to Care. Their outcome in respect of crimes of violence was compared in relation to their length in Care, splitting at the median for time in Care. Of boys who entered Care with one conviction and who stayed less than the median length (for the total Care group), 17/33 had an adult conviction for violence and

sixteen did not. However, of boys who stayed more than the median length, only 2/14 had an adult conviction for violence (Fisher's Exact Test, p<.05, N = 47). For boys with two or more juvenile convictions, 15/24 of those who stayed less than the median length had a conviction for violence, but only 2/10 of boys who stayed longer (Fisher's Exact Test, p = .056). Secondly, we compared the *length* of time boys spent in Care with (a) the proportions committing crimes of violence, and (b) the *number* of violent crimes committed.

Of the quarter of boys from the total Care group who had been in Care longest, only three (fourteen per cent) had convictions for violent crime and it is clear from forensic records that one of these individuals was schizophrenic at the time he committed his crime. By contrast, two-fifths of boys who had been in Care for shorter periods had convictions for violence in adult life ($X^2 = 4.3$, ldf, p<.05).

The proportion of the quarter of boys longest in Care with a conviction for a crime involving violence (fourteen per cent) is only slightly higher than that found by West (eleven per cent) in a sample of working-class boys in London followed up to the age of twenty-four. West's sample (West, 1982) were born in 1951 and 1954. (In addition, one of the boys in our sample was clearly psychotic at the time of his offences.)

In other words, the pattern for crimes of violence to the person followed the pattern which related to adult convictions generally. On the whole, the outcome for boys who had been in Care was significantly worse, but for boys who had been *longest* in Care the outcome was significantly better than for boys who had been in Care for relatively shorter periods, and probably not very different from a working-class population generally.

When we examined the records of boys admitted to Care because of conduct problems (N = 40) there was a significant *negative* association between remaining longer in Care and the number of crimes of violence that were committed in adult life. In other words, the *longer* boys stayed in Care the fewer violent crimes they committed as adults (>16 years) (Spearman's r = −.285 p<.05, N = 40).

Far from making boys more likely to commit violent crimes, the experience of living in Care seemed to have prevented this happening, both in the sense that a not particularly high proportion of boys who lived the best part of their childhood in Care committed violent crimes as adults and, also, that boys who were already delinquent on

admission to Care tended to commit *fewer* crimes of violence the
longer they were in Care.

Family Environment

Factors which we thought might be associated with later crimes of
violence were overcrowding, poverty, poor standards of home cleanliness, social class, parental rejection, parental inability to provide
adequate care because of personal problems, and marital
disharmony.

We found no associations between crimes of violence and coming
from overcrowded homes, living in poverty or coming from homes
with low standards of cleanliness. These failures to disprove the null
hypothesis are not due to small numbers. It could be that the whole
sample was so deprived in a socio-economic sense that it does not contain sufficient opportunity for a real contrast with less crowded living
or greater affluence, e.g. forty per cent of all boys lived in homes
where the income was at or below the National Assistance Benefit
level. The mean average number of children in each family was five
and a half. Another explanation could be that there is no connection
between these factors and crimes of *violence*.

Parental attitudes

There was a very significant association between coming from a
family where the father was described as rejecting, neglectful or unable to provide adequate care and adult crimes of violence. Findings
are presented in Table 10.4.

Table 10.4: *Father's attitude and adult crimes of violence in sons*

	Adult convictions			
Father's attitude	None N (%)	For violence N (%)	For other crimes N (%)	Total
1 Caring	13 (52)	4 (16)	8 (32)	25
2 'Unconcerned'	17 (39·5)	8 (18·6)	18 (41·9)	43
3 Rejecting, neglectful or unable to care	2 (7·7)	14 (53·8)	10 (38·5)	26
Total	32	26	36	94

Note

$X^2 = 17·4$, 4df, p<·01

72 cases missing, because attitude not known or father absent.

When caring fathers are compared with fathers who were rejecting, neglectful or unable to care, for no convictions v. convictions for violence on a 2 x 2 contingency test, $X^2 = 11.47$, 1df, p<.001.

By contrast, there was no *significant* difference in the proportion committing crimes of violence of sons of mothers who were rejecting, hostile or unable to provide adequate care, as compared with the sons of caring mothers. Fifteen per cent (4/27) of the sons of caring mothers committed crimes of violence as adults, as compared with twenty-eight per cent (18/68) of the sons of mothers who were rejecting, neglectful or unable to provide adequate care. 10/27 (or thirty-five per cent) of the sons of caring mothers had no convictions as adults and 16/68 (or 23.5%) of the sons of mothers who were rejecting, neglectful or unable to provide adequate care (X^2 for no convictions v. convictions for violence = 1.723, 1df, .5>p>.1 NS).

Does one caring parent protect a child?

It is possible that having one parent who was, so to speak, 'good enough' might compensate for the other parent being rejecting or inadequate as a parent. There were ninety-five cases in which it seemed possible to make a fair estimate of the parental attitude and we divided these, as in the previous chapter, into three categories: (a) where both parents were hostile or rejecting, or, at least, where neither parent was able to provide adequate care, (b) where one parent provided adequate affection and care and the other was rejecting or unable to provide adequate care, and (c) where both parents seemed to be normally affectionate and caring.

Findings are presented in Table 10.5.

Table 10.5: *Parental attitude and adult crimes*

	Adult convictions			
Parental attitude	None N (%)	For violence N (%)	For other crimes N (%)	Total
1 Neither able to show adequate care	14 (22·6)	23 (37·1)	25 (40·3)	62
2 One able to show adequate care	9 (40·9)	4 (18·2)	9 (40·9)	22
3 Both able to show adequate care	5 (45·5)	2 (18·2)	4 (36·4)	11
Total	28	29	38	95

Note
$X = 5·49$, 4df, $·5 < p < ·2$ (NS)

There seems little difference in respect of adult crimes of violence in the proportions of sons with two caring parents and those with only one caring parent. If these two categories are joined, and the 'caring' and 'mixed' group compared with the group who received inadequate parenting, there is a significant difference in respect of adult *crimes of violence* compared to no convictions ($X^2 = 4.16$, ldf, p<.05).

Parental rejection could be described as a form of *distorted relationships*. Neglect and unconcern are possibly forms of a *lack* of adequate parental care, affection and stimulus. Both distorted relationships and lack of care could be described as forms of parental deprivation.

Another form of distorted relationships is that of living in a home in which the parents are constantly arguing with each other.

The marital relationships of the parents were categorised in the manner described in Chapter 9.

There was a significant difference in the proportions of convictions, particularly for crimes of violence, committed by sons who grew up in homes in which there was considerable marital disharmony. This is shown in Table 10.6.

Table 10.6: *Adult convictions by quality of parental marriage*

Quality of parents' marriage	Adult convictions			
	None N (%)	For violence N (%)	For other crimes N (%)	Total
Normally harmonious	12 (46)	4 (15)	10 (38)	26
Considerable difficulties of worse	16 (22)	26 (36)	30 (42)	72
Total	28	30	40	98

Note
$X^2 = 6.558$, 2df, p < .05

When a comparison is made of males with no convictions and males with convictions for violence, $X^2 = 4.93$, ldf, p<.05). There was little difference in outcome for the two groups in relation to the proportions with convictions for non-violent crimes but, in comparison with boys from harmonious homes, well over twice the proportion of boys from disharmonious homes had convictions for crimes of violence as adults.

Cumulative effect of stresses

Every social worker has the impression that many troubled and troublesome children have experienced a multiplicity of stresses and adversities that possibly act cumulatively. In a crude attempt to measure the sequelae of multiple inadequacies in the home, a score for parenting deficiency was calculated (as described in Chapter 9).

There are at least four disadvantages in such a method: (a) the relative potency of each type of parenting deficiency is not accounted for, (b) there is no acknowledgement of subtler, but still important, deficiencies in parent–child relationships, e.g. lack of adequate communication or the use of 'coercion' in Patterson's sense,.(Patterson, 1982), (c) the role of life events and other traumata are not adequately considered, and (d) the method does not allow for the presence of compensating strengths. In spite of this there was a significant association between the parenting deficiency score and adult crime. Findings are shown in Table 10.7.

Table 10.7: *Parenting deficiency score and adult crimes of violence (%)*

Deficiency Score	Adult crimes			
	None	Violent crimes	Other crimes	(N)
0	60	17	23	(30)
1,2	40	25	35	(57)
3,4	23	26	51	(57)
5+	23	46	32	(22)

Notes
$X^2 = 17.74$, 6df, $p < .01$
For no convictions v. violent convictions, $X^2 = 9.36$, 3df, $p < .05$.

The proportion of men with *more than* one conviction for violent crime rose from 0 per cent, for sons of parents with a deficiency score of 0, to eighteen per cent, for sons of parents with a deficiency score of five or more.

Two details of this table deserve comment. Firstly, the outcome for boys with parents who were not described as showing any marked deficiency in the care of their children was much better than the rest of the sample. This is less surprising once it is borne in mind, for example, that a single mother who severely neglected or rejected her son might only score one point. Secondly, a considerably higher proportion of boys with parents who had multiple deficiencies (i.e. 5+) committed crimes of violence in adult life.

A similar kind of analysis to that carried out in the previous chapter in relation to marital quality and status and adult crime was carried out, focusing on crimes of violence. Numbers are small, but suggest that it made little difference whether marriages remained intact (but were disharmonious) or broke up and, if they broke up, whether the mother remarried or not. Associations seemed to be with marital discord. Results are presented in Table 10.8.

Table 10.8: *Marital status and quality by crimes of violence in sons* (%)

Marital quality and status	None	Crimes For violence	Other	(N)
1 Harmonious and intact	50	25	25	(12)
2 Disharmonious and intact	17	39	43	(23)
3 Separation	8	46	46	(24)

Note
X^2 for 1 v. 2 + 3 combined, for no crimes v. crimes of violence = 3·87, 1df, p < ·05.

Comment

The findings of this chapter suggest even more strongly than those of the previous chapter that many boys from homes characterised by severely distorted relationships are likely to commit crimes as adults, but especially crimes of violence. These crimes are not usually isolated. In fact, the mean number of adult convictions for men committing any crime of violence was 8.4. One possible explanation is that living in distorted relationships affects personality development or at least strongly influences the repertoire of behavioural responses available in certain situations. Our findings on an inverse relationship between the length of time spent in Care and: (a) committing crimes of violence, and (b) the *number* of violent offences committed, strongly suggests that, in some circumstances, removal of children from distorted relationships may reduce the likelihood of their committing violent crimes as adults.

11

The outcome for girls who had been in Care

'*Girls we was all of us, ladies*
We was. . . .'
Don Marquis.

Females always appear to have been generally less delinquent than males. To some extent, this must be the consequence of different socialisation processes, including the greater pressures on males to prove themselves. Constitutional differences may also account for some of the different ways of behaving. Aggression in male mammals seems generally higher than in females. Whatever the cause, little boys seem to be more aggressive than little girls.

Because female crime is relatively rare, adult convictions are a particularly poor index of outcome of girls' upbringing. In addition, there is some evidence that psychiatric disorder and neurological deficits play an obviously larger part in the explanation of female crime than they do in male crime. (Cowie, Cowie and Slater, 1968).

Seventeen girls out of 117 (14.5%) had convictions as adults (>16) and four (3.4%) had three or more convictions, three of them having seriousness-of-crime scores of 4 or more. Fifty-three girls were known to have been admitted to Care, of whom seven (thirteen per cent) had a conviction in adult life. Of the girls in our sample who were not known to have been admitted to Care as children (N = 54), ten (18.5%) had a conviction in adult life. The median length of time spent in Care was five years and ten months and the range was from less than one month to nearly eighteen years. There appeared to be no significant difference in outcome between those girls who were known to have been in Care and those not known to have been. There was a difference which was not significant in the outcome for girls who were in Care for more than the median average in length and girls who were in for shorter periods. As with boys, this difference favoured girls who were in Care for *longer* periods. 6/27 girls who had lived in Care less than the median average length had a conviction as adults (>16 years), as compared with only 1/26 girls in Care over the median (Fisher's Exact Test, p>.1 NS).

Non-parametric ranking tests confirmed that conduct disorder and juvenile convictions have an association with 'adult' convictions in females (in spite of the fact that conduct disorder and delinquency are much less common in girls than boys). We also found that there was a *negative correlation* between the length of time spent in Care and both the number of adult convictions and the seriousness-of-adult-crime scores. Findings for adult convictions are shown in Table 11.1.

Table 11.1 *Spearman's correlation coefficients for number of types of anti-social behaviour recorded, juvenile convictions and length in Care by adult convictions for females*

Independent variables	Adult convictions		
	Spearman's r	Probability level	N
1 Juvenile convictions	·262	·005	117
2 Types of antisocial behaviour	·258	·005	117
3 Length in Care	−·263	·05	53

Numbers were too small to reveal a difference in outcome associated with differences in the reasons why girls entered Care. This was probably because only four girls entered Care because of convictions, on remand or because they were beyond parental control. *None* of these girls had any convictions as adults, compared with 7/42 girls (fourteen per cent) admitted for *other* reasons.

Nor was it possible to detect any association between adult crime and either parental rejection or marital disharmony in the parents. One possible explanation is that the number of women with convictions is too small to permit statistical comparisons to be made. An alternative is that girls are not affected by distorted relationships *in the same way* as boys. Since the total number of females in the study with such parent–child relationships is considerable, it is difficult to avoid this last interpretation. The two explanations are not mutually exclusive.

On the other hand, we did find what appear to be significant associations between an *early* discharge from care and having a conviction in adult life (>16 years) and between the *type* of Care experienced and having an 'adult' conviction (>16 years). When girls discharged before sixteen years were compared with girls discharged at seventeen or eighteen, we found that girls discharged before their sixteenth birthday were more delinquent than girls discharged later, as is shown in Table 11.2.

Table 11.2: *Females: age on discharge by adult convictions (> 16)*

Age on discharge	Adult convictions		
	No N (%)	*Yes N (%)*	*Total*
Under sixteen years	12 (70·5)	5 (29·5)	17
sixteen and over	34 (94·4)	2 (5·6)	36
Total	46	7	53

$X^2 = 3·84$, 1df, p < ·05

Girls were divided according to their 'predominant' type of Care (as described in Chapter 6). No girls who were predominantly fostered, or who lived in small-group homes, had convictions (N = 30), as compared with 7/23 girls (30.4%) who lived mainly in large-group homes ($X^2 = 7.75$, 1df, p<.01). However, it appeared to be even more true of girls than of boys that the only reasons for girls *not* being fostered were: troublesomeness, being older on admission and having experienced fostering disruption or breakdown (often repeatedly).

Brief histories will be presented of the six girls who either committed three or more offences as adults or who committed a crime of violence. The vast majority, of course, were not convicted at all, either as juveniles or adults. It is difficult to draw firm conclusions from six histories. Three girls certainly appeared to have had appalling childhoods, two in their own homes and one in Care – with thirteen placements. A fourth case, Ruby C, was a girl who suffered from Gilles de la Tourette's syndrome.

1 Case 198

Joanne A was referred to Child Guidance at the age of four with rocking, headbanging and overactivity which had been going on for two years. Joanne appeared to be of low intelligence, with an IQ of under 70. Her parents seemed to be fond of her but her mother was described as extremely anxious. Apart from aggressive attacks on other children at four years of age, little in Joanne's background or behaviour really prepares us for her long criminal career of twenty-two offences as an adult (>16), mostly for obtaining money by deception and theft, but including assault occasioning actual bodily harm.

2 *Case 127*

Edwina B was referred to Child Guidance at the age of eight with problems of stealing money outside the home. The house was described as being in a poor structural condition and badly kept. The family were living in overcrowded conditions, with seven people in a 'two-up, two-down' house. Two of Edwina's four brothers had physical handicaps. Edwina was only seen on four occasions, because she was 'unco-operative'. She had a low average IQ but was over two years retarded in reading at eight years of age. Her parents appeared to be caring people and the marriage was said to be happy. She continued to steal throughout her childhood and had five offences as an adult, all for theft.

3 *Case 161*

Ruby C was referred to Child Guidance at the age of twelve with problems of defiance and disobedience at home and school, including deliberate defaecating. She was also described as having fits, grunting, swearing and spitting, and was diagnosed as suffering from Gilles de la Tourette's syndrome. Both her mother and paternal grandmother (who lived with them) appeared completely to reject Ruby. Her father was apparently caring, but committed suicide while Ruby was being treated. She was admitted to a child psychiatric ward for eight months. As an adult she was convicted of seven offences, four of theft and three of dishonesty. She was not known to have been in Care.

4 *Case 28*

Joan D was committed to Care at the age of eight months when her mother was convicted of neglect and put on probation. Joan remained in Care until her eighteenth birthday. In this time she had thirteen placements, including three attempts to board her out, one of which broke down because of the foster mother's ill-health. However, in aggregate, she was fostered for only eight months and spent most of her life in large Children's Homes (i.e. with over twelve children in each home). She had marked conduct problems in adolescence, stealing outside the Home, running away and throwing frequent temper tantrums. She had a low IQ. She was initially discharged to the Army at eighteen. She had two convictions as an adult, one of which was for assaulting the police.

5 Case 201

Ethel E came from a large family (nine children) with an alcoholic father. She was first reported to the Education Department at the age of thirteen for persistent school non-attendance. Her father was described as a violent man who 'terrorised' the children. Two of Ethel's brothers and one sister had juvenile convictions for theft and/or house-breaking. Ethel had, with several of her brothers and sisters, been admitted to Care at the age of eight at her mother's request, as protection from the father. She was discharged after three weeks in Care. As an adult she had twelve convictions, mostly for theft and obtaining money by false pretences.

6 Case 203

Hilda F was admitted to Care on four occasions between the ages of four and fourteen. One the last occasion this was because of her school non-attendance. Her mother was described as anaemic and neglectful of her twelve children, at least five of whom had convictions as juveniles. Altogether Hilda spent fourteen months in Care. She had one conviction for theft as a juvenile and three as an adult, all for defrauding the Social Security Department.

12

Twenty-eight lives

'He who would do good to another must do it in minute particulars.'
Blake.

The statistical analyses we have presented fail to convey the complexities of our subjects' lives and may tend to suggest that they were only numbers and not real children who suffered and who reacted against their frequently painful predicaments. A very brief outline of some of their lives, at least as recorded in Child Care and Child Guidance notes, is a necessary complement to the numerical data. Outlines of 10 boys and six girls have already been given in Chaps. 4 and 11. All of the outlines already given, together with those presented in this chapter, describe only a segment of our subjects' existence, but hopefully they will convey an impression of the considerable deprivation many of our subjects experienced in their own homes, of their experience in Care and of the wrongs they inflicted on others and the penalties they incurred. A minority were allowed little chance of normal development as they moved in and out of Care or, having suffered the consequences of marital conflict, handicap or death in their natural homes, had similar experiences all over again with foster parents. Most of the outlines will be of boys who were admitted to Care at some point in their lives, and we have particularly chosen outlines of children who were first drawn to the attention of 'the Authorities' when they were very young, since it is possible to speculate whether their criminal careers might possibly have been prevented if more had been done for them as young children.

We shall begin with a further eighteen lives of males who were either: (a) convicted of offences as adults, or (b) came from families in which two brothers were committed to Care and one had a conviction. In two pairs of cases, twin brothers were admitted and discharged together but had very different criminal histories. The first eighteen cases will be presented (apart from the first three, which are all from one family) roughly according to the age at which they first entered Care. Where a seriousness-of-crime score is given, this refers to adult offences only.

After these outlines, we shall briefly describe ten lives of males who were not convicted of any offence, either as adults or children, in spite of their socially deprived backgrounds.

Eighteen cases of males with adult convictions (or whose brothers had adult convictions)

1–3 Cases 51, 62 and 29
In this family four of the boys were admitted to Care and three were in the sample selected.

John A (Case 51) was the eldest of thirteen children. He was first admitted to Care when he was six years old, with three younger sisters and a younger brother, because his mother had deserted. The quality of parental care in both a physical and emotional sense seems to have been deficient. His father had severe alcohol problems and was convicted on several occasions, being sent to prison at least four times. There had been frequent fights between his parents. John remained in Care until he was eighteen and in this time had twelve placements. Several foster placements broke down 'because of John's petty theft'. John was intellectually retarded. His mother kept in somewhat sporadic contact and, on his discharge from Care, John returned to live with her. He had one conviction as an adult: for assault occasioning grievous bodily harm, at the age of 20. His seriousness-of-crime score was 3.

George A (Case 62) was the fifth child. He was admitted to Care at eight months when his mother deserted the family. After four years in a residential nursery and small-group homes, he was fostered at the age of five and remained in the same placement throughout his period in Care, in spite of considerable difficulties in adolescence. He stayed with his foster parents on discharge from Care and had no convictions either as a child or as an adult. Matthew A (Case 29) was the seventh child. He was reported to the Education Department for truancy at ten and committed to Care at the age of thirteen, when convicted of theft. As well as stealing and truanting, he was also defiant at home and disruptive at school, and was involved in homosexual play with adults and younger boys. He is not known to have had convictions as an adult but at seventeen he left Care to enter the Army (where he may have had convictions not recorded in the Criminal Records Offices).

4 Case 24

Edward B was admitted to Care at the age of seven months because of his mother's severe incapacity to care for him. She suffered badly from epilepsy and went to live in an epileptic colony when Edward was admitted to Care. He was illegitimate. He had three placements – a residential nursery until two years of age and then a single fostering from two until fifteen years of age, when he went to a training school on a farm for eighteen months. He returned to his foster mother at sixteen and stayed with her after he ceased to be in Care at eighteen years of age.

When he was twelve his foster father died and his foster mother, who was decidedly ambivalent towards Edward, went to live with her own daughter, taking Edward with her. He was not happy with this arrangement and showed many difficulties in adolescence: stealing, being defiant and wetting the bed. He had been given psychometric testing at nine years of age and was deemed to be of low average intelligence.

As an adult he had five convictions, all for burglary and theft, and the last was at thirty years of age. He appears to have had no convictions as a juvenile. His seriousness-of-crime score was 3.

5 Case 19

Albert C was illegitimate and his father never lived with his mother. He was first admitted to Care, at his mother's request, when he was four months of age. (The local authority felt she was neglecting him.) He was returned to his mother again, at her request, when he was six months old and then abandoned by her at eight months of age, when he was placed in a residential nursery. He passed through a succession of foster mothers and had ten changes of placement in a period of less than two years. However, at two and a half years of age he was fostered and, after four years, his foster mother successfully applied to adopt him and he was discharged from Care at the age of six.

The adoption does not appear to have been a complete success, at least in the long term. As a juvenile he had only one conviction, but he committed ten offences as an adult – all for theft, crimes of dishonesty and 'criminal damage'. His last offence was at twenty-eight years of age, so he may well not yet have finished his criminal career. His seriousness-of-crime score was 4.

6 Case 46

Arthur D was first admitted to Care at nine months when his mother abandoned him. He was initially placed in a residential nursery and then fostered at fourteen months. He remained with the same foster parents for fifteen years, but the placement broke down when he was sixteen because of his 'rudeness and defiance' to his foster parents, his stealing and convictions for theft and 'breaking and entering'. He then spent eighteen months in two sets of lodgings. He had had a liver infection and a degree of anaemia as a child, and was excessively small throughout childhood. His foster father seemed to show little interest in him and, although there was little overt conflict in their marriage, his foster mother confessed to considerable dissatisfaction. Her attitude seemed to be one of considerable strictness and overprotectiveness. She seemed a rather over-anxious person.

Arthur had five convictions as an adult, all by the age of twenty-one. They were for handling of stolen goods, taking and driving away, and breaking and entering. His seriousness-of-crime score was 3.

7 Case 232

Joe E was first reported to the Education Department at the age of six for school non-attendance. His father worked on the canal barges. His mother was regarded as possibly retarded and the family was well known to the NSPCC. The marriage was unhappy. Joe was described as very small as a child.

Joe was admitted to Care four times in his childhood (starting at the age of seven years), twice because of his mother's subsequent confinements, once (at ten years of age) when she overdosed following a marital row and, lastly, at fourteen, because of non-compliance with a Supervision Order. He remained in Care for only eight months on that occasion and his total aggregate of time in Care was only fifteen months. His father had been sent to prison on a conviction of assault. He had one conviction as a juvenile and two as an adult – one for theft and one (at the age of twenty) for assault occasioning actual bodily harm. His seriousness-of-crime score was 3.

8 Case 4

John F was the third (and illegitimate) child of five. He was admitted to Care at the age of three, when all five children were admitted because of their mother's neglect. John had five placements, largely owing to unsuccessful attempts to keep the siblings together.

However, at five years of age he was fostered and stayed with his foster parents until he was eighteen, remaining with them even after officially leaving Care. At fifteen and sixteen he was described as very defiant and difficult but the placement did not break down.

He had no juvenile convictions and no adult convictions until the age of twenty-nine when he was convicted of wounding with intent and assault leading to actual bodily harm (i.e. two separate offences). He was diagnosed as schizophrenic and committed to a Special Hospital under Section 65 of the Mental Health Act (1959). His seriousness-of-crime score was 3.

9 Case 20

Robert G was the third of seven children. His father died of lung cancer when he was five. He had already been admitted to Care at the age of three. Altogether, he had six admissions to Care at the ages of 3, 5, 6, 7, 8 and 12. Parental rights were assumed at the age of ten.

His longest period in Care was for three and a half years – from eight until eleven and a half years of age. In aggregate, he spent seven and a half years in Care. When in Care he was in small-group and large-group homes but never fostered.

His mother was described as fond of Robert but grossly inadequate, suffering from poor physical and mental health and having a series of cohabitees. She had recurrent bronchitis, and pneumonia on more than one occasion.

At ten years of age, Robert was described as shy, solitary and withdrawn. He had *no* convictions as a child and only one as an adult – for criminal damage. His seriousness-of-crime score was 1.

10 Case 23

Peter H was first admitted to Care on a voluntary basis at the age of three, when his six older brothers and sisters were evicted and became homeless. Although his older brothers and sisters returned home, his parents left Peter in Care. He was placed initially in a residential nursery. Attempts were made to foster him at four years of age and, again at five, ten and sixteen years of age. All four attempts failed and he had twelve different homes during his fifteen years in Care. It was alleged that the last two placements broke down because of Peter's difficult behaviour, which involved stealing money from the foster parents, temper tantrums and sex play with other boys. He was prone to temper outbursts throughout his childhood, although that is perhaps understandable in the light of his experience.

Neither natural parent appears to have shown any interest in him when he was in Care and there is no record that he was visited at all. His mother was handicapped on one side of her body. The medical reason for this is not recorded. She is described as 'a hard woman' and the marriage of his parents was said to be 'acrimonious', involving several separations.

He had three convictions as an adult; two convictions for larceny and one for non-payment of his fine, for which he was sent to prison. His seriousness-of-crime score was 3.

11 Case 58

Geoffrey I was the second of three siblings and was first admitted to Care at the age of three because of neglect. He went back home at four when his parents applied for a revocation of the Fit Person Order and the Children's Department decided not to oppose them. At five years of age he was readmitted for four months when the family were evicted. He was again committed to Care, because of neglect, at seven years of age and both his parents were sentenced to prison on that occasion because of their neglect.

Although he was the second child, he was born when his mother was only sixteen and his father seventeen. His mother was described as dull and 'inadequate', both as a wife and as a mother. His father had problems with alcohol and spent at least three periods in prison.

Geoffrey lived in Care for just over ten years, of which four were at an ESN residential school. He had a squint and a bald patch. Two foster placements broke down because of Geoffrey's difficult behaviour and stealing. However, he had no convictions as a juvenile.

He was discharged from Care to a Remand Centre at eighteen following two convictions for petty theft and on being charged with a third, for which he was convicted.

He progressed rapidly through Detention Centres, Borstal and prison, to which he was sentenced seven times. He had a total of twenty-three convictions as an adult, all for theft, burglary and other crimes of dishonesty. His seriousness-of-crime score was 6.

12, 13 Cases 11 and 66

Stephen J and Henry J were twins, who were both first admitted to Care at the age of five, following their father's placement in a hospital for the mentally retarded and their mother's incapacity to cope. They remained in Care, fostered together for three years. They returned home at the age of eight when their father was discharged home. Their mother was described as 'moderately retarded in intelligence, fond but inadequate'. The father was committed to a special hospital when they were ten years of age, following a conviction for attempted murder.

At thirteen years of age, both boys were committed to Care after convictions for theft and both returned to the same foster parents and lived with them for the next five years.

Stephen (Case 11) remained with his foster parents at eighteen but had five convictions in the next two years; three for theft, one for taking and driving away a car and one for indecently assaulting an eight-year-old boy. His seriousness-of-crime score was 4.

Henry (Case 66) also remained with his foster parents, but had no convictions.

14 Case 97

Andrew K was first admitted to Care at the age of ten. He was placed for fostering with his aunt and uncle.

As an infant he had had TB meningitis at nine months and been in hospital for nearly a year. He had a squint and was subject to recurrent chest troubles.

His mother had died, possibly of TB, a few months before his admission and he had been cared for by his grandmother, who was bedridden. He was illegitimate.

Prior to his admission to Care, he had been running from home and had been the victim of an indecent assault. He had an IQ of over 125 but was found to be over two years retarded in reading at the age of ten (in relation to his overall IQ).

No problems were acknowledged by his foster parents and he had no convictions as a juvenile. He was discharged to his aunt.

However, as an adult he had fourteen convictions, a high proportion of which (five) were of a sexual nature, including indecent assault. Most of the others involved dishonesty or taking and driving away cars. His last offence was when he was thirty-one. His seriousness-of-crime score was 5.

15, 16 Cases 99 and 79

William L and Henry L were twins and the (joint) fourth of six children. Their mother died of cancer of the bowel when they were ten. Prior to her death, she had been ill for several months.

Their father was chronically unemployed and their parents' marriage was described as characterised by frequent arguments and by the father often deserting the family. After his wife's death, the father abandoned his children and they were admitted to Care. The father was known to have had psychiatric treatment. He showed no interest in his children after their admission to Care and, in fact, disappeared.

After a period in assessment, William was cared for, with his siblings, in a large Children's Home for three years. Little is known about his behaviour at this home, except that he was a 'bully' to smaller children. He was tested by a psychologist while in the assessment centre and found to have an IQ in the high eighties.

At the age of fourteen, he was fostered and presented with serious conduct problems, including persistent disobedience, attacking younger children, theft outside the house, self-injury and a 'hysterical fit'. Owing to his behaviour problems, he had several changes of placement, including discharge to an aunt at fifteen years of age. This, however, did not work and he quickly returned to Care. He continued to injure himself and has been having almost continuous psychiatric treatment ever since, with diagnoses of personality disorder and query schizophrenia. His own children have been briefly in Care. Although he had no convictions as a juvenile, he had eight convictions as an adult, including one for unlawful and malicious wounding, two for assault occasioning actual bodily harm and one for assaulting a policeman. His last conviction was at the age of twenty-eight. His seriousness-of-crime score was 5.

His twin brother, Henry, (Case 79) was also admitted to Care at the same time and was in the sample selected.

He also had serious conduct problems as a boy and was placed in a Residential School for mildly retarded children. On the other hand, he was convicted of only one offence as an adult – for theft. His seriousness-of-crime score was 1.

17 Case 25

John L first entered Care at the age of fourteen when he was committed by the Court for theft. He was an illegitimate child, whose stepfather had been admitted to a mental hospital on several occasions. His diagnosis was not recorded. The mother was described as 'dull' and very dissatisfied with the marriage, although there were few overt rows. John had an IQ of 56 and was involved in prostitution with

older men at the time of his committal to Care. John's mother maintained erratic contact with her son while he was in Care. He had one
placement in a family-group home and was discharged to his mother's
home at the age of eighteen.

As an adult he had fourteen convictions, the last being at the age of
thirty-three, so his criminal career has probably not ended. He had
convictions for practically all types of crime, including three cases of
indecent assault on women and one of assaulting the police. His
seriousness-of-crime score was 5.

18 Case 151

Clarke M was the second and last child of a window cleaner who had
considerable drive and ambition to improve himself socially. The
father seemed interested in and concerned about his son but, by the
time Clarke was referred to Child Guidance at the age of eleven, he
was unable to communicate with him. Clark's mother was anxious,
unhappy and somewhat overprotective towards her son, who was
stealing from the home and had wandered away from the home for
over four years. Clarke had been a diphtheria carrier for two years,
between the ages of six and eight, and had been excluded from school.
His reading was over two years retarded for his IQ, which was
average. The marriage was said to be basically satisfying. Clarke was
remanded into Care at the age of thirteen for three weeks and committed to Approved School for house-breaking. He was committed to
another Approved School at fifteen. At the age of twenty he was
committed to Borstal, following two offences of warehouse-breaking
and theft, and shortly after his release he was sent to prison on a
conviction of unlawful wounding. This was his last conviction (at
twenty-two years of age). He had nine convictions as a juvenile and
four as an adult. His seriousness-of-crime score was 4.

(Clarke is an instance of a boy with apparently caring and
competent parents who was seriously delinquent as a child. His adult
criminal career was slightly less serious than his childhood career).

The childhood experiences of ten subjects who were not convicted of an offence (excluding school non-attendance) either as juveniles or as adults

1 Case 008

James A was his mother's fifth and youngest child and was born to her second husband. His father was a seaman who spent long periods away from home. He seemed unconcerned about his children, even when he was ashore. He was 'violent' and drank heavily, and James's mother also had a serious alcohol problem. She was strongly suspected of being a prostitute. James was committed to the Care of Northtown at nine years of age, because of his mother's neglect, but he had repeatedly been 'reported' for school non-attendance during the previous twelve months.

Although Mrs A did not seem overtly hostile to James, she seemed to lack any maternal concern for him.

The parents' marriage was very quarrelsome and physical violence was not uncommon. The father seemed an explosive personality and the mother apathetic. The house was very dirty, ill-cared for and overcrowded.

James remained in Care for nine years. The relationship with his foster parents was difficult in adolescence and breakdown was predicted by the social worker who visited the family. It never occurred and James remained with them on discharge from Care when he was eighteen.

2 Case 015

Graham B was committed to Care at the age of two because of his mother's neglect. He was the second son of eight (including stepsiblings). His father had deserted and his mother had also disappeared at times before he was committed to Care. After Graham went into Care, she showed no further interest in him. He was placed first in a residential nursery and then fostered, but this placement broke down when he was five years old. After placements in three children's homes, he was again fostered at the age of nine, and he remained with his foster parents for the rest of his period in Care, staying with them after his official discharge. No problem behaviour was recorded about him during his childhood.

3 Case 021

John C was committed to Care on a Fit Person Order at the age of six because he was deemed to be 'in moral danger' (his mother had been convicted of keeping a 'brothel' and sent to prison). His father was recorded as being already dead at the time of his admission to Care, although the cause of death was not recorded. His six brothers and sisters were also committed to Care at the same time. Prior to the

Court proceedings, the family had already been the subject of several case conferences on neglected children. John's mother continued to visit for several years while he was in Care.

He had ten placements, including four foster placements, only the last of which 'survived'. He started this at the age of nine and was adopted by his foster parents when he was fifteen.

4 Case 026

Peter D was 'admitted to Care', with his younger sister, at the age of twelve and fostered with his own maternal grandmother for the next six years. His mother had deserted them both. His father was in the regular army and showed no interest in his children. The records give no reason for his mother's desertion. She had previously given cause for public and neighbourly concern because of her inadequate parenting of Peter. Neither Peter nor his sister presented with any marked problems in adolescence.

5 Case 042

Brian E was first admitted to Care at the age of eighteen months, his mother having died shortly after child-birth. He remained in Care until he was eighteen and had ten placements during his childhood. His father, who appears to have struggled to care for him until he was received into Care, died when he was seven. He never visited Brian in Care (and had been sentenced to prison when Brian was three years old).

Brian was fostered three times and the first placement broke down when he was five years of age, allegedly because of Brian's soiling and wetting. Brian was also said to have poor speech at that age. He was fostered again and this placement ended when his foster mother died when Brian was ten. He was then placed in a small-group home but was moved because of his difficult behaviour. At thirteen years of age he was admitted to the Reception Centre/Assessment Unit because of his tempers, defiance and theft, both inside and outside the Home.

His IQ, as measured by Raven's matrices, was 93. He was fostered again at the age of thirteen, but his third foster placement also broke down as a result of the foster mother's death. It follows that Brian was 'orphaned' at least three times. He was discharged from Care to lodgings.

6 Case 068

Duncan F was admitted to Care briefly at the age of two years, when his mother was confined for a subsequent child. His father was a docker who had alcohol problems. Several social workers and Education Welfare Officers commented on his mother's dullness. She seemed constantly tired and the house was 'revoltingly' dirty. He had six brothers and sisters. Marital strife seems to have been the rule rather than the exception and the father often deserted. At one point he was committed to prison for non-payment of an affiliation order.

Duncan's parents were prosecuted for his school non-attendance when he was five years old and again when he was eight. On this occasion he was committed to Care because of his school non-attendance. He had seven placements in Care before discharge back to his mother at the age of sixteen. A year before his discharge, his houseparents complained of his stealing in the Children's Home and from shops.

7 Case 119

William G was referred to the Child Guidance Clinic at the tender age of five years by the 'school doctor' after having broken at least three crucifixes in churches. The family took William to the clinic only once and the reason for his bizarre behaviour was never discovered.

The home was described as 'badly cared for' and the children (including William) had been subjects of case conferences on neglected children. (William's younger brother was, in fact, committed to Care because of neglect.) The psychiatrist described the mother as depressed. The father had a contracted right hand and was unemployed for long periods. The social worker felt he was 'hostile to authority'. However, the marriage seemed to be satisfying to both partners and was not overtly disharmonious.

8 Case 124

Thomas H was referred to the Child Guidance Clinic at the age of eight with problems of over-anxiety and primary enuresis. He had an average IQ but had not yet begun to read. Thomas's father had died of stomach ulcers when Thomas was three and had been ill for two years prior to his death. Thomas's mother was described as decidedly-over-anxious but strict. She brought Thomas to the clinic weekly for almost a year. He was discharged as being 'much improved'.

9 Case 141

Derek I was referred to the Child Guidance Clinic at the age of nine for failure to read. He was judged to have a reading age of less than seven and overall IQ of 141 on the WISC Scale. His father had separated from his mother when Derek was only twelve months of age and had no further contact with the boy. His mother was intending to remarry at the time of the referral. She seemed to be capable of managing Derek and a generally competent person. No specific reason was discovered for Derek's failure to learn to read. The family attended the clinic only four times.

10 Case 236

Charles K was reported for truancy at the age of seven. The Education Welfare Officer felt his parents condoned his absence.

He was committed to care for truancy when he was twelve, remained in Care for seven months and was then discharged home. Whilst in Care, he was caught attempting sexual intercourse with a girl of his own age. He was known to have committed burglary. Because of his high IQ (156) it was recommended that he should go to a special residential school but this recommendation was never implemented. His brother was convicted of theft as a juvenile.

Comment

It is not apparent why the ten boys who were free from official convictions should have remained so. Their backgrounds seemed very similar to those who became delinquent and this impression is strengthened when we compare the outcome of the two sets of twins in the study, Stephen and Henry J (Cases 11 and 66) and William and Henry L (Cases 99 and 79). In both pairs, each of the twins had a very different outcome. (It is not known if the twins were identical.)

Although retrospective speculation cannot carry much scientific weight and our evidence is woefully limited, it is tempting to try to find reasons why these ten boys were not convicted, especially as adults. The first six may have been protected by being in substitute Care, although it has to be conceded that two of them (John C. and Brian E) experienced very inadequate and disrupted care, and four were admitted to Care 'for good' when they were relatively older (James A when he was nine, Peter D, to his grandmother, when he was twelve, Brian E when he was seven and Duncan F when he was eight.

Thomas H and Duncan I were not known to have shown severe conduct problems as boys. On the other hand, the behaviour of five of the boys appeared at times to be quite seriously antisocial (James A, Brian E, Duncan F, William G and Charles K). The latter was perhaps saved from being convicted by his intelligence; on one occasion at least, he committed an offence without being caught.

We have found no single explanation as to why these boys avoided officially recorded crime.

13

Discussion, comments and implications

'The quality of Care a child receives could be expected to be reflected in the quality of life upon leaving Care.'
Parker, 1980.

The findings reported in this study will, we suspect, be strongly resisted by some because they run contrary to most current ideologies and policies in relation to children 'at risk', which are in favour of helping children 'in the community' and against their removal into Care. One particular attitude which may colour people's reactions is the current suspicion of 'treatment' in relation to delinquents and even the rejection of a 'welfare approach' as being contrary to their best long-term interests (Jones, 1983). We feel it important to stress that our main intention has *not* been to study the effectiveness of Care as the means of *treating* delinquents, nor even, in the first place, as a means of *preventing* delinquency.

Our primary aim has been to follow up children living in socially and often emotionally deprived circumstances, including children admitted to Care, and to compare their adult outcome with some of the more salient features of their childhood experiences and environments. A major subsidiary aim has been to examine the outcome for children who were brought up in Care, using, as an index of outcome, their recorded offences, with a view to testing an attitude widely held by professional workers with children: that the admission of children to Care, and keeping them there long-term, frequently does more harm than good. Part of the case for this view is that associations have been found between living in Care as a child and later becoming delinquent.

For nearly half the boys in our total Care sample, and for almost all the quarter of boys longest in Care, there was no intention on the part of Social Workers or the Courts of either dealing with recent crime or preventing future delinquency in admitting them to Care. Nearly all the boys longest in Care had been either: (a) severely neglected, abandoned or deserted by their parents, (b) had had mothers who were unable to care for them because they had died or had chronic illnesses and handicaps, or (c) they originally had been admitted to Care because their families were homeless. In all the cases in the quarter of the boys longest in Care, homelessness was unlikely to have been the only factor determining whether they remained in Care, since their brothers and sisters returned home within a few weeks of admission, but the subjects of our study remained behind. Only one of the twenty-two boys longest in Care officially entered Care for behaviour problems, and this boy had previously been in Care as a baby because of his mother's inability to cope with him.

Owing to the way in which our original Care sample and its comparison groups were chosen, both the original Care sample and the 'total group' of boys who came into Care are, in one respect, untypical of children admitted to Care, either now or a generation ago. Both 'samples' probably fail to contain a typical proportion of children admitted for short periods because of family crises. By definition, the original Child Care sample excluded children in Care for less than two years and, by the choices of comparison groups, the only children who entered the total Care group in addition to the original sample were children who were eventually seen as problematical in a broad sense (although in many cases it was clear in the non-attenders' group, and even in the Child Guidance group, that the original pathology lay in the parents and in their lack of ability to provide adequate parenting, even though there may have been contributory factors in the child).

As we have seen, Packman, Randall and Jacques (1986) categorise the reasons for admission into Care into three groups: victims, villains and volunteeered. Milham *et al.* (1986) adopt a similar categorisation, without the same terminology.

The children in our sample could also be divided roughly into three categories: (a) children whose parents were unable or unwilling to provide adequate care (and for this reason the children were unlikely ever to return home), (b) boys who were eight years and above on admission to Care and who were either officially delinquent or beyond parental control, and (c) other children, who in our sample are only a small group, consisting of about a fifth to a sixth of the total Care group (N = 90), and made up mainly of school non-attenders and a few other children originally admitted because of the mother's confinement for a subsequent child, temporary homelessness or the parents' temporary illness. However, it would be a mistake to assume, in assessing our study or most other studies of children in Care, that there is a large proportion of children admitted to Care from homes where their parents have been providing perfectly adequate parenting but have been temporarily incapacitated by some crisis, whether it be confinement, acute illness or material or emotional stress. This will be true of a minority of cases, but studies a generation ago by Schaffer and Schaffer (1968) and Mapstone (1969) have shown that a poor quality of parental care and a considerable level of material deprivation are very widespread in the families of children who enter Care, whatever the official reason for their admission. More recent studies by Quinton and Rutter (1984) and Isaac, Minty and Morrison (1986) have shown that the families of children entering Care are characterised not only by material poverty but also by considerable personal problems in the parents, including a great deal of mental disorder, in a broad sense.

In cases of desertion or abandonment, or gross physical or sexual abuse, admission to Care, on either a voluntary or compulsory basis, is often inevitable. Faute de mieux, it is inevitable that the Care system will continue to be used for adolescents who are either delinquent or beyond control. However, in addition, there should remain a Child Care service to parents who, for a variety of reasons, are unable to provide adequate parenting because of temporary, or sometimes permanent, incapacity to cope with children, or with the particular children they have.

It is difficult to deny the validity of Packman's categorisation (Packman, Randall and Jacques, 1986) of there being, crudely, three groups of children and adolescents who need Care: victims, villains and the volunteered, although it has to be accepted that some children fall into two, or even three, categories and that children may move from one category to another as they grow through childhood and adolescence; e.g. in our sample there are clearly cases of children who were initially victims of neglect, hostility and distorted relationships but who later became 'villains.' There are known to be associations between living in such relationships and later delinquency (the evidence being discussed in Chapters 1 and 9). At first sight, it would seem to follow that if such children were removed from these relationships their delinquency would diminish. Studies on adolescent delinquents have not confirmed this conclusion (Clarke and Cornish, 1972) and there are anxieties that the deficiencies of the Care 'system', and contamination by children already delinquent or very troublesome, may make matters even worse for juvenile delinquents who are admitted to Care in order to check their downward drift into repeated offending.

There is a good deal of evidence in this monograph that once young males get into repeated trouble with the law, there is a considerable chance that they will go on to commit multiple offences as adults, often in spite of attempts at either treatment or punishment. There is also evidence that children who came from homes characterised by arguments, hostility and lack of care were more likely to become multiple and serious offenders. On the other hand, children who were virtually brought up in Care were relatively less likely to be recidivists or to commit serious crimes as adults. Among the quarter of boys longest in Care, half had been brought up predominantly in foster homes and the other half either in residential living or in a mixture of fostering and residential care. Both groups did equally well. At this point it is appropriate to discuss our findings.

Length of Care and outcome

It could rightly be objected that our study does not compare the outcome for the boys who stayed longest in Care with a representative sample of apparently trouble-free boys drawn from the community. For reasons already given, it proved impossible to find such a comparison group. On the other hand, the quarter of boys who were longest in Care were not significantly more delinquent as adults than those boys who had attended the local Child Guidance with entirely emotional problems and who could be considered, on the basis of Robins' study (1966), to be likely to have an outcome no worse than controls drawn from the ordinary population.

A further objection might be put that the study does not compare like with like, in that it so happened that the boys admitted to Care for short periods were much more likely to be admitted for reasons of conduct and delinquency or were later found to have conduct problems. It has to be accepted that the study does not compare the long-term outcome of children who remained in Care for lengthy periods with a representative sample of children who stayed in Care for only short periods. That study has still to be done. However, one of the clearest findings of our study was that coming into Care for reasons of delinquency, *whatever* the length of time spent in Care, was associated with a poor outcome.

In our view, the current assumption that boys in Care do badly after leaving Care, although correct, fails to take into account two facts: (a) that many boys are already troubled and troublesome when they enter Care, and (b) that inadequate support has often been offered to boys on leaving Care.

On all comparisons in our study, boys longest in Care did better (and usually significantly better) than boys admitted later and for reasons of delinquency. They also did better, although not significantly so, than boys admitted for shorter periods for non-delinquent reasons. The thesis of this study is not that staying a long time in Care is in itself a good thing for children, but that, on our limited criterion of adult offences, it is a better upbringing than living in some very inadequate homes. The boys who virtually grew up in Care had a better outcome than either boys who were first admitted to Care later in childhood, when they were already delinquent, or boys who were admitted very early in life, but who then returned home. These boys may not have been representative of all short-term admissions to Care but they are instances of childhoods where it is arguable that it would have been better for them to have remained in Care. Our outcome index is admittedly very limited but it cannot be assumed that the outcome for these boys in other respects was any better than that of boys who remained in Care.

Our findings are: (a) that those boys who stayed longest in Care did relatively well, (b) that those boys who came into Care later, for reasons of delinquency, did poorly, and (c) that there was a group of children who were admitted to Care early in life and then discharged home who did very poorly.

On the basis of the above it seems reasonable to argue that it is likely that some of the boys admitted later, when already delinquent, would not have had such a poor outcome if they had been admitted earlier.

Age on first and subsequent admissions

We found that when boys who were admitted to Care before the age of four were divided into those who remained in Care and those who returned home, a poor outcome was almost exclusively confined to those who had returned home – even though sometimes, after a gap of several years, they came back into Care again. This suggests strongly that for many boys who have been in Care, the damaging factors do not usually lie in the Care experience itself (in spite of all its deficiencies) but in factors in the home and wider social environment before, and after, Care.

There could well be other boys who had been admitted to Care for short periods at an early age and who were discharged home without either being later readmitted to Care or referred to Child Guidance or picked up by the Education Welfare Service. While this may be true, it is incontrovertible that the *excess* of delinquency and conduct problems in boys who were in Care for *shorter* periods, including boys who were admitted early and returned home only to come back into Care again, appears prima facie to be due to factors *outside* the Care system. This is confirmed by our evidence that criminality in adult life (> 16 years) was associated with various parenting deficiencies and marital discord in the natural home.

Care as a remedy for pre-existing delinquency

The most obvious reason why being longer in Care appeared to be associated with fewer crimes of violence is that such boys were removed for longer periods from living in natural homes where there was often discord, sometimes rejection and not infrequently violent parental models. Living in such environments may well have had a long-term adverse effect on their personality development and the removal from such homes may have diminished this process.

Such reasons may explain our finding that the longer boys lived in residential Care, the fewer crimes of violence they tended to commit in adult life. Another factor, which may be of considerable importance here, is that while in Care they probably had stricter oversight and this may have lessened their chances of embarking on serious criminal careers, especially between the ages of sixteen and eighteen.

Sadly, for most boys who were already delinquent or largely beyond parental control, admission to Care did not lead to the entire absence of a criminal record in adult life or even (for a majority) avoiding 'recidivism' in our sense, i.e. having three or more convictions.

Changes of placement

One of our more surprising findings was that when we confined analysis to the original sample of boys in Care, there was no association between having a greater than average number of placements in Care and having more convictions in adult life, and this was true even when we excluded boys already delinquent on admission. When we examined the total Care group, boys with *more* than an average number of placements had significantly *fewer* convictions as adults than boys with a small number of placements.

The likeliest explanation for this is that, within the total Care group, the majority of boys with a *lower* number of placements consisted of boys who were in Care for relatively *shorter* periods. Boys who had a greater than average number of placements had nearly always spent a considerable period of their childhood 'in Care'. On the other hand, living through a succession of placements, spread out over several years, seemed less criminogenic than living *outside* Care for most of one's childhood in damaging family environments. This has some implications in relation to the evaluation of the damage done by the breaking of attachment bonds, followed, possibly, by having more neutral relationships with care-givers in the genesis of delinquency, as compared with living in distorted relationships and experiencing lax controls.

We are not suggesting at all that changes of placement are in themselves generally a good thing, even though it is sometimes better for a child that a particular placement that has gone sour should break down and allow for a fresh start. In fact, in keeping with the common-sense view that stability of Care is helpful in personality development, we found: (a) that there was a significant *negative* association between the length of the longest foster placement (for boys who were fostered) and the number of convictions our (male) subjects 'acquired' in adult life, and (b) that boys who had more than the average number of placements also tended to have *longer* placements. It is also our impression that comparatively more of these 'broke down' prematurely because of illness or other problems in the foster family, and not usually because of conduct problems in the child. In fact, the majority of the longest foster placements for each boy which ended in disruptions 'broke down' for reasons of ill health, death or other family difficulties, rather than because of difficulties in the child, although, sadly, in four cases long-term placements which had survived several years until adolescence did break down in that period, allegedly because of the boys' difficult behaviour.

There are obvious dangers in assuming that adults who grew up in Care will look back on the longest placements they had as being the most influential – for good or bad. This may not always be the case. Measuring the length of placements is at best an inadequate approach to evaluation.

It could be argued that, in so far as Social Services Departments accept the arguments put forward by Goldstein, Freud and Solnit (1979), and researchers into child care such as Rowe and Lambert (1973), Mass and Engler (1959), Emlen and Cascaito (1978), and Adcock (1981) about the need for stability and permanency in substitute parenting and the feasibility of achieving this, then proper decisions will be made relatively early in children's lives about permanent substitute care and this will do away with frequent changes in placement. Nobody would do other than try to achieve permanency and stability for children, but there are various reasons why it is impossible to prevent a certain number of changes of placement in substitute care: (a) the more attempts are made at preventing admission, the more likely it is that, in some cases, social workers will only postpone admission into Care. This will make it both harder to find the right foster and adoptive parents (since some children will have become quite difficult to manage) and perhaps less desirable to use adoption, since the child will have strong links with his natural family, in spite of their inadequacies, (b) it is not always apparent at first contact that some parents are chronically unable to provide a particular child with adequate affection and care. This too will delay plans for permanency and possibly increase disturbance in a child, perhaps making a family placement inappropriate, (c) what are intended to be permanent substitute placements sometimes rapidly turn out not to be so – in spite of careful selection, and (d) substitute families are subject to all the vulnerabilities of natural families and are almost certainly often subject to additional stresses.

Destination on discharge

We found that the young men who were discharged from Care neither to their own homes nor to foster parents but to lodgings, residential types of work, farming or hostels were more likely to be sentenced to prison, even though their seriousness-of-crime scores did not indicate that they had committed particularly serious crimes. There were other young men with apparently much more 'serious' criminal careers (who returned to their natural parents or remained with foster parents) who were not given prison sentences. The numbers involved are small (4/9 cases) and possibly not representative. It is also a fact that two of the four received only suspended sentences and these sentences were possibly effective in preventing further offending – they marked the apparent end of their criminal careers. However, they are 'risky' sentences, since further serious offending would inevitably have led to committal to prison. It could be that magistrates and judges felt they were more restricted in the penalties available to them in dealing with young men who had no relatives and possibly no fixed abode. Such young men may have been less likely to know how to obtain proper legal representation a generation ago and suffered as a consequence, especially without older friends who could provide money or advice.

It is probable that young men and women discharged from residential Care at eighteen years of age may suffer not so much from the experience of Care but from the lack of any semi-permanent emotional and physical base, such as is available for most other young people in the community.

On the evidence presented here, it would be unjustifiable to urge great changes in policy. However, other studies confirm the trend of our findings and it would seem inherently wrong to expect that young people of eighteen should survive on their own resources without an emotional or physical base. Human beings do not seem made for complete independence, and how many natural parents would expect their late teenage children to fend entirely for themselves? Two studies of children leaving Care strongly support this view. Mann (1984) interviewed in depth a number of children who had been in long-term Care. A frequent comment was that *leaving* Care was a very difficult time. Some young people were very angry at what they felt was the lack of social-work concern for them in that period. Stein and Carey (personal communications) who followed up a much larger sample of children leaving Care (N = 79) came to similar conclusions, finding a good deal of loneliness, frequent movement and difficulties in finding accommodation, employment or income.

Two other studies which looked at the parenting capacities of women (including women who had been in Care as children) found that parenting capacities tended to be good in those who had current support (from spouses or their own parents) and poor in those without (Rutter, Quinton and Liddle, 1983; Kruk and Wolkind, 1983). One implication of these studies (and our own) is that what happens to young people when they leave Care may well depend on the quality of their material resources and personal supports. Some training for self-care is no doubt essential for children leaving Care, but it is not sufficient in itself.

Foster v. residential care

Our findings suggest that (by our very limited criteria) both fostering and small-group living might be an adequate upbringing for children. While it is true that boys who were fostered did better than boys who lived mainly in small-group homes, fostering was nearly always the preferred method of care, so that only boys who had failed in fostering tended to stay in small-group homes. However, the outcome for the subgroup within the quarter of boys longest in Care who were brought up largely in small group-homes suggests that small-group living may be an adequate preparation for adult life – at least as judged by our limited criteria.

These findings will surprise some social workers for whom both fostering and residential care, but especially the latter, are seen as discredited.

Perhaps what matters most is that a Children's Home is really home for the children who live there and are likely to continue to live there, and that they know that there will always be at least a temporary place for them when they return – even after leaving Care. 'Home' says Robert Frost 'is the place where when you have to go they have to take you in.' Having met some of the staff in charge of the small-group homes in which some of our subjects spent several years, we feel it is likely that they were encouraged to think of the Home as theirs in many respects and we know that some continued to have contact with their house-parents after leaving. Of course, it will always be true that a major advantage for long-term fostering over residential care is that when fostering works, children tend to remain with foster parents on leaving Care.

Poor natural homes

Our findings require little explanation and suggest that professionals working with children cannot afford to dismiss the possible long-term adverse consequences for boys of growing up in an atmosphere of hostility and conflict. It was also clear that the more deficient the home, the greater the likelihood that boys would commit multiple offences and crimes of violence as adults.

As a guide to practice, these findings have limited value, since practitioners will often be faced with the dilemma that early intervention to remove a child will not be justifiable, particularly since predicting the future is so very unsure. On the other hand, by the time a child is seriously delinquent, it may be too late to prevent a long subsequent career in crime. Social workers cannot avoid considering the consequences of leaving a child in his natural home if other methods of intervention have not succeeded.

Comparison with other studies

How far does our research show results comparable with other studies? Our findings in relation to the associations between: (a) severe conduct disorder in boys and later delinquency, and (b) living in distorted relationships in the home and later delinquency are entirely in line with previous findings. We also found that, measured by criminality, the outcome for boys who had been in Care was significantly *worse* than for boys not known to have been in Care, which tends to confirm the findings of certain previous studies (e.g. Ferguson, 1966) and the widespread impressions of social workers. Crime is a particularly poor index of outcome for females since they are much less delinquent. The use of other measures of outcome for women (e.g. poor parenting) suggests that some forms of residential care (Rutter, Quinton and Liddle, 1983) and *some* forms of foster care (Murphy, 1974) may be a poor preparation for parenthood. In one respect, our study goes beyond what has been examined in most previous studies and has discovered that boys who came into Care when they were very young and who stayed in Care did significantly better than boys who were admitted later, often for reasons of difficult behaviour.

In this respect, our findings are exactly in line with Otterström's study in Sweden (1956). However, it is likely that, unintentionally, the design of both studies was such that they lacked sufficient numbers of relatively trouble-free children who come into Care for brief periods. However, we are not claiming that long-term Care is always better than short-term Care, which would be a monstrous proposition, but that in some circumstances it may be better and that some social workers should question their often automatic assumption that it is invariably worse. Our own view would be that staying in Care would only be better for a child if it kept him from returning to a home that was not good enough to meet his basic needs. The implications of this point of view sometimes leave practitioners with difficult questions. When are parents not good enough? Although there will be situations which are agonisingly difficult, there has also been a strong suspicion that some social workers have been so blinkered by the ideology of maintaining the family as to fail to recognise parenting which could never be regarded as adequate. A line of child abuse disasters from Maria Colwell (Howells, 1975) through to Jasmine Beckford (Brent, 1985) have suggested an inability on the part of some social workers to understand the extent and consequences of parental hostility and ambivalence, even at a crude physical level, or appreciate the quality of life endured by some children in appalling homes.

The validity of our criteria of 'Damage'

Throughout this monograph, we have conceded that convictions in adult life ($<$ 16 years) are only one possible index of outcome. Some might want to deny them even that limited validity. They could point to the two large gaps that are to be found between 'cleared-up' offences and offences which are never cleared up, and between reported and unreported offences, arguing that this makes our findings meaningless. There would have been a great advantage if our study of officially recorded crime could have been supplemented by a self-report study, but it remains true that, by and large: (a) the more 'serious' offences are reported, (b) the police make more effort to clear up the more 'serious' offences, including crimes of violence, (c) self-report studies are often inflated with relatively trivial offences, and (d) most young men who report persistent criminal activity appear to get caught eventually (Belson, 1975; Shapland, 1978; West, 1982).

We cannot argue that the convictions reported in this study are the only crimes committed by our subjects and it is likely that intelligence and chance will play a considerable part in determining who gets caught. Some of those without a known criminal career in our study are likely to have committed crimes. Still less can we argue that children who were *not* convicted as adults were necessarily well-adjusted, productive people, nor that those with convictions were totally unsuccessful as adults. However, it is unlikely that most of those with multiple convictions, or who committed the more serious types of crime, were either well-adjusted or contented members of society. As Robins (1979) says: 'Serious anti-social behaviour' in childhood 'in many cases presages life-long problems with the law, inability to earn a living, defective interpersonal relationships and severe personal distress. In fact, if we could successfully treat the antisocial behaviour of childhood, the problems of adult crime, alcoholism, divorce and chronic unemployment might be significantly diminished'. We would largely agree with Robins, except that changing social mores and the present economic situation have made divorce and chronic unemployment less robust indices of poor outcome. Evidence from the Cambridge Study in Delinquent Development (West, 1982) confirms that what is true of the USA also appears to be true of Britain. Persistent recidivists (i.e. men who continued to reoffend through young adult life) were found also to be much more likely than either temporary recidivists or non-offenders: (a) to have spent more than eight weeks unemployed during a two year period, (b) to have 'poor home conditions', (c) to have unpaid debts, (d) to have separated from their children because of marital difficulties or imprisonment, and (e) to have been involved in a fight in the previous two years (West, 1982).

Other complications

There are further complicating factors, such as the fact that this study was quite unable to take into account genetic, neurological and temperamental factors which might well influence behaviour in both childhood and/or adult life. Some of the boys in our study are likely to have had an adverse genetic loading. One example is that some mothers were known to be schizophrenic. One young man (John K, Case 4), with a schizophrenic mother, committed no offences until he was twenty-nine years old, when he was convicted of two crimes of violence, both of which appeared to be connected with the fact that he was himself schizophrenic and, as a result, he was committed to a secure special hospital/prison. A further serious deficiency is that we have been unable to study current circumstances and their relationships to convictions in adult life.

It is likely that the experience of having been brought up by inadequate, quarrelsome and rejecting parents manifests itself in a variety of ways in adult life, and not just in recorded crime. Wadsworth (1979) pointed out that there were likely to be alternative consequences to delinquency for boys who had experienced poor parenting, and that some boys who were not delinquent appeared to have psychiatric or psychosomatic problems as young men. Other outcomes for a serious lack of proper care and affection in childhood are likely to be depression, for which there appears to be evidence in women (Brown, G. W. – personal communication), and social inadequacy (Brown and Madge).

Although these findings strengthen the case for a more vigorous approach to helping and protecting children who lack good enough parenting, they may appear to weaken our own findings since they imply that, although the children who grew up for many years in Care may not have turned out as delinquents, they may have become depressed or socially inadequate instead. This may be so, but we would then need to ask (a) whether children brought up in Care are more or less likely to become socially inadequate or depressed than children brought up in poor natural homes, and if so, why; and (b) what would need to be done in relation to Care and after-Care, and to children living in their own homes, so as to provide a good enough environment for them to grow up in. What would be feasible? There is the further important question of whether recidivism, psychiatric illness and disturbance, and psychosomatic problems are mutually exclusive alternatives, or often exist side by side, and of the extent to which society's responses to disturbed behaviour are always the most appropriate. Whether some older boys with delinquent behaviour are pushed into the criminal system or treated by the local Child Guidance Clinic is likely to be a matter partly of social class and locality of residence (Gath *et al.*, 1977), and perhaps a matter of chance. There are similar problems in relation to whether some young men with problems of mental disorder and criminal behaviour end up in prison or in a psychiatric hospital.

It is clear that, whatever dependent criterion is used, there is far from a one-to-one correlation between the quality of parenting experienced in childhood and adolescence and the indices of outcome. There are many reasons for this, to which we have already referred. Children have their own individual vulnerabilities and strengths, including temperament and intelligence. Many contemporaneous happenings and opportunities in adult life will affect outcome. In relation to officially-recorded crime, as West (1982) points out, the extent of police vigilance and the number of unlocked cars or poorly secured houses in particular neighbourhoods will all have an influence on whether an adolescent boy – or girl – will enter the penal system. Of equal importance for young men and women are the quality of the relationships they enter into and maintain, including their sexual relationships. The importance of these factors for a group of women brought up in Care was highlighted by Rutter, Quinton and

Liddle (1983).

Our claim, based on the findings of many studies, is that firstly, on the whole, the less adequate the parenting, the worse the outcome. Secondly, that for boys, officially-recorded crime is one crude index of the level of parenting. We would accept that there are many causes for crime, just as there are likely to be many causes for depression and for 'social inadequacy'. Thirdly, it appeared to us, on the basis of our study, that growing up in Care, with all its deficiencies, was less likely to be associated with recidivism than growing up in grossly deficient families, with hostile fathers and parents who were continuously rowing.

Generalisability

How generalisable are our findings? Care is not a single entity. Within the spectrum of different types of care-giving the quality of each home varies and its excellence eventually depends on the individual characteristics and commitment of care-givers, on the match of care-giver and child and on changing policies in relation to residential care, foster care and adoption – all of this being under the oversight of publicly accountable agencies. Levels of crime also vary from area to area and generation to generation.

In our view, the factors in the Care experience itself that are the most important, and perhaps the most difficult to grasp by objective measurement, are whether the care-givers are understanding, affectionate people with the capacity to control their charges. It is hard to say whether such people are equally distributed throughout the child-care system and remain 'the same' from one generation to another, and whether they are equally likely to have power and influence in Children's Homes or on Social Services' policies. No matter how caring individual foster or house parents are, they will not be able to help individual children very much if the Care systems stand in their way. Tizard and Tizard (1974) found that in 'particular residential establishments characteristic patterns of function tend to remain relatively constant over long periods of time, despite changes in staff and inmate population. . . . An institution tends to function in one way rather than another not simply because of personal factors associated with particular individuals, or idiosyncratic circumstances, but because of the characteristics of its organization'. We would like to add that it is of no use a particular house-parent welcoming back and befriending young people he or she has cared for, if the Social Services Department closes the Home and reallocates the staff to other duties.

We would expect that certain aspects of our study are likely to be generalisable for boys currently at risk. We believe that boys who stay in substitute Care for many years would do relatively well, at least in terms of freedom from convictions, provided they are not seriously antisocial on entering Care. We would like to believe (on the basis of our findings) that this would be as true of boys living in small group Homes as of boys who are fostered, except that such Homes are rapidly disappearing, or used increasingly for older, more troubled and troublesome children and adolescents, which can drastically alter the atmosphere of the Home. We would still believe that, on the whole, the earlier children are admitted, the better, especially if they can be given permanency of placement. However, in relation to our indices of outcome, it appears that a few changes in placement, even though undesirable, would seem to be within the resilience of most boys to withstand. In view of the fact that female crime is much less common than male crime, we have found it difficult to comment on the outcome for women, except to say that: (a) they are less likely to be seriously involved in crime, even though there has been a trend for female crime to increase, and (b) it seemed that for girls, as for boys, length in Care was inversely related to the number of convictions.

It has to be accepted that, in comparison with the period in which our subjects grew up, alternatives to having to admit a child to Care are now much more available in the form of day nursery care, family centres for the under-fives and their families, and intermediate treatment and cautioning for delinquent adolescents. One effect of these trends is that children in Care are generally older and, in many cases, more delinquent on admission than they were. The increasing reluctance to admit children to Care and the closing of a number of residential homes have probably contributed to this tendency. The proportion of children committed to Care in England and Wales because of offences rose in the period 1966–76 from nine per cent to twenty-five per cent, partly as a result of changes in Child Care legislation which abolished Approved School Orders in the 1969 Children and Young Persons Act and replaced them with Care Orders (Parker, 1980). In the same period, the proportion of under-fives fell from twenty-two per cent to twelve per cent. Since, in disposing of juvenile delinquents, magistrates are tending to use committal to Care only as a response to serious offending, we would expect that committal to Care would be even less effective today as a remedy for delinquency than it was in the period of our study.

Alternatives to admission to Care, such as day care, attendance at family centres or better family casework, can sometimes prevent the reception of some children into Care, but it is clear that this may not *always* be in the child's best long-term interests. While we would not wish to see our data used (or rather *abused*) to hold back on the development of effective alternatives to Care, we do feel that our findings suggest a need seriously to question the almost unequivocally negative evaluation of Care which is currently prevalent in parts of social work, the helping professions and society at large. We should also like to reiterate our view that the admission of some children to Care and their retention in Care long-term is sometimes less harmful than allowing a child to remain in a damaging home. Whether it is better for a particular child suffering severely from emotional neglect or persistent hostility to be admitted to Care will always depend on a number of factors, e.g. (a) the severity of that neglect and hostility, (b) whether day care, group work or skilled help for the family will produce any real change, (c) whether there are factors in the family that will lead to positive change or spontaneous growth (which is sometimes hard to predict), and (d) whether the substitute Care actually available in and through local statutory and voluntary bodies is likely to be any more adequate as a form of upbringing.

Another major, and welcome, difference in child-care practice since the time we studied has been the increasing use of adoption and the search for permanent placements. This must tend to remove one of the greatest deficiencies of substitute Care previously available. We are also suggesting, on the basis of our findings, that: (a) long term fostering, with the inevitable risk of several changes in placement, may be better than a return to some homes (at least judged by the admittedly limited criteria of adult convictions), and (b) some forms of residential care, especially small-group homes, could lead to a better outcome. (Almost half of the quarter of boys in our sample who were longest in Care had experienced a mixed type of Care for most of their stay in Care.) It does not help the effectiveness of residential Care if it is assumed that it is *necessarily* damaging and that any commitment to keeping some children in residential Care fairly long-term is always a serious mistake.

Implications for practice

On the basis of this one study, particularly when it has used limited criteria of outcome, it would be wrong to push strongly for massive changes in Child Care policy. On the other hand: (a) our findings are consistent with those of Otterström (1956) who also found (on the basis of very complete public registers) that children who were admitted to the Care of Welfare Agencies in Sweden tended to have a better long term outcome in *many* respects the longer they stayed and the earlier they were admitted, and (b) much of current Child Care policy is itself based on inadequate evidence and questionable assumptions. We believe our findings throw doubt on four assumptions that are at present fairly widely held:

1 It is assumed that most long-term substitute Care (with the exception of adoption) is seriously deficient and often damaging. While our life histories show that the Care received by many of our subjects was very far from ideal, we also found that boys and girls who lived longest in Care had a significantly better outcome in terms of freedom from multiple convictions and violent crime than boys and girls in our sample who stayed for shorter periods. This suggests that, in spite of its deficiencies, the Care received by our subjects a generation ago might in *some* respects, have been a better upbringing than that received by some children living in very inadequate homes.

2 It is assumed that long-term foster care will almost inevitably involve several changes of placement (as we found) and that these changes are damaging. Such changes are in *general* very undesirable, but our inability to find that boys with a *greater* than average number of placements did any worse suggests that we need to do more research on the relative damage incurred by passing through discontinuities of parenting, as compared with living in distorted relationships. It is assumed that it is morally indefensible to intervene in a radical way to remove a child from its natural home only to subject it to an upbringing which may well consist of a succession of substitute parents. However, it may be even more detrimental to the child to allow it to continue to live in severely distorted relationships.

It might, of course, be held to be self-evident that living long-term in Care is a worse upbringing for a child than finding permanent substitute care elsewhere. Such would probably be the view of Goldstein, Freud and Solnit (1979) and of advocates of the so called 'permanency principle' in relation to children requiring substitute care (e.g. Emlen and Cascaito, 1978; Lahti *et al.*, 1978). We accept that a long-term commitment is part and parcel of all parenthood but we do not see permanency as being self-evidently the only important principle in parenting. A small minority of natural parents are not fit parents. Not all adoptions are successful; follow-up studies suggest that about a fifth involve considerable dissatisfactions on one side or the other. Nor would we wish to restrict a long-term commitment to only natural or adoptive parents. Some long-term foster placements appear to be very successful and the provision of custodianship for long-term foster parents offers an element of permanency. Some children in Care want neither fostering nor adoption and some have links with their families that the traditional form of adoption, and certain types of fostering, would effectively break. We would accept, sadly, that with the exception of organisations with a religious or philosophical ethos, residential care all too often lacks long-term commitment. This needs to be remedied. None of these facts should prevent social workers trying to take long-term decisions as early as possible in relation to children who come into Care and whose natural parents would appear either to reject them or to have such personal deficiencies as to make them unlikely ever to be adequate parents. However, this is an area where our understanding is often too inadequate to allow professionals to make precise predictions, and the legal system, at least in Britain, does not permit effective advocacy on behalf of some children who suffer emotional and sexual abuse in their own homes.

The fact that a rather large number of placements in childhood (four or more) was not associated with more convictions in adult life may mean that most children are more resilient than we suppose or that the consequences of changes of home show themselves in other ways. On the other hand, it may be that the children studied by us were more fortunate than some children in Care. Social workers have told us of children whose number of placements is more than twenty or even thirty, and this seems to us to be frankly scandalous.

3 It is assumed by many social workers and magistrates that natural parents who persist in asking for the return of children who have

been in Care for a considerable period (e.g. over a year) should usually be given 'another chance', however inadequate their previous care, unless there has been quite unacceptable physical or sexual abuse. We found that there was a group of boys who had been admitted to Care as infants, usually on the grounds, that their single young mothers were quite unable adequately to care for them. They had stayed in Care for between five months and two and a half years and had then returned home. In five of the eight cases, the Child Care Department had no legal power to prevent this. In a further two cases, it did not oppose parents applying for a revocation of 'Fit Person Orders' and, in the last case, the court overruled the Department's objections. The outcome for these boys was significantly worse than that for boys who remained in Care.

4 Society and social workers act as if they assumed that too little is known about severe conduct disorder and delinquency to justify vigorous intervention in a child's early years to try to prevent a recidivist and sociopathic way of life developing. In fact, it is known that boys who grow up in families in which there is a high level of overt hostility, rejection and harshness, with frequent marital rows, and in which parents themselves have a criminal record and provide inadequate oversight for their children, are at much greater risk of becoming seriously delinquent.

Although it was the case that when delinquent boys were kept longer in Care, i.e. several years, they seemed to commit fewer crimes as adults, and especially fewer crimes of violence, than boys committed for shorter periods, the Care experience did not dramatically reduce the chances of juvenile delinquents becoming either offenders or multiple offenders.

We live in a society which is reluctant to separate younger children from their parents on the grounds of parental failure, inadequacy and hostility, but which has much less reluctance about committing troublesome adolescents to Care because of persistent delinquency. This study found that taking severely delinquent boys into Care, even at the tender age of eight to twelve years, did not usually prevent them going on to commit several more crimes. This suggests that there is a strong case for some form of intensive intervention in early school years and even at the pre-school stage (in extreme cases with legal sanctions) to try to improve the quality of parental understanding, care and control. This intervention should usually fall short of

admission to Care but, if it seems highly likely that a boy will eventually *have* to be admitted, the sooner this is done, the better. At least
our findings cast some doubt on the almost unqualified assumption
made by many in the helping professions that admission to long-term
care will almost always be the most detrimental of all alternatives.
This kind of objection to the use of Care should no longer be made
with the absolute confidence and certainty with which it has often
been made in the past and still is being made.

It is likely that, if early and sound decisions were taken in relation to
children who do need to come into substitute Care and if good
material, housing and emotional support were available for young
people who leave Care in their late teens, the outcome for children
who have been in Care would greatly improve. This, in turn, would
affect decisions relating to the use of Care and so, hopefully, set in
motion a spiral that is genuinely beneficial to children at risk.

The deficiencies of the Care system are all too apparent and it is not
our intention to avoid acknowledging them or to deny that they must
have some effect on children in Care. On the other hand, some form of
substitute care is inevitable and in some situations there is no choice
but to admit a child to Care. In others, the question is 'which is the
"least detrimental alternative" for the child?' Our own limited findings and those of Otterström (1956) suggest that it is sometimes less
harmful for a child to be admitted into Care and to remain long-term
in substitute care. So much emphasis has been placed on preventing
admission to Care that possibly inadequate efforts have been made to
make substitute care as good as possible for the small minority of
children whose natural homes will never be adequate. We would
include within the category of substitute care the increasing use of
adoption and long-term fostering with a view to custodianship.

Too often, social workers have found themselves in a position in
which they feel they have either to support and help parents whose
level of caring may never really be good enough for their children's
needs *or* use substitute Care, which is known to be often inadequate
and which is unlikely to improve in quality. Support and help to the
natural parents should not be given at the child's expense and, if a
child is admitted to Care long term, there should be a reasonable
expectation that substitute care will be adequate. To make all substitute care adequate will require an injection of resources and training
that are particularly hard to come by in many countries at the present
time. However, commitment to these objectives will not occur as long

as many professionals working with children assume that substitute care will inevitably be seriously deficient.

The studies reviewed by Skuse (1984) and Rushton and Treseder (1986) demonstrate that some appallingly deprived children can make good severe developmental delays if they are moved to a more normal and caring environment. It is often assumed by social workers that the experience of Care will necessarily be bad, when, in fact, it could be very remedial for some children. Unfortunately, in practice it tends to be much less good than it could be. It is also apparent from the studies of young people who have left Care, especially Ferguson (1966), Mulvey (1977), and Stein and Carey (1986), that the level of after-Care is often very poor. It has to be accepted that some young people who leave Care have had quite enough of social workers and Social Services Departments. However, the studies quoted suggest that many would have been only too happy to receive a measure of both material help and emotional support; but that often these things were either not offered, or only offered very sparingly. Although the Care system itself leaves much to be desired, the provision of an adequate after-Care service for those young people who appear to want help seems an even more urgent priority. Young people will always have to learn by their own mistakes, but do they have to do it entirely on their own?

Appendix 1 Seriousness-of-crime scale

A. Instructions to raters of seriousness-of-crime scale

You are being asked to judge the relative seriousness of the criminality of a number of people: (a) as juveniles (< 17 years), and (b) as adults (> 16 years). You have two sets of evidence, from: (a) the local Criminal Records Office, and (b) the Criminal Records Office in London.

You should assume that whichever office records the greater amount of crime, that record is likely to be the most correct.

To guide you in your rating you have: (a) your own internal logic and view of what constitutes seriousness of criminality, (b) the definitions of each point in the scale, (c) descriptions of what constitutes a criminal record appropriate to a particular point, and (d) two other rules: (i) offences t.i.c. (taken into consideration) should be counted at about 1/3 the normal seriousness of convictions, and (ii) the differences between levels become greater the higher one moves up the scale.

You should not be influenced by the sentences imposed. In fact, I strongly suggest you try to cover up the record of penalties column, where this is possible.

Please confine yourselves to the scale 0 to 7.

B. Definitions

0 – No criminal record.
1 – A minimal record. Normally, this should only include *one* 'appearance' and usually only one conviction of a relatively minor nature. However, some 'appearances' in court almost invariably include two charges and, therefore, two convictions, e.g. TADA (taking and driving away) is almost always accompanied by 'driving without insurance' and *one* such appearance should be regarded as minimal. (However, if the defendant were also convicted of driving

without a licence, this should qualify for a score of 2.) Similarly, a conviction of being 'drunk and disorderly', together with a conviction for *criminal damage* on what appears to be the same appearance, would, by itself, qualify for a score of *1* and not 2.

2 – Has committed more than a minimal 'amount' of crime without having a serious criminal record.

3 – Appears to be on the verge of serious criminality.

4 – Has a definitely serious criminal record.

5 – Very serious criminal record, but not the most serious.

6 – The most serious degree of criminal record, excluding murder.

7 – Murder, with or without other crimes.

C. Seriousness-of-crime scale

Sellin and Wolfgang's scale (1964) includes only crimes of dishonesty/theft, destruction of property and violence against persons. The scale created by us included all indictable and serious crimes committed by subjects in this study. It has not been validated. Eleven social work colleagues were asked to rate most crimes on a randomly ordered list, using a 7 point scale. The criterion of seriousness was 'how seriously do you believe most people view typical instances of these crimes'.

Seriousness-of-crime scale

0 – No criminal record.

1 – Very mild degree of criminality, e.g. one conviction or, at the most, one appearance and that of a relatively minor nature, e.g. either: (a) one instance of theft to the value of less than £5, or (b) one instance of criminal destruction (unless considerable damage is known to have resulted, or (c) one instance of criminal deception involving a value of £5 or less, or (d) receiving stolen goods to the value of less than £5, or (e) being drunk and disorderly, or (f) one instance of TADA or (g) one instance of possession of drugs, or (h) one common assault (not involving bodily harm).

2 – Either two or more instances of any of the above, or combinations of them, or one instance of any one of the following: (i) theft to the value of over £5, or (j) serious wilful damage, e.g. (k) arson leading to serious destruction, or (l) USI (unlawful sexual intercourse), or (m) sexual interference (on an adult – if a juvenile, level 3), or (n) selling drugs, or (o) receiving stolen goods to the value of over £5, or (p) breaking and entering, or (q) driving under the influence of drink, or (r) importuning.

3 – Either combinations of four or five minor crimes at Level 1 or two or three crimes at Level 2, or (s) one instance of robbery, or (t)

assaulting a policeman, or (u) assault causing actual bodily harm, or (v) living off immoral earnings.

4 – Either combinations of four to six offences at Levels 1 and 2, or two or three offences at Level 3, or (w) one instance of wounding, or (x) assault causing grievous bodily harm.

5 – Either combinations of seven to twelve offences found at Levels 1 and 2, or four to six offences at Level 3, or two to three at Level 4, or (y) rape, or (z) homicide.

6 – Combinations of crime each more serious than Level 4.

7 – Murder.

Appendix II Checklist of types of anti-social behaviour problems

1. Serious and repeated temper outbursts in children over five years.
2. Abnormal and persistent defiance or disobedience (at home or school).
3. Abnormal destructiveness.
4. Stealing inside and outside the home (not food inside the home), with or without a conviction.
5. Arson, persistent fire-lighting.
6. Bullying younger children.
7. Abnormal cruelty to animals.
8. Abnormal aggression (within/outside the family or both).
9. Self injury/poisoning in the apparent absence of depression.
10. Persistent running away from home.
11. Overactivity (as diagnosed by a psychiatrist).
12. Truancy (not school refusal).
13. Deliberate urinating or defaecating.
14. Abnormal sex play in pre-pubescence (not masturbation).
15. Lying.
16. Fantastic lying.
17. Persistently demanding/attention-seeking behaviour.
18. Swearing.
19. Abnormally sadistic fantasy play.

Bibliography

Adcock, M., 'The right of a child to a permanent placement' in *Rights of Children*, ed. D. Rawstron, London, British Association for Adoption and Fostering, 1981.

Ainsworth, F. and Fulcher, L. C., *Group Care for Children: Concepts and Issues*, London and New York, Tavistock, 1981.

Andry, R. G., *Delinquency and Parental Pathology*, London, Methuen, 1960.

Baldwin, J., 'Ecological and area studies in Great Britain and the United States', in *Crime and Justice, an annual review of research*, 1, pp. 29–66, ed. N. Morris and M. Tonry, Chicago and London, University of Chicago Press, 1979.

Barclay Report, National Institute of Social Work, *Social Workers, Their Role and Tasks*, London, Bedford Square Press, 1982.

Barton, R. *Institutional Neurosis*, Bristol, F. Wright and Sons, 1959.

Belson, W. A., *Juvenile Theft: The Causal Factors*, London, Harper & Row, 1975.

Berry, J., *Daily Experience in Residential Life: A Study of Children and their Care Givers*, London, Routledge & Kegan Paul, 1975.

Block, J. H., Block, J. and Morrison, A., 'Parental agreement – disagreement on child rearing orientations and gender related personality correlates in children', in *Child Development*, 52, pp. 965–74, 1981.

Bohman, M., *Adopted Children and their Families. A follow-up study of Adopted children, their Background, Environment and Adjustment*, Stockholm, Proprius, 1970.

Bowlby, J., *Forty-four Juvenile Thieves. Their characters and Home Life*, London, Baillere, Tindall and Cox, 1946.

Bowlby, J., *Maternal Care and Mental Health*, Geneva, World Health Organisation, 1951 and 1957 (2nd edn).

Bowlby, J., Ainsworth, M. *et al.*, 'The effects of mother–child separation. A follow-up study', *British Journal of Medical Psychology 29*, pp. 211–47, 1956.

Bowlby, J., *Attachment and Loss*, Vol. 1: Attachment, Harmondsworth, Middx, Penguin Books, 1969.

Bowlby, J., *Attachment and Loss*, Vol. 2: Separation, Anxiety and Anger, Harmondsworth, Middx., Penguin Books, 1973.

Bowlby, J., *Attachment and Loss*, Vol. 3: Loss, Sadness and Depression, Harmondsworth, Middx., Penguin Books, 1980.

Bowley, A. H., *Child Care*, London, E. & S. Livingstone, 1951.

Brearly, P., 'The experience and process of leaving', in Brearly P., Black, J., Gutridge, P., Roberts, G. and Tarran, E., *Leaving Residential Care*, London and New York, Tavistock, 1982.

Brent, *A Child in Trust, The report of the panel of inquiry into the circumstances surrounding the death of Jasmine Beckford*, London Borough of Brent, 1985.

Bronfenbrenner, U., 'Reaction to social pressure from adults versus peers, among Soviet day school and boarding school pupils in the perspective of an American sample', in *Successful Group Care*, ed. M. Wolins, Chicago, Aldine, 1974.

Bronfenbrenner, U., *The Ecology of Human Development: Experiments by Nature and Design*, Cambridge, Mass., Harvard University Press, 1979.

Brown, G. W., Brolchain, M. N. and Harris, T., 'Social class and psychiatric disturbance among women in an urban population', in *Sociology*, 9, pp. 225–54, 1975.

Brown, G. W. and Harris, T., *The Social Origins of Depression: A study of psychiatric disorders among women*, London, Tavistock, 1978.

Brown, M., and Madge, N., *Despite the Welfare State*, London, Heinemann, 1982.

Burgess, C., *In Care and into Work*, London, Tavistock, 1981.

Butler, N. R. and Alberman, E. D. (eds.) *Perinatal Problems*, Edinburgh, E. and S. Livingstone, 1969.

Cadoret, R. J. and Cain, C. 'Sex differences in predictors of antisocial behaviour in adoptees', in *Archives of General Psychiatry*, 37, pp. 1171–5, 1980.

Central Statistical Office, *Social Trends*, No. 16, London, HMSO, 1986.

Clarke, A. D. B. and Clarke, A. M., 'Cognitive changes in the feeble-minded', *British Journal of Psychology*, 45, pp. 173–9, 1954.

Clarke, A. M. and Clarke, A. D. B., *Early Experience: Myth and Evidence*, London, Open Books, 1976.

Clarke R. V. G., and Cornish, D. B., *The Controlled Trial in Institutional Research*, Home Office Research Studies, London, HMSO, 1972.

Cline, H. F., 'Criminal behaviour over the life span', in *Constancy and Change in Human Development*, Brim, O. G. & Kagan J. (eds.), Cambridge, Mass., Harvard, 1980.

Conger, J. J. and Miller, W. C., *Personality, Social Class and Delinquency*, New York, Wiley, 1966.

Cornish, D., and Clarke, R., 'Residential treatment and its effects on delinquency', *Home Office Research Study*, 32, London, HMSO, 1975.

Cowie, J., Cowie, V. and Slater, E., *Delinquency in Girls*, London, Heinemann, 1968.

Craig, M. M. and Glick S. J. 'Ten years experience with the Glick Social Prediction Table', in *Crime and Delinquency*, 9, pp. 249–61, 1963.

Crellin, E., Pringle, M. L. K. and West, P., *Born Illegitimate: Social and Educational Implications*, Windsor, NFER, 1971.

Crissey, O. L., 'Mental development as related to institutional residence and educational achievement', *University of Iowa Studies*, 13, No. 1, 1937.

Curman, H., and Nylander, I., 'A ten year follow-up of 2268 cases seen at child guidance clinics in Stockholm', in *Acta Paediatrica, Supplement 260*, pp. 5–71, 1976.

'The Curtis Report', in *Report of Care of Children Committee*, Cmnd. 6922. London HMSO, 1946.

Davis, A. *The Residential Solution*, London, Tavistock, 1981.

Department of Health and Social Security, *Report of the Committee on One-Parent Families* (Finer Report), London, HMSO, 1974.

Department of Health and Social Security (Social Work Service), *Boarding Out Regulations*, London, HMSO, 1982.

Dinnage, R. and Pringle, M. L. K., *Residential Child Care: Facts and Fallacies*, London, Longman, 1967a.

Dinnage, R. and Pringle, M. L. K., *Foster Home Care: Facts and Fallacies*, London, Longman, 1967b.

Douglas, J. W. B., 'Early hospital admissions and later disturbances of behaviour and learning, in *Developmental Medicine and Child Neurology*, 17, pp. 456–80, 1975.

Durkin, R. P., and Durkin, A. B., 'Evaluating residential treatment programs for disturbed children', in *Handbook of Evaluation Research*, Vol. 2, ed. M. Guttentage and Struening, Beverly Hills, Sage, 1975.

Eisenberg, L., 'The sins of the fathers: Urban decay and social pathology', *American Journal of Orthopsychiatry*, 32, pp. 5–7, 1962.

Elliott, D. S. and Voss, H. L., *Delinquency and Dropout*, Toronto and London, Lexington Books, 1974.

Elmer, E. and Gregg, G. S., 'The characteristics of abused children', *Paediatrics 40*, pp. 596–602, 1967.

Emlen, A. C. and Cascaito, J., *The Oregon Project County by Country. Outcome of permanency planning for children in foster care*, Portland State University, 1978.

Essen, J., Lambert L. and Head J., 'School Attainment of children who have been in Care', *Child: Care, Health and Behaviour*, Vol 2 (6), pp. 339–51, 1976.

Essen J. and Wedge P., *Continuities in Childhood Disadvantage*. Heinemann Educational Books, London, 1982.

Fanshel, D. and Shin, F. B., *Children in Foster Care – A Longitudinal Study*, New York, Columbia University Press, 1978.

Farrington, D. P., 'The family background of aggressive youths', in *Aggression and Antisocial Behaviour in Childhood and Adolescence*, ed. L. Hersov, M. Berger and D. Shaffer, Book Supp. No 1 for *Journal of Child Psychology and Psychiatry*, Pergamon, Oxford, 1979.

Farrington, D. P. 'The prevalence of convictions', *British Journal of Criminology*. 21, pp. 173–5, 1981.

Ferguson, T., *Children in Care – and After*, London, Oxford University Press, 1966.

Fernald G. M., *The Mental Examination of 75 Children at the 'Y' House, Sacramento*, California State Board of Control, 1918.

Ferri, E., *Growing up in a One-Parent Family*, Slough, NFER, 1976.

Finer Report 1974: see Department of Health and Social Security.

Fisher, M., Marsh, P., Phillips, D., and Sainsbury, E., *In and Out of Care*, London, Batsford/BAAF, 1986.

Fuller, R. and Stevenson, O., 'Policies, programmes and Disadvantage', in SSRC/DHSS *Studies in Deprivation and Disadvantage*, No. 9, London, Heinemann Educational Books, 1983.

Gath, D., Cooper, B., Gattoni, F. and Rockett, D., *Child Guidance and Delinquency in a London Borough*, Oxford, Oxford University

Press, 1977.

George, V., *Foster Care: Theory and Practice*, London, Routledge and Kegan Paul, 1970.

Gibbens, T. C. N., *Psychiatric Studies of Borstal Lads*, London, Oxford University Press, 1963.

Gladstone, F. J., 'Vandalism among Adolescent schoolboys', in *Tackling Vandalism*, ed. R. V. G. Clarke, Home Office Research Study No. 47, London HMSO, 1978.

Glueck, S. and Glueck, E., *Juvenile Delinquents Grown Up*, New York, Commonwealth Fund, 1940.

Goffman, E. *Asylums*, Harmondsworth, Penguin, 1961.

Goldfarb, W., 'The effects of early institutional care on adolescent personality', *Journal of Experimental Education* 12, pp. 106–29, 1943.

Goldfarb, W., Psychological privation in infancy and subsequent adjustment, *American Journal of Orthopsychiatry* 15, pp. 247–55, 1945.

Goldfarb, W., Variations in the adolescent adjustment of institutionally reared children, *American Journal of Orthopsychiatry*, 17, pp. 449–57, 1947.

Goldstein, J., Freud, A. and Solnit, A. J., *Before the Best Interests of the Child*, London, Free Press, 1979.

Goodwin, D. W., Schulsinger, F. Hermansen, L., Guze, S. B. and Winokur, G., 'Alcohol problems in adoptees raised apart from biological parents', *Archives of General Psychiatry*, 28, pp. 238–43, 1973.

Goodwin, D. W., Schulsinger, F., Moller, N., Hermansen, L., Winokur G., and Guze, S. B. 'Drinking problems in adopted and non-adopted sons of alcoholics', *Archives of General Psychiatry*, 31, pp. 164–9, 1974.

Hall, J. W. 'Inter-rater reliability of ward rating scales', *British Journal of Psychiatry*, 125, pp. 248–55, 1974.

Healey, W., and Bronner, A., *Delinquents and Criminals: their making and unmaking*, New York, Macmillan, 1926.

Henke, D., 'Child care in crisis', The Guardian 3 November 1982.

Hetherington, E. M., 'Children and divorce', in *Parent–Child Interactions: Theory, Research and Prospect*, ed. R. Henderson, New York, Academic Press, 1981.

Hewitt, L. E., and Jenkins, R. L. *Fundamental Patterns of Maladjustment. The Dynamics of their origin*, Illinois, Michigan Child

Guidance Institute, 1946.

Heywood, M., *Children in Care: The Development of the service for the deprived child*, London RKP, 1959.

Hobbs, N., 'The reeducation of emotionally disturbed children, in *Behavioural Science Frontiers in Education*, ed. E. M. Bowes and W. G. Hollister, New York, John Wiley, 1967.

Hodgkin, R., Penn, H., Streather, J., and Tunstill, J., 'The case for Prevention', *Community Care*, 13 October 1983, No. 483, pp. 31–2, 1983.

Hoghughi, M. *Troubled and Troublesome: Coping with Severely Disordered Children*, Worcester and London, Burnett Books, 1978.

Holman, R., *Trading in Children*, London, RKP, 1973.

Home Office, *Children in Care 1955*, London, Cmnd 9881, 1956.

Howells, J. G., *Remember Maria*, London, Butterworths, 1974.

Hutchings, B. and Mednick, S. A., 'Registered criminality in the adoptive and biological parents of registered male adoptees', in *Genetics, Environment and Psychopathology*, pp. 215–17, ed. S. A. Mednick, F. Schulsinger, J. Higgins and B. Bell, Amsterdam – North Holland, 1974.

Isaac, B. C, Minty, E. B. and Morrison, R. M., Children in Care – the association with mental disorder in the parents. *British Journal of Social Work*, 16 pp. 325–39, 1986.

Jenkins, S., 'Separation experiences of parents whose children are in Care', *Child Welfare*, 48, Part 6, 1969.

Jones, K., 'The Development of institutional care', *New Thinking about Institutional Care*, London, Association of Social Workers, 1967.

Jones, R., 'Justice, social work and statutory supervision', in *Providing Criminal Justice for Children*, ed. A. Morris and H. Giller, London, Arnold, 1983.

Kadushin, A., *Adopting Older Children*, New York, Columbia University Press, 1970.

Kahan, B., *Growing up in Care: Ten people talking*, Oxford, Basil Blackwell, 1979.

King, R. D., Raynes, N. V. and Tizard, J., *Patterns of Residential Care*, London, Routledge and Kegan Paul, 1971.

Kohn, M., *Social competence, Symptoms and Underachievement in Childhood: a longitudinal perspective*, London, Wiley, 1977.

Kolvin, I., Garside, R. G., Nicol, A. R., Macmillan A., Wolstenholme, F. and Leitch, I. M., *Help Starts Here: The maladjusted child in the ordinary school*, London, Tavistock, 1981.

Kruk, S. and Wolkind, S. 'A longitudinal study of single mothers and their children', in *Families at Risk*, ed. N. Madge, London, Heinemann Educational Books (SSRC/DHSS Studies in Deprivation and Disadvantage, 8), 1983.

Kvaraceus, W. C., *Anxious Youth: Dynamics of Delinquency*, Columbia, Ohio, C. E. Merrill, 1960.

Lahti, J. Green, K. and Emlen, A., *Follow-up Study of Oregon Project*, Regional Research Institute for Human Services, Portland State University, 1978.

Lambert, L., Essen, J. and Head, J., 'Variations in behaviour ratings of children who have been in Care', *Journal of Child Psychology and Psychiatry*, 18, pp. 335–46, 1977.

Lane, H., *Talks to Parent and Teachers*, London, Allen & Unwin, 1928.

Lavik, N. J., 'Urban–rural differences in rates of disorder. A comparative psychiatric population study of Norwegian adolescents', in Graham, P. J. (ed.), *Epidemiological Approaches in Child Psychiatry*, London, Academic Press, 1977.

Lefkowitz, M. M. *et al.*, *Growing Up to be Violent*, New York, Pergamon, 1977.

Leslie, S. A., 'Psychiatric disorder in the young adolescents of an industrial town', *British Journal of Psychiatry*, 125, pp. 113–24, 1974.

Levine, A. S., 'Substitute child care. Recent research and its implications', *Welfare in Review*, 10, 1, 1972.

Levy, D. M., *Maternal overprotection*, New York, Columbia University Press, 1943.

Lewis, H., *Deprived Children*, London, Oxford University Press, 1954.

Lynch, M. A. and Roberts, J., *Consequences of Child Abuse*, New York, Academic Press, 1982.

Maas, H. S., 'The young adult adjustment of twenty wartime residential nursery children', in *Successful Group Care*, ed. M. Wolins, 1963.

Maas, H. S. and Engler, R. E., *Children in Need of Parents*, New York, Columbia University Press, 1959.

McClintock, F. H. and Avison, N. H., *Crime in England and Wales*, London, Heinemann Educational, 1968.

McCord, J., 'A longitudinal view of the relationship between paternal absence and crime', in *Abnormal Offenders, Delinquency and the Criminal Justice System*, ed. J. Gunn and D. P. Farrington, New York, John Wiley and Sons, 1982.

McCord, W., and McCord, J., *Origins of Crime*: A new evaluation of the *Cambridge Somerville Study*, New York, Columbia University Press, 1959.

McWhinnie, A. M., *Adopted Children: How they grow up*, London, Routledge and Kegan Paul, 1967.

Maluccio, A. N., Fein, E. and Olmstead, K. A., *Permanency planning for children*, Tavistock, New York and London, 1986.

Mann, P., *Children in Care Revisited*, London, Batsford Academic and Educational, 1984.

Mapstone, E. 'Children in Care', *Concern* 3, pp. 23–28, 1969.

May, D., 'Juvenile offenders and the organisation of juvenile justice; an examination of juvenile delinquency in Aberdeen, 1959–67', Unpublished Ph.D. thesis, University of Aberdeen, 1975.

'Mehmadagi, Maria', *Report of an Independent Inquiry*, London, Borough of Southwark, 1981.

Meier, E. G. 'Current circumstances of former foster children', *Child Welfare*, 44, pp. 196–206, 1965.

Milham, S., Bullock, R. and Cherrett, P., *After Grace – Teeth: A comparative study of the residential experience of boys in Approved Schools*, London, Human Context, 1975.

Milham, S., Bullock, R., Hosie, K. and Haak, M., (1986): *Lost in Care: The problems of maintaining links between children in Care and their families*, Aldershot, Gower, 1986.

Mitchell, S. and Rosa, P., 'Boyhood behaviour problems as precursors of criminality: a fifteen year follow-up study', *Journal of Child Psychology and Psychiatry*, 22, pp. 19–34, 1980.

Morris, C., *The Permanency Principle in Child Care Social Work*, Social Work Monograph 21, Norwich University of East Anglia, 1984.

Morris, P., *Put Away: A sociological study of institutions for the mentally retarded*, London, Routledge and Kegan Paul, 1969.

Mortimore, J., and Mortimore, P., 'Benign or malignant? The effects of institutions', *Child: Care, Health and Development*, 11, pp. 267–80, 1985.

Moss, P., 'Residential care of children: a general view', in *Varieties of residential experience*, ed. J. Tizard, I. Sinclair and R. G. V. Clarke, London, Routledge and Kegan Paul, 1975.

Moss, P. and Plewis, I., 'Mental distress in mothers of pre-school children in Inner London', *Psychological Medicine*, 7, pp. 641–52, 1977.

Mulvey, T., 'After care – who cares?', *Concern*, 26, pp. 26–30, 1977.

Murphy, H. B. M., 'Long-term foster care and its influence on adjustment in adult life, in *Children at Psychiatric Risk*, ed. E. J. Anthony and C. Koupernik, Vol. 3 of The Child and his Family, 1974.

Naess, S., 'Mother–child separation and delinquency: further evidence', *British Journal of Criminology*, 2, pp. 361–74, 1962.

Naess, S., 'Mother–child separation and delinquency', *British Journal of Delinquency*, 10, pp. 22–35, 1979.

Neill, A. S., *Summerhill: a radical approach to education*, London, Gollanz, 1962.

Oliver, J. P. J., Knight, D. J., 'An evaluation of an inpatient psychiatric unit for children', *Child Care, Health and Development*, 10, pp. 141–55, 1984.

Olweus, D., 'Stability of aggressive reaction patterns in males', *Psychological Bulletin*, 86, pp. 852–75, 1979.

Osborn, S. G. and West, D. J., 'Conviction records of fathers and sons compared', *British Journal of Criminology*, 19, pp. 120–33, 1979.

Oswin, M., *The Empty Hours*, London, Allen Lane, 1971.

Oswin, M., *Children Living in Long Stay Hospitals*, SIMP Research Monograph 5, London, William Heinemann Medical Books, 1978.

Otterström, E., 'Delinquency and children from bad homes', *Acta Paediatrica Scandanavica*, 33, Suppl. 5, 1956.

Ouston, J., 'Delinquency, family background and educational attainment', *British Journal of Criminology*, 24, pp. 2–26, 1984.

Packman, J. *Child Care: Needs and Policies*, London, Allen & Unwin, 1968.

Packman, J., *The Child's Generation: Child Policy from Curtis to Houghton*, Oxford, Blackwell, 1975.

Packman, J., Randall, J. and Jacques, N., *Decision Making on Admissions of Children to Local Authority Care*, Report to DHSS, London, HMSO, 1984.

Packman, J., Randall, J. and Jacques, N., *Who needs Care?*, Oxford, Blackwell, 1986.

Page, R., and Clarke, G. A. (eds.), *Who cares?*, London, National Children's Bureau, 1977.

Parker, R., *Decision in child care*, Allen & Unwin, 1966.

Parker, R., ed, *Caring for Separated Children*, London, Macmillan Press for National Children's Bureau, 1980.

Patterson, G. R., *Coercive Family Processes*, Eugene, Oregon, Castalia, 1982.

Pease, K., Ireson, J. and Thorpe, J., 'Additivity assumptions in the measurement of delinquency', *British Journal of Criminology*, 14, pp. 256–63, 1974.

Porter, B. and O'Leary, K. D., 'Marital discord and childhood behaviour problems', *Journal of Abnormal Child Psychology*, 8, pp. 287–96, 1980.

Power, M. J., Ash, P. M., Schoenberg, E. and Sorey, E. C., 'Delinquency and the family', *British Journal of Social Work* 4, pp. 13–38, 1974.

Pringle, M. K. and Bossio V., 'Prolonged separation and emotional adjustment', *Journal of Child Psychology and Psychiatry*, 1, pp. 37–48, 1960.

Prosser, A., *Perspectives in Residential Child Care*, Windsor, NFER, 1976.

Prosser, A., *Perspectives in foster care*, Windsor, NFER, 1978.

Quinton, D. and Rutter, M. 'Parents and children in Care, I', *Journal of Child Psychology and Psychiatry*, 25, pp. 211–230, 1984a.

Quinton, D. and Rutter, M., 'Parents and children in Care, II', *Journal of Child Psychology and Psychiatry*, 25, pp. 231–250, 1984b.

Quinton, D. and Rutter, M., 'Family pathology and child psychiatric disorder: a four-year prospective study', in *Longitudinal Studies in Child Psychiatry*, ed. A. R. Nicol, New York, John Wiley and Sons, 1985.

Redl, F. and Wineman, D., *The Aggressive Child*, New York Free Press, 1957.

Reymert, M. L., and Hinton, R. T., 'The effects of a change to a relatively superior environment upon the IQs of one hundred children', *National Society for the Study of Education*, Yearbook 39 (II), Bloomington. Public School Publishing, 1940.

Richman, N., Stevenson, J. and Graham, R. J., *Preschool to School, a Behavioural Study*, London Academic Press, 1982.

Roberts, R., *The Classic Slum*, University of Manchester Press, Manchester (and Pelican Books), 1971.

Robins, L., *Deviant Children Grown Up*, Baltimore, Williams and Wilkins, 1966.

Robins, L., 'Follow-up studies in behaviour disorders in children', in *Psychopathological Disorders in Childhood*, ed. H. C. Quay and J. C. Werry, New York, John Wiley, 1979.

Robins, L. N., 'An actuarial evaluation of the causes and consequences of deviant behaviour in young black men', in *Life History Research in Psychopathology*, Vol. II, ed. M. Roff, L. Robins and Pollack, 1972.

Robins, L. N., 'Sturdy predictors of adult antisocial behaviour: replications from longitudinal studies', *Psychological Medicine*, 8, pp. 611–22, 1978.

Rose, G. N. G., 'Concerning the measurement of delinquency', *British Journal of Criminology*, 6, pp. 414–21, 1966.

Rowe, J. and Lambert, L., *Children who wait. A study of children needing substitute families*, London, Association of Adoption Agencies, 1973.

Roycroft, B., 'The biggest form of child abuse is indifference', *Community Care* 12/5/83, pp. 30–33, 1983.

Rushton, A., and Treseder, J., 'Developmental recovery', *Adoption and Fostering*, 10 (3), pp. 54–6, 1986.

Rutter, M., Parent–child separation: psychological effects on the children', *Journal of Child Psychology and Psychiatry*, 12, pp. 233–60, 1971.

Rutter, M., 'Family, area and school influences in the genesis of conduct disorders', in *Aggression and Antisocial Behaviour in Childhood and Adolescence*, ed. L. A. Hersov and M. Berger, Oxford, Pergamon, 1978.

Rutter, M., *Maternal Deprivation Reassessed* (2nd edition), Harmondsworth, Penguin, 1981.

Rutter, M., Tizard, J. and Whitmore K. (eds.), *Education, Health and Behaviour*, London, Longmans, 1970.

Rutter, M., Cox, A., Tupling, C., Berger, M. and Yule W., 'Attainment and adjustment in two geographical areas. 1. The prevalence of psychiatric disorder', *British Journal of Psychiatry*, 126, pp. 493–509, 1975.

Rutter, M., and Madge, N., *Cycles of Disadvantage: A review of research*, London, Heinemann, D. 1976.

Rutter, M., Maughan, B., Mortimer, P., Ouston, J., with Smith A., *Fifteen Thousand Hours: secondary schools and their effects on children*, London, Open Books, 1979.

Rutter, M. and Giller N., *Juvenile Delinquency, Trends and Perspec-*

tives, Harmondsworth, Penguin, 1983.

Rutter, M., Quinton, D. and Liddle, C., 'Parenting in two generations', in *Families at Risk*, ed N. Madge, SSRC/DHSS Studies in Deprivation and Disadvantage No. 8, London, Heinemann Educational Books, 1983.

Sameroff, A. J., and Chandler, M. J., 'Reproductive risk and the continuum of caretaking casualty', in Horowitz, F. D. (ed.), *Child Development Research*, Vol. 4, Chicago, University of Chicago Press, 1975.

Schaffer, H. R. and Schaffer, E. B., 'Child care and the family', *Occasional Papers in Social Administration* No. 25, London, G. Bell and Sons, 1968.

Scull, A., *Decarceration: Community Treatment and the Deviant – A radical view*, Cambridge, Polity Press, 1984.

Seglow, S., Pringle M. K. & Wedge P., *Growing up adopted: a Long Term National Study of Adopted Children and their Families*. Windsor, NFER, 1972.

Sellin, T. and Wolfgang, M. E., *The Measurement of Delinquency*, New York, Wiley, 1964.

Shapland, J., 'Self-reported delinquency in boys aged 11 to 14', *British Journal of Criminology*, 18, pp. 255–66, 1978.

Shaw, M., and Hipgrave, T., *Specialist Fostering*, London, BAAF and Batsford Academic, 1983.

Sinclair, I., 'The influence of Wardens and Matrons on probation hostels: a study of a quasi family-institution in *Varieties of Residential Experience*, ed. J. Tizard, I. Sinclair and R. V. G. Clarke, London, RKP, 1975.

Skeels, H. M. 'Adult status of children from contrasting early life experiences: a follow-up study', *Monographs of the Society for Research in Child Development*, 31, No. 3, 1966.

Skuse, D., 'Extreme deprivation in early childhood – II: theoretical issues and a comparative review', *Journal of Child Psychology and Psychiatry*, 25 (4), pp. 543–72, 1984.

Spitz, R. A., 'Hospitalism; a follow-up report', *Psychoanalytic Study of the Child*, 2, pp. 113–17, 1946.

Spitz, R. A., and Wolf, K. M., 'Anaclitic depression', *The Psychoanalytic study of the child*, 2, pp. 313–342, 1946.

Sroufe, L. A., Fox, N., and Pancake, V., 'Attachment and dependency in developmental perspective', *Child Development*, 55, pp. 17–29, 1983.

Stein, M. and Carey, K., *Leaving Care*, Blackwell, 1986.

Stein, T., Cambrill, E. and Wiltse, K., *Children in Foster Homes: Achieving Continuity of Care*, Praeger Publishers, 1978.

Steiner, R., *Practical Advice to Teachers (Fourteen lectures given at the Waldorf School)*, London, Steiner Press, 1919.

Tennent, T. G., 'Truancy and stealing', *British Journal of Psychiatry*, 116, pp. 587–92, 1970.

Tennent, T. G., 'School non-attendance and delinquency', *Journal of Educational Research*, 13, pp. 185–90, 1971.

Terman, L. M. and Wagner, D., 'Intelligence quotients of 68 children in a Californian orphanage', *Journal of Delinquency*, 3, pp. 115–21, 1918.

Theis, S. Van S., *How Foster Children Turn Out*, New York, State Charities Association, 1924.

Thomas, A., Chess, S., and Birch, H. G., *Temperament and Behaviour Disorders in Children*, New York, University Press, 1968.

Thorpe, R., 'The experience of children and parents living apart: implications and guidelines for practice' in *New Developments in Foster Care and Adoption*, ed. J. Triseliotis, London, Routledge & Kegan Paul, 1980.

Timms, N., 'The Child Guidance Service – a pilot survey', in *Problems and Progress in Medical Care*, ed. G. Mclachlan, London, Oxford University Press, 1968.

Tizard, B., and Tizard, J., 'The institution as an environment for development', in *The Integration of a Child into a Social World*, ed. M. P. Richards, Cambridge University Press, 1974.

Tizard, B. and Hodges, J., 'The effects of early institutional rearing on the development of eight year old children, *Journal of Child Psychology and Psychiatry*, 19, pp. 99–118, 1978.

Tizard, J., 'Results and summary of the Brooklands experiment, in Clarke, A. D. B., and Tizard, B., (eds.) *Child Development and Social Policy: the Life and Work of Jack Tizard*, Leicester, British Psychological Society, 1983.

Townsend, P., *The last refuge: A survey of residential homes for the aged in England and Wales*, London, Routledge and Kegan Paul, 1962.

Trasler, G., *In place of parents: A study of foster care*, London, Routledge, 1960.

Triseliotis, J., 'Growing up in foster care, and after', In *New Developments in Foster Care and Adoption*, ed. J. Triseliotis, London, Routledge and Kegan Paul, 1980.

Triseliotis, J. and Russell, J., *Hard to Place. The outcome of adoption and residential care*, Heinemann Educational Books, London, 1984.

Vernon, J., 'Preventing long-term care', *Concern*, 56, pp. 6–7, 1985.

Vernon, J. and Fruin, D., *In Care: A Study of Social Work Decision Making*, National Children's Bureau, London, 1986.

Wadsworth, M., *Roots of Delinquency*, Oxford, Martin Robertson, 1979.

Wagner, H. and Pease, K., 'On adding up scores of offence seriousness', *British Journal of Criminology*, 18, pp. 175–78, 1978.

Wallerstein, J. S. and Kelly, J. B., *Surviving the Breakup*, London, Grant McIntyre, 1980.

Walton, R., and Heywood, M., *The Forgotten Children: A study of children in Care*, Extra mural Department, University of Manchester, 1971.

Wardle, C. J., 'Two generations of broken homes in the genesis of conduct and behaviour disorders in childhood', *British Medical Journal*, 2, pp. 349–54, 1961.

Weinstein, E., *The Self Image of the Foster Child*, New York, Russel Sage Foundation, 1960.

West, D. J., *Delinquency: Its Roots, Careers and Prospects*, London, Heinemann, 1982.

West, D. J., and Farrington, D. P., *Who Becomes Delinquent?*, London, Heinemann, 1973.

West, D. J. and Farrington, D. P., *The Delinquent Way of Life*, London, Heinemann, 1977.

Whitaker, J. K., *Caring for Troubled Children: Residential Treatment in a Community Context*, San Francisco, Jossey Bass, 1979.

Wilson, H., *Delinquency and Child Neglect*, London, George Allen and Unwin, 1962.

Wilson, H., 'Parenting in poverty', *British Journal of Social Work*, 4, pp. 241–54, 1974.

Wolfgang, M. E., 'Crime in a birth cohort', in *Crime, Criminology and Public Policy*, ed. R. Hood, London, Heinemann Educational Books, 1974.

Wolins, M., 'Group care. Friend or foe', *Social Work*, 15, pp. 35–53, 1969.

Wolins, M., 'Young children in institutions – some additional evidence', *Development Psychology*, 2, pp. 99–109, 1970.

Wolins, M., 'Maimonides revisited', in *Successful Group Care*, ed. M. Wolins, Chicago, Aldine, 1974.

Wolkind, S. N. 'A child's relationships after admission to residential care', *Child Care, Health and Development*, 3, pp. 357–62, 1977a.

Wolkind, S. N., 'Women who have been "in Care": psychological and social status during pregnancy', *Journal of Child Psychology and Psychiatry*, 18, pp. 179–82, 1977b.

Wolkind, S. N. and Rutter, M., 'Children who have been "in Care" – an epidemiological study', *Journal of Child Psychology and Psychiatry*, 14, pp. 97–105, 1973.

Wolkind, S. N. and Renton, G., 'Psychiatric disorders in children in long-term residential care', *British Journal of Psychiatry*, 135, pp. 129–35, 1979.

Wootton, B., *Social Science and Social Pathology*, London, Allen & Unwin, 1959.

Yule, W., and Raynes N. V., 'Behavioural characteristics of children in residential care', *Journal of Child Psychology and Psychiatry*, 13, pp. 249–58, 1972.

Zimmerman, R., 'Foster care in retrospect', *Tulane Studies in Social Welfare*, 14, pp. 1–119, 1962.

Index of names

Index of subjects